Revolutionary Feminisms

Revolutionary Feminisms

Conversations on Collective Action and Radical Thought

Edited by Brenna Bhandar and Rafeef Ziadah

London • New York

First published by Verso 2020

1 3 5 7 9 10 8 6 4 2

Verso
UK: 6 Meard Street, London W1F 0EG
US: 20 Jay Street, Suite 1010, Brooklyn, NY 11201
versobooks.com

Verso is the imprint of New Left Books

ISBN-13: 978-1-78873-776-0
ISBN-13: 978-1-78873-778-4 (US EBK)
ISBN-13: 978-1-78873-777-7 (UK EBK)

British Library Cataloguing in Publication Data
A catalogue record for this book is available from the British Library

Library of Congress Cataloging-in-Publication Data
A catalog record for this book is available from the Library of Congress

Typeset in Minion by Biblichor Ltd, Edinburgh
Printed and bound by CPI Group (UK) Ltd, Croydon CR0 4YY

This book is dedicated to the memories of our grandmothers, Ranjit Kaur Sran and Malakeh Hajjar.

And to the young ones, Kira, Zadie, Kalen, Ami, Mai, Joseph and Esha.

Contents

Acknowledgements ix
Introduction 1

Conversations 31

Diaspora/Migration/Empire 31
Avtar Brah 33
Gail Lewis 55
Vron Ware 73

Colonialism/Capitalism/Resistance 93
Himani Bannerji 95
Gary Kinsman 119
Leanne Betasamosake Simpson 139
Silvia Federici 149

Abolition Feminism 159
Ruth Wilson Gilmore 161
Avery F. Gordon 179
Angela Y. Davis 203

Afterword: Revolutionary Feminisms in a Time of Monsters
by Lisa Lowe 217

Acknowledgements

We write a few days into an apparent 'lockdown' in the city of London, as the government attempts to mitigate the effects of the global pandemic. One third of the world's population is now effectively quarantined to some degree. As the effects of ten years of cuts to the National Health Service are now revealing the true cost of austerity for society in its entirety, it is imperative to insist on a vision of healthcare as a universal social good, not as a marketised commodity that has to be re-nationalised in order to effectively cope with intense stress. We have seen increased racist attacks on Asian people in the weeks preceding the lockdown, the hoarding of basic necessities by individuals, sweeping emergency powers being brought swiftly into force; we are at the same time, also witnessing the ability of the government, with the stroke of a pen seemingly, to provide unprecedented amounts of financial support for workers who will be unable to earn a living during these months, and to re-nationalise various elements of the national transport network. Our employers will for the first time it seems, be forced to confront the inconvenient fact of socially reproductive labour as they grapple with how those of us who are able to, will continue to 'work from home'. Mutual aid networks are springing up everywhere, as people try to support one another in their local communities, particularly the most vulnerable. Extraordinary times, deeply unsettling, and perhaps a moment when we can continue to think, alone and together, about how to radically transform what we value and how we value those things; how we want to organise healthcare, work, the care of children and the elderly, food security. We hope that as the crisis subsides, whenever that is, that we find the collective will and desire not to continue 'as usual' in the aftermath of this pandemic.

This project, which has stretched over more than a few years, has reached fruition due to the generosity of many people. First and foremost are the interviewees, who generously and patiently agreed to collaborate with us. Their work has long been an inspiration to both of us and so many others. We are deeply grateful to Lisa Lowe for writing the afterword, opening up new horizons to consider as we complete this project. We would also like to thank our editor at Verso, Rosie Warren, for her support and encouragement. Sam Smith did a wonderful and meticulous copy edit for which we are thankful. We are grateful to Rashmi Varma for her thoughtful and constructive feedback on the introduction. We would like to acknowledge the support of SOAS, University of London for allocating transcription funds. Brenna would like to thank all of her feminist friends, and particularly on this occasion Haneen Naamnih, who regularly prompts her to question things taken for granted. She gives heartfelt thanks to Alberto Toscano, for discussing each and every aspect of this project over a lengthy period of time with great care, enthusiasm and insight. Rafeef thanks her family for their love and support, Laleh Khalili who continues to be a brilliant friend and mentor, and Adam Hanieh for his unfailing support and encouragement for this project.

Introduction

> I use the term *radical* in its original meaning – getting down to and understanding the root cause. It means facing a system that does not lend itself to your needs and devising means by which you change that system.
>
> Ella Baker, 1969[1]

The feminisms that we explore in this book are rooted in various political contexts and situated within a variety of political traditions. In fact, they are too diverse to easily name under a single heading. 'Black feminism', 'Indigenous feminism', 'socialist feminism', 'communism', 'Third World feminism', 'queer feminism': all of these terms and others could be used to describe the political work and thought of the people we have interviewed. At the same time, despite the range of differences that mark each of the revolutionary scholars interviewed here, their scholarly works also share a number of qualities that create a common ground for their political thought and activism. Namely, each of them has devised anti-capitalist, anti-imperialist and anti-racist feminist frameworks of analysis. All of the individuals interviewed here, along with ourselves, may not agree on every detail – but we share the belief that freedom requires revolutionary transformation in the organisation of the economy, social relations, political structures, and psychic and symbolic worlds, and that this must take place across multiple scales – from intimate relations between individuals to those among individuals, communities and the state.

In this introduction, our aim is to map some of the feminist lineages that appear in the book, as a means of drawing out the common ground shared by the interviewees and identifying what we consider to be absolutely crucial for feminist politics in our current conjuncture. When we write 'our' current conjuncture, we mean an explicit location: a postimperial metropolis, in which the mainstream political scene has jolted (again) to the right, with a highly developed neoliberal economy and mode of governance unfolding hand in hand with an ever-emboldened racist nationalism. Although the global financial crisis of 2008 shook the very foundations of the economic system, capital quickly recalibrated to offload the crisis onto ordinary people

---

1 As quoted in Barbara Ransby, *Ella Baker and the Black Freedom Movement: A Radical Democratic Vision* (Chapel Hill: University of North Carolina Press, 2003), 1.

through long-term austerity politics, intensifying its assault on public services and living standards. This is consistent with the longer-standing neoliberal capitalist project, in the making for several decades, that has entailed the restructuring of capital on a global scale, the rise of new centres of accumulation, the weakening of trade unions, and the flexibilisation of labour. As we explore below, this has disproportionately affected people of colour and women workers.

The conversations included in this book are part of feminist genealogies rooted in Black feminist engagements with communist politics in the United States and the UK; feminist engagements with Marxism and communism in Italy, India and beyond; Indigenous feminisms grappling with the specifically gendered aspects of racial, settler colonial capitalism; and diasporic and queer feminisms confronting the racial caste hierarchies of labour markets and borders in postcolonial and settler colonial states. Fundamentally, these feminisms are formed by – and formative of – diverse histories of radical thought and action. Going against the contemporary obsession with novelty and newness in academic and related media environments, our aim in this introduction is more or less the opposite: it is to explore the collective memory and histories of struggle that shape the very possibilities of radical change in our present and near future.

While based in the academy, the scholar-activists interviewed here have long-term engagements with social movements and have consistently worked to maintain archives of resistance – indeed, ones which are often excluded from mainstream accounts. We thank them for the time they so generously gave to this project, engaging with our questions and believing in the aims of the book. We opted early on, in the tradition of community building and collaboration, to develop this volume in conversation with them, rather than writing about their work. It was more in line with the praxis we discuss below to collectively think through earlier periods of resistance, past political trajectories and lessons learned, and to recognise how they continue to shape our present. As Angela Y. Davis eloquently noted in her 2016 Steve Biko Memorial Lecture, 'Legacies and Unfinished Activisms':

> Students are now recognising that the legacies of past struggles are not static. If these legacies mean anything at all, they are mandates to develop new strategies, new technologies of struggles. And these legacies, when they are taken up by new generations reveal unfulfilled promises of the past and therefore give rise to new activisms. As an activist of Steve Biko's generation, I have to constantly remind myself that the struggles of our contemporary times should be thought of as productive contradictions because they constitute a rupture with past struggles, but at the same time they reside on a continuum with those struggles and they have been enabled by activisms of the past. They are unfinished activisms.

In the following discussions, we aim to collectively grapple with this continuum of 'unfinished activisms' – the continuities and discontinuities, complexities and contradictions of anti-racist and Indigenous feminist resistance.[2] We assemble a small group of authors to critically engage with movement histories, to examine useful conceptual tools and forms of praxis for feminist, anti-capitalist and anti-racist movements. We hope this makes a contribution to contemporary struggles.

As we think through collective memory of struggle, we want to do more than make direct connections between oral histories, conventional archives, and the written work produced by feminists over the past several decades. We want to emphasise that our political inheritance exceeds and stretches far beyond what is typically understood as 'history' and lineage. It is transmitted to us through the stories we grow up listening to, in what we come to recognise, retrospectively, in ourselves and others as ways of surviving the daily onslaught of racism, patriarchy, heterosexism and ableist forces that structure our everyday – as well as the shared forms of leisure, pleasure and joy that are also a source of our collective resilience. We were struck by the interviewees' detailed recollections of early life experiences and observations on domestic life as they reflected on their intellectual and political formations. For us, the making of this volume is itself the result of a diverse set of experiences – some lived directly, others inherited, some observed in others, and all of them *felt* (in the way that one's emotional and psychic life tells us something about social and political cultures) – of migration, estrangement, displacement, settlement, exile and differentiated belongings.[3] We should also add that we are keenly aware of the geopolitical limits of this project. Certainly the inclusion of Latin American and African feminists, for instance, would have greatly enriched the terrain covered in this volume. The interlocutors included here are based primarily in North America, the UK, and Europe, and while they are nowhere near representative of left, anti-racist feminisms as they exist globally, the ideas and analytic frameworks they have developed have undoubtedly had a very wide and influential reach.

Lee Maracle, a leading Indigenous feminist scholar from the Sto:lo First Nation in British Columbia, Canada, illuminates a complex notion of memory – one that is transgenerational, biophysical (i.e., carried in our bodies and psyches), transmitted through song and orality. Memory, for Maracle, is intensely bound up with language (written and oral, English and Salish). She writes:

---

2 The interviews in this volume have been lightly edited by interviewees and interviewers for clarity and length.

3 See the interview with Gail Lewis in this volume.

> Memory is powerful. It can twist us in knots, but the imagination can untwist the knots, unravel the memory, rework it into blankets that protect us, designs that promote, carry, and create new being. Re-membering is significant, holy in its duty, recollecting bits of engagement, social interaction, success and failure. The imagination can transform memory from depression to a simple incident . . . from perverse to natural or from failure to opportunity if you are moving toward the good life. It can inspire us to re-evaluate our intervention, alter our course, and create a new beginning.[4]

Memory, and the act of *re-membering*, as theorised by Maracle, rearticulates several concepts that are often held apart; the desire to resist, to survive, coalesces with an embodied will in a movement towards freedom. In stating that her 'memory begins with an imagined world' – that is, her vision of a world free from war, violence, poverty and racism – Lee begins to describe a method for decolonising our ways of thinking and seeing the world. This radical imagining of freedom finds common ground with the thought and praxis of feminists who have grasped the complexity, and indeed the enormity, of intergenerational political struggles for freedom from the oppression of globalised racial colonial capitalism. In what follows, we map out some of the diverse intellectual and political terrain that has given rise to the scholarly and political work explored in the interviews, with particular attention to the points of contact among these different feminisms.

Anti-racist and Indigenous feminists have long analysed the international character of colonial and settler violence, carceral violence and police brutality.[5] While it has become more common to speak of a 'boomerang effect' of military and security policies 'returning' to the West, there is hardly newness to this: there has always been fluidity and learning from such processes of exploitation, as well as resistance to them, across borders and empires. However, as Lisa Lowe has argued, these connections 'between the emergence of European liberalism, settler colonialism in the Americas, the transatlantic African slave trade, and the East Indies and China trades in the late eighteenth and early nineteenth centuries' are often obscured by dominant understandings of the development of the liberal individual subject. Significantly, Lowe utilises the term 'intimacies' to grasp such links among a constellation of political economic, literary, philosophical and sociocultural meanings of interiority. She deploys the concept to investigate, 'against the grain', how the figure of the liberal individual, and attendant political formations of freedom

---

4 Lee Maracle, *Memory Serves: Oratories* (Edmonton: NeWest Press, 2016), 31.

5 On the relationship between transatlantic slavery and contemporary surveillance practices, see Simone Browne, *Dark Matters: On the Surveillance of Blackness* (Durham: Duke University Press, 2015).

and democracy, have been produced through imperial forces of worldmaking and according to logics (such as commodity fetishism) that work – structurally, affectively and psychically – to abstract from and mask the imperial 'details' of their formation.[6]

Grappling with the aftermath of decolonisation and continuing forms of neo-imperialism, many of the feminisms explored in this volume have been shaped by the violence of partitions, the 'pitfalls' of anti-colonial nationalism, and itineraries of migration and exile. Third World, postcolonial and diasporic feminisms speak to the complexities of life for migrant women who carry with them radical political traditions from their countries of origin, and who have long confronted religious fundamentalism, patriarchy and racism as these formations change over time, reflecting geopolitical, cultural specificities. However, the oft-repeated linear division of feminist thought into first, second and third waves elides the complex geographies and travelling theories within feminism itself. This division has the tendency to obscure the much longer histories of feminist praxis within communities of colour, and commonalities across struggles – underplaying the conceptual tools developed through specifically feminist anti-capitalist praxis. As postcolonial scholar Rashmi Varma notes, 'dissident histories' of feminism are 'rooted in trajectories of anti-colonial struggle' and have multiple 'diasporic genealogies'.[7] One of the motivations of this book is to acknowledge and learn from the political and intellectual labour of Black, Indigenous and socialist feminisms that have attempted to capture and theorise the complexity and multiplicity of lived experience.

Each of the feminists interviewed in this book has, at one time or another, sustained a serious engagement with anti-capitalist politics, whether as a communist, a critic of Marxist thought from the left, or an acute observer of the effects of poverty and socioeconomic inequality on racialised communities (locally and globally). As noted above, despite the diversity of political and intellectual formations of the interviewees, their feminisms share some contact points that we aim to emphasise as crucial for our contemporary political moment: the understanding that radical thought emerges in conjunction with social and political movements; that the individual is, at a fundamental level, constituted through relations with others and that this entails an ethical and political responsibility, which is the basis for solidarity[8]; and that radical

6 Lisa Lowe, *The Intimacies of Four Continents* (Durham: Duke University Press, 2015), 84–5.

7 Rashmi Varma, 'Anti-Imperialism', in *The Bloomsbury Handbook of 21st-Century Feminist Theory*, ed. Robin Truth Goodman (London: Bloomsbury, 2019), 463.

8 These themes and the political positions that emerge from them have been explored at great length over the course of decades in the work of philosopher Judith Butler. Beginning with *Subjects of Desire: Hegelian Reflections in Twentieth-Century France* (New York: Columbia University Press, 1987), through her path-breaking work on gender, sexuality, and performativity,

feminist thought and praxis must necessarily be internationalist in its solidarities, alliances and outlook.

Black feminism as it emerged in the early twentieth century in the United States was not, of course, a homogenous enterprise. Differences among activists and intellectuals formed along lines of ideology and class, as Black Communist women 'modified or rejected certain aspects of the politics of respectability because they were neither seeking legitimacy from whites for their institution building, nor were they women trying to reconstruct black images through proper etiquette or accomplished midwifery'.[9] While it would take some decades for sexuality to make its way into Black left feminist discourse, it is clear that radical Black working-class women rejected the norms and ideals of white bourgeois feminine respectability and their middle-class sisters' attempts to reform their behaviour.[10] What is clear from this earlier period of radical Black feminism is that the brilliant and bold work of the likes of Angela Y. Davis, Barbara Ransby, June Jordan, Audre Lorde and the Combahee River Collective, just to name a few prominent Black feminists to emerge in the 1960s and '70s, was most certainly situated in a lineage of Black left feminism and more specifically, Black feminist involvement in the Communist Party USA and internationalist, Third World socialist movements.[11]

Angela Y. Davis has often, and from early on, located her own political and scholarly work within this trajectory. For instance, in her autobiography, Davis recalls her vital connection to Claudia Jones, a militant anti-racist Communist activist. Born in Trinidad in 1915, Jones immigrated to the United States at an early age. Persecuted for her political activities, she was arrested and detained in prison no fewer than three times between 1948 and 1953; she was eventually convicted under the Smith Act and sentenced to a year in prison.[12] When Jones was deported from the United States in 1955, she went

to her exploration of ontology, politics and the constitution of subjects through the optics of grievability and mourning, to her more recent works *Notes Towards a Performative Theory of Assembly* (Boston, MA: Harvard University Press, 2015) and *The Force of Non-Violence: The Ethical in the Political* (London: Verso, 2020) Butler has produced a body of work that invites us to consider, in these times of genocidal violence and authoritarianism, the ways in which we are fundamentally relational beings and the implications of this for individual and collective responsibility and solidarity.

9 LaShawn Harris, as quoted in Erik S. McDuffie, *Sojourning for Freedom: Black Women, American Communism, and the Making of Black Left Feminism* (Durham: Duke University Press, 2011), 10.

10 See Saidiya Hartman, *Wayward Lives, Beautiful Experiments: Intimate Histories of Social Upheaval* (New York: W.W. Norton & Company, 2019); McDuffie, *Sojourning*, 11.

11 See David F. Gore, Jeanne Theoharis and Komozi Woodart, eds., *Want to Start a Revolution? Radical Women in the Black Freedom Struggle* (New York: New York University Press, 2009); McDuffie, *Sojourning*.

12 The 1940 Smith Act, formally titled the Alien Registration Act, was used to criminalise anyone who advocated or organised the violent overthrow of the government or belonged to a

to London, where she resided in exile until her death in 1964. During her time in London, she cofounded the *West Indian Gazette and Afro-Asian Caribbean News*, the West Indian Workers and Students' Association, as well as the Carnival in West London. She was a trenchant critic of UK immigration policies and worked as part of an international solidarity movement for the end of apartheid in South Africa. Jones's outlook was fundamentally feminist, anti-imperialist, anti-capitalist and internationalist, as evident in her political activism, essays and poetry.[13]

Writing about the few books that were held in the prison library in New York where she was detained following months underground (which included 'a book on the Chinese Revolution by Edgar Snow, the autobiography of W.E.B. Du Bois and a book on communism written by an astonishingly objective little-known author'), Davis describes their 'enigmatic presence', and realisation that the pages of those books had likely been read by 'Elizabeth Gurley Flynn, Claudia Jones or one of the other Communist leaders who had been persecuted under the Smith Act during the McCarthy era'.[14] While Davis writes about 'feeling honoured to be following in the tradition of some of this country's most outstanding heroines, Communist women leaders', we find Davis's words remarkable in another way: namely, in their articulation of a kind of connection and memory, a felt proximity provoked through the pages of a book and by the physical and emotional experience of confinement. As noted above, this connection, both imagined and real, is crucial for understanding the conditions under which revolutionary struggle, radical thought and praxis can and do emerge. While we use Davis's words as an example of the vital need to recognise and remember such connections to our radical feminist lineages, this mode of remembering, recalling, of memory work, is a significant aspect of much critical race theory, from the work of Patricia J. Williams and Derrick Bell[15] to the scholarship of Avery F. Gordon, whose book *The Hawthorn Archive: Letters from the Utopian Margins* finds company with other works that do not adhere to strict divisions and conventions of genre.

Among other shared concerns, US- and British-based Black feminisms both engage transgenerational and transcontinental perspectives. While we do not aim to provide a genealogy of the development of Black feminism in

---

group that did so. The act was used to prosecute members of the Socialist Workers Party and the Communist Party of the United States of America.

13 See Carole Boyce Davies, ed., *Claudia Jones: Beyond Containment* (Banbury: Ayebia Clarke Publishing, 2011); and Marika Sherwood, ed., *Claudia Jones: A Life in Exile* (London: Lawrence & Wishart, 1999).

14 Angela Y. Davis, *Angela Davis: An Autobiography* (New York: Random House, 1974), 51

15 See, for instance, Patricia J. Williams, *The Alchemy of Race and Rights: Diary of a Law Professor* (Cambridge, MA: Harvard University Press, 1991); Derrick Bell, *And We are Not Saved: The Elusive Quest for Racial Justice* (New York: Basic Books, 1987).

the UK,[16] which, moreover, is not a homogenous group or school of feminism, we will note that it emerged in the wake of large-scale migration from the former British Empire in the postwar period. Confronting myriad forms of racism and sexism in the fields of employment and work, immigration law, healthcare, housing, education and social welfare, and of course, faced with endemic police violence, collective feminist struggles for justice arose in the crucible of decolonisation, anti-imperialism and resistance to state-based racism in the UK. The formation of a political identity of Blackness was based on shared experiences and political objectives among Asian, Afro- and Indo-Caribbean, and African descent.[17] We want to explore the immense amounts of intellectual and emotional labour involved in the creation of such solidarities, a concrete history that serves, in our view, as a vital and exemplary instance of the kind of praxis required to deal with the current conjuncture of neoliberal, extractivist and militarised global capitalism.

If Black feminism as it emerged in the nineteenth and twentieth centuries in the United States was internationalist in the trajectories that many women followed, Black feminism as it developed in the UK was diverse in its very composition, owing to the history of the British Empire. Women from Africa, the Caribbean and Asia, in all their diasporic richness, found common ground as they struggled against a neo-imperialist and racist state formation in Britain. In the 1960s and '70s, Black feminists in the UK were at the forefront of resistance to racist violence, both at the hands of the Far Right (who were encouraged by politicians such as Enoch Powell), the private and public sectors (in relation to unemployment and racist working conditions) and state racism (in relation to education, health services and social welfare policy). Some of the most poignant industrial action that took place during those decades saw women workers striking, after struggling for union recognition, over unfair and discriminatory working conditions at the Grunwick photo-processing factory, the Chix bubblegum factory in Slough, the Imperial Typewriters in Leicester and elsewhere.

The militancy of trade unionism, particularly among large groups of immigrant workers of colour, was deeply affected by Margaret Thatcher's brutal assault on the miners and on industrial relations more generally. The compound effect of highly restrictive labour laws governing industrial action, coupled with a long history of trade unions' failure to adequately represent the interests of racialised workers, can be seen in the Gate Gourmet strike of 2005. In that case, a workforce comprised of largely South Asian women workers arrived at their airport catering jobs one day to find employment agency workers in the workplace, in the midst of a long process of restructuring the

16 See Heidi Safia Mirza, *Black British Feminism: A Reader* (London: Routledge, 1997).

17 Nydia Swaby, 'Disparate in Voice, Sympathetic in Direction: Gendered Political Blackness and the Politics of Solidarity', *Feminist Review* 108 (2014), 11–25.

company. Over the course of two days, over 670 workers would be fired, giving rise to weeks of strike action.[18]

Two male shop stewards of the Transport and General Workers' Union (TGWU), Pat Breslin and Mark Fisher, were sacked for organising a wildcat solidarity strike that saw British Airways baggage handlers stop work for two days, costing the airline between 30 and 40 million pounds. The Gate Gourmet workers, originally employed by British Airways until they contracted out their catering services to Gate Gourmet in the 1990s, were part of a South Asian (and largely Punjabi) community in Southall who have long ties as employees with British Airways and Heathrow Airport, and these baggage handlers, who were also TGWU members, were very upset by the treatment of their colleagues. Under labour legislation such solidarity actions are illegal, and the two TGWU stewards were fired for organising them. They were, however, eventually awarded very large compensatory settlement payments by TGWU and the airline, under conditions of confidentiality. The former shop stewards were 'allegedly following union orders'[19] (presumably, as they had been following union orders to take illegal action), and if they had successfully proven that, the ripple effects of liability for the union would have been potentially disastrous.[20]

The outcomes of the strike action by the Gate Gourmet workers left many of the women workers feeling betrayed by their union.[21] The TGWU negotiated a settlement that enabled the company to achieve many of its desired objectives – such as the reinstatement of some of the striking workers, but on worse terms (less sick leave, less pay for overtime and other changes). Some workers took voluntary redundancy. But fifty-six of the women refused to accept voluntary redundancy or compensation and continued their struggle for several years. By 2009, all but a handful of workers had had their unfair dismissal claims rejected by the Reading Employment Tribunal.[22] The strike is both a testament to the ongoing militancy of women of colour workers and a reflection of the particularly punitive consequences they face due to outsourcing, privatisation, and restrictive labour legislation.

In other employment sectors and institutions populated by relatively more privileged workers, such as the civil service, universities, or museums and galleries, sociologist Nirmal Puwar argues 'we are witnessing an unflagging

18 Daniel Pimlott and Suneal Housley, 'FT Briefing: Gate Gourmet Dispute', *Financial Times*, 23 August 2005, ft.com.

19 David Hencke, '£600,000 for Shop Stewards Fired over Gate Gourmet Strike', *Guardian*, 17 September 2006, theguardian.com.

20 'Gate Gourmet – Chronology of Events', University of Leeds official website, leeds.ac.uk/strikingwomen/gategourmet/chronology.

21 Sundari Anitha and Ruth Pearson, 'The Gate Gourmet Dispute', Striking Women, striking-women.org.

22 'Gate Gourmet – Chronology of Events'.

multicultural hunger within the drive for diversity'. 'Alongside this shift', she notes, 'long-standing traditions seem to be alive and well, as the spiritual, authentic, exotic, religious, ceremonial, innocent and barbaric continue to be the dominant ways in which diverse bodies are received.'[23] She shows, with great nuance, the complex and ambivalent status of the racialised body in spaces that have hitherto been closed to the presence of these 'space invaders'. Our experiences in the workplace continue to be shaped by hyper-surveillance, rigid and reified categories of legitimate speech, and the steadfast grip of 'somatic norms' which render racialised bodies out of place vis-à-vis a universal subject who remains white and male.

As with today's austerity policies and the cuts to councils and local governments that followed the 2008 financial crash, a disproportionate number of women and people of colour were affected by Thatcherite labour policies as they held jobs in sectors affected by budgetary cuts.[24] And thus it is crucial to recognise, as Akwugo Emejulu and Leah Bassel argue, the 2008 crisis intensified, rather than produced anew, the effects of a racialised social and economic order that has always operated to the disadvantage of women of colour workers.[25] And while it is also imperative to recognise the vast differences in the conditions of work for working-class women of colour and middle-class professionals, the pressures of austerity and cuts to funding, along with the increasing precarity of work across practically all public sectors of employment, have certainly impacted even relatively privileged women of colour workers.

The concrete issues around which Black and anti-racist feminists organised from the 1960s onwards included housing, health, social welfare and immigration. The work done by organisations such as OWAAD (Organisation of Women of African and Asian Descent, founded in 1978) and Southall Black Sisters (founded in 1979), among many others[26] would lay the groundwork for feminist resistance to austerity and discriminatory immigration policies that continue today (see, for instance, the work of Focus E15, or Sisters Uncut UK).

Of course, there were omissions, exclusions and difficulties in Black feminist movements in the UK. Sexuality was largely absent in the political positions and concerns they articulated. In a collective conversation titled

---

23 Nirmal Puwar, *Space Invaders: Race, Gender and Bodies Out of Place* (London: Berg Publishers, 2004), 69.

24 See Beverly Bryan, Stella Dadzie, and Suzanne Scafe, *Heart of the Race: Black Women's Lives in Britain* (London: Virago Press, 1985; London and New York: Verso, 2018). Citations refer to the Verso edition.

25 Akwugo Emejulu and Leah Bassel, 'Women of Colour's Anti-Austerity Activism: They Cut, We Bleed', in *The Violence of Austerity*, ed. Vickie Cooper and David Whyte (London: Pluto Press, 2017), 117–22.

26 See Julia Sudbury, *'Other Kinds of Dreams': Black Women's Organisations and the Politics of Transformation* (London: Routledge, 1998).

'Becoming Visible: Black Lesbian Discussions' published in the 1984 OWAAD issue of *Feminist Review*, four lesbian women (one of whom, Gail Lewis, features in this volume) discuss the intense difficulties and challenges they contended with in the process of coming out, both within Black feminist organisations such as OWAAD and in relation to family and community. Deeply entrenched homophobia and heterosexism, compounded by racist notions that white, liberal social and familial spaces were somehow more enlightened in relation to sexuality than Asian and Black communities, made coming out a very fraught process for Black lesbians.[27]

It was therefore a groundbreaking development when Black lesbian and queer feminists in the 1970s and '80s managed to put sexuality on the agenda at major women's conferences, including the OWAAD conference in 1983. In spite of such victories, as Roderick Ferguson reminds us in *One Dimensional Queer*, dominant queer histories have not ceased to fall prey to the erasure of their multiracial and coalitional character. Our interview in this volume with Gary Kinsman traces some of the ambiguities and contradictions of activism from the 1970s onwards that sought to bring together anti-racist, queer and anti-capitalist critique with resistance to militarism and many other forms of state violence. This early political work, and all of the labour it entailed, set the scene for the development and reception of a queer of colour critique. A queer of colour critique, as defined by Ferguson, seeks to place the figure who has been routinely marginalised in radical Western epistemologies – the queer of colour, the sex worker, the vagrant – as the central subject in our theoretical frameworks and political concerns. Methodologically, it means engaging 'nonheteronormative racial formations as sites of ruptures, critiques, and alternatives'.[28]

This is especially pertinent for thinking through the task of cultivating critical, creative and oppositional positions in relation to contemporary nationalisms and global capital. Moreover, Ferguson argues that in reformulating culture and agency, and opposing nationalism and the state form, women of colour feminisms 'helped to designate the imagination as a social practice under contemporary globalisation. In a moment in which national liberation movements and Western nation-states disfranchised women of colour and queer of colour subjects, culture, for those groups, became the obvious scene of alternate agency.' Culture became the field from which to imaginatively work against the disfranchisements of nationalism and the debilities of global capital. [29] Many of the interviewees in this volume are poets,

---

27 Carmen, Gail, Shaila et al., 'Becoming Visible: Black Lesbian Discussions', *Feminist Review* 17 (July 1984), 53–72.

28 Roderick Ferguson, *Aberrations in Black: Towards a Queer of Colour Critique* (Minneapolis: University of Minnesota Press, 2004), 18.

29 Ibid., 117.

fiction writers or photographers, and have engaged other media (such as film) as part of their praxis, providing many rich examples of how cultural and artistic practices are central dimensions of radical thought.

Of course, another major difficulty with which Black feminists in both the UK and the United States have had to contend is the racism of mainstream or white feminist movements (whether liberal or socialist).[30] Julia Sudbury, in her groundbreaking book *'Other Kinds of Dreams': Black Women's Organisations and the Politics of Transformation*,[31] utilises the term 'womanist' as a means of recognising how fraught the term 'feminist' was for some Black women activists in the 1990s. She writes:

> Womanism is also symbolic of my accountability to a community of Black women activists for whom the term 'feminism' is associated with daily struggles against racist exclusion by white women's organisations. The interviewee whose funding application for a Black women's refuge had been undercut by the local [white] women's refuge claiming to serve 'all' women. The organisation which had been allocated a white feminist project officer by the local authority only to discover that the latter was opposed to 'Black separatism' and consistently sought to undermine their work. The black women who have had to oppose white feminist calls for increased policing in primarily black neighbourhoods, in the name of 'women's safety' . . . For many black women in 1990s Britain, 'sisterhood' with white feminists is a luxury which may be afforded at an abstract level, but when issues of funding and power are at stake, it would be naïve to assume that sisterly solidarity will determine white women's actions.[32]

One may query how much has changed since the 1990s on this score. While the term 'intersectionality' rolls off the tongues of many white feminists with quotidian frequency, it is clear that the lack of meaningful solidarity between women of colour and white feminists has not been ameliorated.

Oftentimes, Marxist and socialist (feminist) events and spaces, even when well intentioned, involve groups of people who are poorly informed about histories of colonialism and issues of race, and, one surmises, deeply attached

---

30 Our use of the term 'whiteness' is heavily informed by, among others, the analysis of David R. Roediger, *The Wages of Whiteness: Race and the Making of the American Working Class*, 2nd ed. (London and New York: Verso, 2007), wherein, drawing on the work of W.E.B. Du Bois and others, whiteness is understood, like other racial categories, as fabricated and unstable, yet absolutely central to capitalist forms of labour exploitation, slavery and colonisation. As Vron Ware and Les Back discuss in *Out of Whiteness: Color, Politics and Culture* (Chicago: University of Chicago Press, 2001), giving meaning (economic, social, psychic) to whiteness involves cultural and political processes that are specific to each place (be that a particular nation-state or geopolitical region).

31 Sudbury, *'Other Kinds of Dreams'*.

32 Ibid., 47.

to their refusal to think through the ways race is central to capitalist social and political orders. Thus, for many women of colour feminists, to engage with them is an exercise in frustration, at best – and at worst, requires subjecting oneself to a kind of invisibility and erasure. While this project itself was initially motivated by a justifiable sense of plaintiveness, and fatigue, at the continual marginalisation of left, anti-racist feminist thought and praxis, that sense of complaint was fairly quickly overwhelmed by a satisfying sense of the peripherality of 'white feminism' to the thought and praxis explored in this volume.

Nonetheless, it remains crucial to note that the institutionalised power of white feminism remains an obstacle for those of us who centre race and colonialism in our work; many of us have experienced the nonrecognition of white feminist colleagues (particularly in academia) who refuse to even acknowledge our work as 'feminist'.[33] Recently, several feminist scholars have critiqued the way the discourse of intersectionality has been appropriated by white feminists without sufficiently acknowledging or engaging with the feminists of colour who developed the concept.[34] In a not dissimilar fashion, we have also seen socialist feminists criticising the concept of intersectionality without taking the time, we would argue, to adequately study the diverse body of scholarship that evolved the concept and its associated forms of praxis, prematurely dismissing it as inadequate to challenge contemporary forms of capitalism.

Methodologies: Historical Materialism and its Feminist Instantiations

If there is a common thread among the feminists interviewed in this book, it is their long-standing and critical engagement with historical materialism. What is historical materialism? At its most elemental level, it can be understood as a form of critique that situates itself within social relations.[35] Marx understood 'social relations of production' to be the totality of relationships that encompass our personal and family lives, our interactions in the workplace and with the state, and our associations with communities or groups of people.

Capitalist social relations, the form that has come to dominate the globe, have always been differentiated by forces generated by colonial history, imperialism, war economies, and the patriarchal, racial and heteronormative nature of those formations. More than 'stretch' Marxism to account for

33 See Patricia Hill Collins, 'Learning from the Outsider Within: The Sociological Significance of Black Feminist Thought', *Social Problems* 33:6 (Autumn 1986): 14–32.

34 For debates on the misappropriation of intersectionality by white feminists, see Sirma Bilge, 'Intersectionality Undone: Saving Intersectionality from Feminist Intersectionality Studies', *Du Bois Review* 10:2 (2013): 405–24; and Jennifer C. Nash, *Black Feminism Reimagined: After Intersectionality* (Durham: Duke University Press, 2019) for a complex engagement with Black feminists' response to the uptake of intersectionality by mainstream academic feminists.

35 Ferguson, *Aberrations in Black*, 4.

colonialism (as Frantz Fanon did), feminists have had to remake Marxist categories of analysis to more fully account for the centrality of race, gender and sexuality to capitalist social relations.

These critical feminist engagements with historical materialism have taken many different forms.[36] One is the trajectory of work that emerged in the 1970s in Italy, shaped by the defeat of fascism and the aftermath of the Second World War. Silvia Federici, Mariarosa Dalla Costa, Leopoldina Fortunati and others undertook highly significant critical interventions into Marxist theory and practice by emphasising the centrality of women's reproductive labour in the home to the reproduction of capitalist social relations – a massive absence in Marx's and Marxist labour theories of value. Fortunati's *The Arcane of Reproduction: Housework, Prostitution, Labor and Capital* (1981) embodies a form of immanent critique whereby the value of women's labour is thought of in terms of Marx's critique of capitalist social relations. Here, she shows how women's housework is a process of value creation by demonstrating that it is a process of commodity production: it is only through the socially reproductive labour of women in the home that the individual male worker is able to reproduce himself as labour power, as use value for value.[37] Fortunati's work shows how women's housework is fundamentally *productive labour*, in Marx's own definitions of the term.

The difficult question of how to value such productive labour, given the temporality, duration and nature of reproductive housework – it is, after all, work that never ends – is one Fortunati took up at a theoretical level. At a political level, it was taken up by the Wages for Housework (WFH) campaign, also rooted in the idea that housework is productive, value-producing labour which both capital and the state rely upon to function. In terms of its 'methodology', the WFH campaign reflected a form of praxis influenced by a diverse range of critical engagements with Marxist thought and political work. The campaign occupied a very ambivalent, if not divisive, place in feminist organising. One of the critiques pertinent to our concerns in this volume is the early one rendered by Angela Y. Davis, namely, that WFH utterly failed to account for the histories of Black women's servitude and domestic labour, both unpaid and paid.[38] The same could be said for

36 Above, we discussed the intellectual and political trajectories of some Black feminists both in the United States and the UK, which can be understood as a long history of critical engagement with communist politics and historical materialism as a method, more generally.

37 Leopoldina Fortunati, *The Arcane of Housework: Housework, Prostitution, Labor and Capital*, trans. Hilary Creek (New York: Autonomedia, 1995), 78.

38 Angela Y. Davis, 'The Approaching Obsolescence of Housework: A Working-Class Perspective', in *Women, Race and Class*, ed. Angela Y. Davis (London: The Women's Press, 1981). For critical engagements with social reproduction feminism that take into account racialisation, colonialism and globalisation, see 'Dossier: Social Reproduction Theory', in *Radical Philosophy*,

Fortunati's work, published a decade after Davis's critical work on Black women and reproductive labour.

In Italy during the 1960s and '70s, the work of Mario Tronti and the concept of *operaismo* (workerism) rose to some prominence in Europe.[39] In particular, the idea of the 'social factory' – which articulated the view that capitalist forms of production seen in the factory would increasingly extend outwards, eventually encompassing all of social life – was quite influential on the work of Silvia Federici and other Italian feminists. However, Federici's intellectual work and political experiences took her in radically different directions from operaismo; as explored in her interview in this volume, her time in both the United States and Nigeria shaped her understanding of reproductive labour to account for global political economies of labour, and histories of colonisation and racism. Federici's method was influenced in part by the work of Tronti, particularly with regard to the idea that radical change always begins with workers themselves rather than exogenous forces.[40] This remains embedded in her theorisation of socially reproductive labour, which does not begin with the abstract but is resolutely grounded in the productive work and activities of people who are usually invisibilised within mainstream political economic work. Despite the critiques of WFH, the crucial need to recognise and value the productive work of women in the home (both paid and unpaid) remains an essential part of efforts to abolish racialised patriarchy, and gender as we currently know it.

If it is not clear by now, let us emphasise that the methods developed by the feminists interviewed in this volume prioritise as their points of departure the grounded, place- and site-specific, phenomenal (i.e., experiential), and embodied, lived realities of differently situated subjects. For instance, the 'diasporic' method[41] developed by Avtar Brah emphasises the spatial dimension of the performance and embodiment of racial identification and subjectivisation, gender relations, and class-consciousness in particular sites of migration and movement. The spatial politics of migration and dislocation typify Brah's method and find points of contact with other leading critical race feminists, such as Sherene Razack, who have established new pathways of thought in relation to the spatial politics of race, gender, class and colonialism.[42]

---

series 2, 2:4 (2019), with articles by Sara Salem and Mai Taha, Alessandra Mezzadri, Kalindi Vora and Silvia Federici.

39 See Mario Tronti, *Workers and Capital*, trans. David Broder (London and New York: Verso, 2019), originally published as *Operai e capitale* (Torino: Einaudi, 1966).

40 See George Souvlis and Ankica Čakardić, 'Feminism and Social Reproduction: An Interview with Silvia Federici', *Salvage* [2017], salvage.zone.

41 See the interview with Avtar Brah in this volume.

42 See Sherene Razack, *Looking White People in the Eye: Gender, Race and Culture in the Courtrooms and Classrooms* (Toronto: University of Toronto Press, 1998); 'Gendered Racial Violence and Spatialized Justice: The Murder of Pamela George', *Canadian Journal of Law and*

The spatial dynamics of capitalism – the mainstay of critical Marxist geography – have, in the words of Ruth Wilson Gilmore, 'everything to do with human-environment interactions . . . the social, and the scale and organisation of capitalist and anti-capitalist space'.[43] Gilmore, part of a group of radical Black geographers, has expanded the bounds of her discipline in conjunction with decades of activism for the abolition of the prison industrial complex. In *Golden Gulag*, she analyses the spatial and financial abstractions that determined where and how prison expansion was planned in California in the 1990s; moreover, she brings these geographies into direct confrontation with the lived realities on the ground – the specific places, people and communities that bear the material consequences of the violence of abstraction. Her work is an object lesson in how to think about scale, and how to investigate the mutually constituting relationships between domestic spheres, local government, the state, and the global economy. Her work reflects an acute sensitivity to recent and longer histories of struggle against racial capitalism that are present in the urban and rural, and significantly, challenges this divide itself.

To begin with actual, existing social relations and not with the abstract requires an immense amount of intellectual labour. Our interviews with Himani Bannerji, Gail Lewis and Vron Ware explicitly illuminate how in the context of feminist organising and political work in the 1970s and '80s, one was expected to do the work of informing oneself about a range of issues of geopolitical import that lay outside their own immediate range of concerns. This was what building solidarity required: taking the time to do the research, to read, engage with, listen to people whose experiences and conditions of work and life were sometimes radically different to your own. This was the essence of creating shared and common political ground for collective action. While debates continue to rage about the perils of appropriation – of 'speaking for' others from a position of privileged ignorance, of adopting a lazy cultural relativism in approaching the conditions of people who live according to norms, cultural practices and philosophies that are not liberal, Western or secular[44] – these earlier feminist commitments to the expansion of one's understanding of people in other parts of the world, or in other parts of the city one inhabits, for that matter, were undertaken with the aim of building solidarity.

Throughout, there was an emphasis on the challenges of building such solidarity within the existing hierarchies that characterise the differences between feminists. As Brah writes:

Society 15:2 (August 2000): 91–130; and Razack, ed., *Race, Space and the Law: Unmapping a White Settler Society* (Toronto: Between the Lines Press, 2002).

43 See the interview with Ruth Wilson Gilmore in this volume.

44 See Saba Mahmood, *The Politics of Piety: The Islamic Revival and the Feminist Subject* (New Jersey: Princeton University Press, 2011).

> Is this not one of the most difficult things to do, positioned, as each and every one of us is, in some relationship of hierarchy, authority or dominance to another? How do we construct, both individually and collectively, non-logocentric political practices – theoretical paradigms, political activism, as well as modes of relating to another person – which galvanize identification, empathy and affinity, and not only 'solidarity'?[45]

Brah breaks open the notion of political solidarity to include terms that could loosely be described as affective – empathy and affinity. Her provocation also posits the individual and collective character of the challenges that critical race scholars and Third World, Marxist feminists have been working through for decades: the challenges of creating political spaces and intellectual frames of analysis that account for the complex reality of power relations between and among women. The desire to construct non-logocentric political practices also reflects the desire to refuse (or at least, to make visible) symbolic and linguistic orders that constrain our political imaginaries, and the very real, concrete ways in which we make sense of the world around us.

Asserting voice and claiming space

The authors of the pathbreaking *Heart of the Race: Black Women's Lives in Britain* (first published in 1985) note, in their introduction, that what matters to them is the *way* Black women have challenged [their] state of triple bondage:

> Black women in Britain today are faced with few positive self-images and little knowledge of our true potential. If we are to gain anything from our history and from our lives in this country which can be of practical use to us today, we must take stock of our experiences, assess our responses – and learn from them. This will be done by listening to the voices of the mothers, sisters, grandmothers and aunts who established our presence here. And by listening to our own voices.[46]

They proceed to frame their intervention into contemporary issues of racism, sexism and class exploitation with a history of labour relations, resistance and revolt. The history of slavery and indentureship, throughout the Caribbean in particular, and the modes of resistance employed by the colonised inform their understanding of contemporary Black politics in the UK. As they note, writing in relation to 'the massive political upheaval throughout the 1930s', in Jamaica, Saint Kitts, Barbados and elsewhere in the Caribbean, the militant strike actions of workers – 'dockers, sugar workers, shop girls, street cleaners, domestic workers and casual labourers' – would serve the

---

45 Avtar Brah, 'The Scent of Memory: Strangers, Our Own, and Others', *Feminist Review* 61:1 (1999), 15.

46 Bryan et al., *Heart of the Race*, 2.

workers well later on in England.[47] The authors put the agency of the enslaved, and in the aftermath of slavery, the colonised, populations of the Caribbean at the forefront of their understanding of the prehistory of the large-scale migration to the UK after World War II. And, following that, they trace the more recent modes of resistance into present struggles in the UK in relation to employment and labour, health services and housing. They show how discriminatory practices are historically embedded in the state apparatus. The book is exemplary in the method it employs: it is historically grounded from the perspective of Afro-Caribbean women, women who are workers, mothers, carers and a part of transcontinental and intergenerational communities.

Among Black feminist organisers, an emphasis on finding and asserting the political voice of their communities was certainly prominent throughout the 1980s and '90s. But this was not primarily rooted in a concern about impacting white-dominated spaces and discourses in pursuit of inclusion; it was a reflection of a demand to be seen and heard – both historically and in the present – as active agents and makers of their own lives.[48] They were not merely the victims or objects of racist state practices who needed to assert their voices in order to be 'heard' and 'listened to' in an ordinary sense. The demand 'to be listened to rather than examined or spoken for' was about creating a space where Black women could collectively 'define their own realities', based on their experiences as active agents of change.[49] These demands were never about some kind of liberal move towards reconciliation or mutual understanding, to be reached through dialogue with white people; rather, these were powerful assertions of autonomy.

It is a common misunderstanding that Black feminism stressed racial identity and fetishised difference to the detriment of structural change. This reading ignores the very nuanced writing and rich organising undertaken which insisted on grounding analysis in the lived reality of racism *within and against* capitalist social relations – studying how class itself is raced, while race is historically constructed and utilised to differentially insert communities into the economic system. The anti-racist critique was not a one-dimensional grievance around the inclusion of race, but an analytical intervention that detailed how a lack of attention to race produces a flawed analysis that does not adequately expose or help us to challenge the realities of capitalist exploitation. The interviewees in this book also point to the importance of rejecting culturalist essentialism and the commodification of racial identity into its most visible and 'colourful' aspects. In the Canadian context, Himani Bannerji has written powerfully about the co-optation of

47 Ibid., 14–15.

48 See Amrit Wilson, *Finding a Voice: South Asian Women in Britain* (London: Virago Press, 1978); and *Dreams, Questions, Struggles* (London: Pluto Press, 2006).

49 Hazel Carby, quoted in Sudbury, *Other Kinds of Dreams*, 16.

anti-racist organising into a liberal multiculturalism which reified static notions of culture and promoted diversity at the expense of social justice and economic equality. There are indeed stark differences between liberal notions of cultural diversity and those initially articulated by anti-racist feminisms, which ultimately aim to challenge institutionalised racism and dismantle structural oppression.

This is not to say that the diverse bodies of critical race feminist work have not been subjected to critiques, particularly with a notable shift in the 1990s to more identity-driven and individualistic tendencies. Julia Sudbury, for instance, charts a movement away from the emphasis on collective organising by Black women and towards engagements with race and racism that seemed to reify racial identity in ways that worked against collective action across differences:

> By the 1990s black women intellectuals who were at the forefront of national black women's organising in the 1980s were beginning to feel a sense of disillusionment with the methods of that very movement. Experience of the more excessive and essentialising forms of identity politics, 'guilt tripping' of white women, aggressive comparisons of oppression in a hierarchy of 'isms' all led to a questioning of the assumptions underlying black women's organisations.[50]

It is notable, therefore, that reissues of texts foundational to Black and critical race feminisms have become increasingly prevalent, and that many of these centre questions of solidarity and collective action. Importantly, their modes of praxis (discussed in more detail below) are rooted in critiques of individual leadership (a structure that often glorifies male leaders). The focus is on democratic grassroots organising that empowers every member to be able to do their part in movements, building from the ground up. As Angela Y. Davis notes in this volume, it has been heartening to see the reemergence, in the Black Lives Matter movement and contemporary Indigenous resistance to the intensification of dispossession through resource extraction, different models of collective organising that are not focused on the singular charisma of an individual (male) leader and that are coalitional in nature.

Indigenous Methodologies

It would be impossible to make generalisations about Indigenous methodologies of research, teaching and political activism, whether in the context of the Americas, Asia or more globally. We wish to briefly introduce two dimensions of Indigenous feminist methodologies emanating from Indigenous scholar-activists in what is now known as North America, and more specifically, Canada. The first is the notion of what some Indigenous scholars have termed

---

50 Ibid., 17–18.

'land-based pedagogy'.[51] The second is the importance of language in recovering and centring Indigenous ontologies and epistemologies.

Indigenous feminists – including Patricia Monture-Angus, Lee Maracle, Leanne Betasamosake Simpson, Audra Simpson, Bonita Lawrence, Theresa Nahanee, Emma LaRocque and, in Australia, Irene Watson and Aileen Moreton-Robinson, among many others – have emphasised the centrality of their relationship to land to the ontologies and epistemologies, and the survival, of First Nations. Indeed, land is their basis for learning about law, kinship, economy and social relations. In the words of Glen Coulthard, First Nations territories have 'associated forms of knowledge';[52] reflecting upon this idea, it becomes clear that colonisation is not only about settler states' desire for the land itself as a resource (or territory, in the sense of the Westphalian state form), but that the colonial dispossession of Indigenous land was and remains central to attempts to destroy First Nations communities. The genocidal intentions of settler states lie not only in the wide range of measures used to diminish, contain and destroy First Nations people, but in the suppression of Indigenous knowledge, ontologies and ways of living that are carried through and in the land. We understand this way of knowing to be radically relational, not simply with other human beings but with nonhuman life and land. This is a radically embodied practice of knowledge formation, for one needs to be on the land to learn.

Leanne Betasamosake Simpson offers a crucial point about children and parenting. In the Dechinta Bush University, which takes place on land of the Yellowknives Dene First Nation, children are welcome and included in the programme. This goes beyond recognition of the socially reproductive labour that many Indigenous and other parents (mainly women) undertake: here, 'children are co-learners and co-instructors'.[53] The collective nature of parenting at Dechinta Bush University, as in many non-Anglo and non-bourgeois communities, is an antidote to the poverty of the nuclear family form and also creates a richer and more dynamic learning environment for all present. There is a contact point here with the direction taken by scholar-activists, such as Federici, who see the health and well-being of children and the elderly as key aspects of the challenges of social reproduction under capitalism.

As mentioned above, an emphasis on learning, reviving and using Indigenous languages has long been central to anti- and de-colonial movements, and this remains the case in contemporary First Nations scholarship

51 Matthew Wildcat, Mandee McDonald, Stephanie Irlbacher-Fox et al., 'Learning from the Land: Indigenous Land-Based Pedagogy and Decolonization', *Decolonization: Indigeneity, Education and Society* 3:3 (2014): i-xv.

52 Eric Ritskes, 'Leanne Simpson and Glen Coulthard on Dechinta Bush University, Indigenous Land-Based Education and Embodied Resurgence', *Decolonization: Indigeneity, Education and Society* (2014).

53 Ibid.

and activism. Political scientist Noenoe K. Silva offers exemplary research on how the use of native language – in her case, Hawai'ian – can challenge imperial historiographies of dispossession.[54] Taking up long-standing critiques of the colonial archive, as formulated by Gayatri Spivak and others, Silva's commitment to completely reframing the history of Indigenous Hawai'ian political formations and resistance to colonisation is subtended by a close reading and analysis of sources in Hawai'ian. It becomes clear in her scholarship that the work of making native agency visible in the historical record, the work of recentring Indigenous Hawai'ian worldviews with a view to supporting Indigenous sovereignty movements, is intimately connected to, perhaps even dependent upon, her excavation and use of political concepts in Hawai'ian.

Ngũgĩ wa Thiong'o's 1986 essay collection, *Decolonising the Mind*, written from the locus of postcolonial East Africa, begins with a reflection on the issues facing African writers at the time of independence. At the forefront of his concerns was the primary place of language in the enunciation of an anti-colonial politics, and in the continuation of the epistemic violence of colonisation into the postcolonial moment:

> Berlin of 1884 was effected through the sword and the bullet. But the night of the sword and the bullet was followed by the morning of the chalk and the blackboard. The physical violence of the battlefield was followed by the psychological violence of the classroom . . . In my view language was the most important vehicle through which that power fascinated and held the soul prisoner.[55]

We can consider, on the one hand, how the question of language was and remains central in its relation to culture and cultural practices – and intimately bound to the way we see the world, and our shared priorities about how to live. On the other hand, as African and Caribbean writers have long argued, it is also true that people have made the language of their former colonial masters their own, bending, reshaping and appropriating it in ways that produce new dialects and alternate lexicons pertinent to their particular locations and lifeways.

Whatever one's position, it is clear that First Nations are engaged in a long-standing and continuous struggle to revive and use Indigenous languages as a part of a larger, global, anti-colonial struggle that has no clear end in sight.

---

54 See Noenoe K. Silva, *Aloha Betrayed: Native Hawaiian Resistance to American Colonialism* (Durham: Duke University Press, 2004); and *The Power of the Steel-Tipped Pen: Reconstructing Native Hawaiian Intellectual History* (Durham: Duke University Press, 2017).

55 Ngũgĩ wa Thiong'o, *Decolonising the Mind: The Politics of Language in African Literature* (London: East African Educational Publishers, 1986), 9.

Radical Imaginaries and Praxis

While there has been a general taming of the mainstream feminist movement, through its professionalisation and institutionalisation at UN conferences and within nongovernmental organisations, along with forms of glass ceiling feminism, a common thread among those interviewed in this book is a commitment to a transformative feminist praxis and collective action that aims for systemic and radical change. The term 'praxis' itself implies an organic interconnectedness of theory and practice in challenging ongoing inequalities and confronting histories of colonial and imperial domination. In this sense, radical knowledge production, the development of new methodologies and political activism are not in reality separable, and they do not exist as distinct categories.

Here, we understand the term 'radical' in the sense that Ella Baker, a central figure in the civil rights movement in the US who played a pivotal role in the Southern Christian Leadership Conference, and the Student Nonviolent Coordinating Committee, uses it: understanding and resisting the root causes of economic, social and cultural oppression embedded in racial capitalism. The aim of such praxis is not simply to reform aspects of the current system, but to radically transform the totality of social relations through oppositional and coalitional politics. It is steeped in the long histories of Indigenous, Black, and Third World resistance to colonialism and imperialism, and radical imaginaries for a better world that were forged in relation to and dialogue with each other.

Ella Baker famously emphasised the importance of education to develop every individual's leadership capacity, allowing every person to be a full participant in their own liberation rather than an observer waiting for orders from the top of hierarchical structures. Every social movement and/or campaign mentioned in the following interviews utilised a variety of strategies, tactics, research, alliances and modes of outreach and internal education. They produced knowledge, debated methods and made their fair share of mistakes, as well, while holding a deep belief in the ability of ordinary people to both understand and translate daily conditions into radical demands for change. Each experience deserves a book in its own right, to excavate the modes of knowledge production and community building that took place, and continue to take place, in its respective geographic and historical contexts. As social movements scholar Aziz Choudry notes, oftentimes, 'given the academic emphasis on whether an action, campaign, or movement can be judged a "success", the intellectual work that takes place in movements frequently goes unseen, as do the politics, processes, sites, and locations of knowledge production and learning in activist settings.'[56] In light of this, we use the space that

56 Aziz Choudry, *Learning Activism: The Intellectual Life of Contemporary Social Movements* (Toronto: University of Toronto Press, 2015), 1.

remains here to simply highlight a few common threads among the forms of praxis that are relevant to ongoing struggles.

The praxis emerging from collectives like the Combahee River Collective, the Brixton Black Women's Group, the Organisation of Women of African and Asian Descent, and Southall Black Sisters focused on the complex reality of the lived experience of class oppression and gendered racism within and beyond the workplace. This pushed against some strands within left politics that saw radical action as taking place only at the so-called point of production, thus fetishising the industrial male worker. Their understanding of the totality of social relations as located within the body, home, community and workplace, in turn, opened up important avenues for organising in multiple sites. For example, in the UK context, Asian and Black women's collectives were at the forefront of a number of long industrial struggles, and they also organised against racist anti-immigration campaigns such as the infamous virginity tests, while at the same time tackling issues of domestic violence and actively organising against fascist violence targeting their communities.

This multi-scalar organising was vital to building coalitions between Black and South Asian feminists – coalitions that worked to tackle state-sponsored racism and sexism while openly discussing how communities and individuals are differentially racialised. This required very patient and conscientious work to study how class, race and gender operate in specific historical conjunctures. The analytic link they drew between class and race helped to articulate an inclusive and militant Black political identity. As we have noted, there were tensions and contradictions in this form of coalitional politics – yet it remains an important moment that foregrounded political unity.

This political identification was also reflected in novel forms of organising. Specifically, cultural production took on a vital role, as discussed above. Our interlocutors, in the following pages, invoked the potent work of poets and authors like June Jordan, Audre Lorde, Toni Morrison and Dionne Brand, among many others, in helping to shape their politics, while powerfully naming racism as a lived reality. As Bannerji has put it elsewhere, 'the greatest gain, was meeting with young Black women, whose experience and politics matched with mine, whose poetry along with mine named our world'.[57] Theatre, music, poetry, poster art and spaces of leisure, as well, helped to create a sense of common struggle and community, but also to address challenging subjects. For example, in her interview, Brah explains the importance of community theatre productions in tackling taboo topics like domestic violence.

There are important lessons to draw from this mode of organising, whereby campaigns were orchestrated not from above but in collaboration, utilising varied repertoires of oppositional practices while continuously

57 Himani Bannerji, *Thinking Through: Essays on Feminism, Marxism and Anti-Racism* (Toronto: Women's Press, 1995), 59.

reassessing the political situation, allowing for shifts in tactics and multiple entry points for campaigners, as well as room for mistakes. As Brah puts it, 'we must take politically thought-through positions. Because I don't think we can have blueprints for all situations' (49). Thus, organising can develop with sensitivity to particular contexts, foregrounding community voices and needs. The prison abolition organisation Critical Resistance is a good example of a formation that has incorporated important aspects of this praxis, ensuring a multiplicity of tactics. Apart from more attention-grabbing legal cases against government departments, the group also produces a variety of media for outreach and builds grassroots coalitions whose aim is to stop prisons from being built in the first place.[58] Some of the most crucial work is mundane and hidden from public view – from setting up regular meeting times and places to ensuring continuity and access to the organising space.

Finally, a critical aspect of the praxis we are discussing is its internationalist orientation, and the struggle to build feminisms that stretch across national borders and mobilise against multiple imperial interventions. As noted above, anti-colonialism and anti-imperialism are foundational to Black, Indigenous and postcolonial feminism(s), and an internationalist stance continues to inflect their organising. Historically, its influence is evident in the profusion of statements and practical support for international solidarity campaigns against militarism and military occupations, including the anti-apartheid movement, solidarity with Palestine, and anti-imperialist opposition in Central America and Southern Africa. In more recent times, this has included a feminist response to the more overt racialisation of Arabs and Muslims under the guise of the War on Terror. The opposition to direct regional military interventions in Afghanistan and Iraq, long-term support for the state of Israel, and the internationalisation of racialised surveillance practices aimed at Arabs and Muslims have generated a rich body of feminist literature from within North Africa, West Asia, Europe and North America.[59] In Europe and North America, anti-racist feminists have advanced an anti-imperialist analysis and worked tirelessly to build multiracial anti-war coalitions and, especially, to add Palestine to the agenda of the progressive feminist movement. They have argued for a feminist praxis that centres support for anti-colonial struggles and understands solidarity with Palestine as a feminist issue.[60] More recently, this

---

58 Rose Braz et al., 'The History of Critical Resistance', *Social Justice* 27:3 (2000).

59 Rabab Abdulhadi, Nadine Naber and Evelyn al-Sultany, eds., *Arab American Feminisms: Gender, Violence and Belonging* (Syracuse: Syracuse University Press, 2011); Nadine Naber, *Arab America: Gender Politics and Activism* (New York: New York University Press, 2012); Nisha Kapoor, *Deport, Deprive, Extradite: 21st-Century State Extremism* (London and New York: Verso, 2018).

60 David Lloyd, 'It is our belief that Palestine is a Feminist Issue', *feminists@law* 4:1 (2014); Nadera Shalhoub-Kevorkian, 'Palestinian Feminist Critique and the Physics of Power: Feminists Between Thought and Practice', *feminists@law* 4:1 (2014); Rana Sharif, 'Bodies, Buses and Permits: Palestinians Navigating Care', *feminists@law* 4:1 (2014); Brenna Bhandar, 'Some Reflections on

has included advancing the Palestinian-led Boycott, Divestment and Sanctions (BDS) campaign, which in turn has galvanised discussions within the feminist movement. As Palestinian scholar-activist Rabab Abdulhadi has asserted however, this work was underpinned by much-longer-standing solidarities, built through decades of anti-imperialist and anti-capitalist organising in different contexts.[61] In other words, there is nothing spontaneous about solidarity; it is historically rooted and comes about through consistent dialogue, learning /unlearning, and joint struggle.

It is common to present the contemporary moment as one of multiple crises and ongoing emergencies; as Lauren Berlant puts it, 'politics is defined by a collectively held sense that a glitch has appeared in the reproduction of life. A glitch is an interruption within a transition, a troubled transmission. A glitch is also the revelation of an infrastructural failure.'[62] If we are to face this 'infrastructural failure', the reimagining and revitalisation of anti-capitalist and anti-racist feminist politics is crucial. It is no coincidence, then, that we are seeing social movements take on multiple issues and make the links between political, economic, environmental and social demands. Various movements, from Black Lives Matter, Idle No More and the Women's Marches to the teachers' strikes, the square occupations across southern Europe and the Arab uprisings, have brought with them critical questions about forms of organising and sustainability, as well as a growing interest in radical anti-colonial and anti-imperialist feminisms. This surge in interest has not been based on abstract theory but has originated overwhelmingly with people in movements who are interested in learning from past resistance.

As we confront the impending climate catastrophe, which is becoming more widely understood among different layers of the population, this broader movement desperately needs to centre feminist anti-racism in its analysis.[63] As many anti-racist activists have pointed out, ignoring the fact

---

BDS and Feminist Political Solidarity', *feminists@law* 4:1 (2014); Nadine Naber, 'A Call for Consistency: Palestinian Resistance and Radical US Women of Color', in *Color of Violence: The Incite! Anthology* (Durham: Duke University Press, 2006); Linda Tabar and Chandni Desai, 'Decolonization Is a Global Project: From Palestine to the Americas', *Decolonization: Indigeneity, Education and Society* 6:1 (2017): i–xix; Nada Elia, 'Justice Is Indivisible: Palestine as a Feminist Issue', *Decolonization: Indigeneity, Education and Society* 6:1 (2017): 45–63.

61 Rabab Abdulhadi, [plenary] American Studies Association Conference 2014: 'Black Radicalism, Insurgency in Israel/Palestine and the Idea of Solidarity', [Posted July 2015] YouTube, youtube.com.

62 Lauren Berlant, 'The Commons: Infrastructures for Troubling Times', *Environment and Planning D: Society and Space* 34:3 (2016), 393.

63 See for instance, the work of Laura Pulido: Laura Pulido and Juan De Lara, . 'Reimagining "Justice" in Environmental Justice: Radical Ecologies, Decolonial Thought, and the Black Radical Tradition', *Environment and Planning E: Nature and Space* 1:1–2 (2018): 76–98; Laura Pulido, 'Geographies of Race and Ethnicity II: Environmental Racism, Racial Capitalism and State-Sanctioned Violence', *Progress in Human Geography* 41:4 (2017): 524–533.

that the climate emergency is racialised leads to very troubling conclusions, steeped in neocolonial formulations. With only 10 per cent of the world's population responsible for 50 per cent of all global emissions,[64] the class and racial hierarchies of the climate crisis are unmistakable, as well as the inequalities between the global North and South, or what feminist geographer Doreen Massey identified as the 'power geographies' of globalisation. From this perspective, there is urgent need to consider the interconnections of struggle and to link campaigns for environmental, economic and racial justice, rather than operate within self-constructed silos. The revolutionary feminisms explored in this volume have the potential to help us tackle the root causes of the climate crisis – how resources are used and distributed, and to what ends, within an economic system based on extractivism, militarism and the drive for profit. Taking this critical approach would necessarily include an analysis of the social sorting process codified in immigration policy, whereby those fleeing the impacts of climate change, war, poverty and gender violence are deemed a threat to be contained, while capital moves freely and so-called golden visas allow for the purchase and protection of citizenship.[65]

As anyone who has spent time in organising spaces knows well, collectively (re)imagining a process as all-encompassing as climate change is easier said than done, especially in such a fragmented landscape of resistance and given the hyper-atomisation of individuals within neoliberalism. From the intensely classed and racialised spaces we inhabit, to the decimation and privatisation of public services, finding the grounds to think and act collectively is challenging. Yet, from within this very material and political fragmentation there have emerged inspiring acts of resistance that we can build upon. The challenge, in part, is how to bring these often-disparate campaigns together and how to sustain them for the long term. Here, it is useful to draw from the lessons of political resistance emanating from earlier moments in time – not because they entail fully formulated programmes or answers, but because we navigate a collective repertoire of struggle; its lessons – be they positive, negative, difficult or, indeed, painful – are crucial if we are to make headway towards (re)building what sociologist Alan Sears has termed 'infrastructures of dissent'.

An infrastructure of dissent, Sears writes, is 'the means through which activists develop political communities capable of learning, communicating and mobilising together'. He stresses the importance of the role of theatres, bookstores, choirs, education and sports as integral to movements, rather than external elements. This view of the totality of political and cultural

64 AFP, 'World's Richest 10% Produce Half of Global Carbon Emissions, Says Oxfam', *Guardian*, 2 December 2015, theguardian.com.

65 Adam Hanieh, 'The Contradictions of Global Migration', *Socialist Register* 55 (2018).

mobilisation is one which today's social movements are working hard to recapture and revitalise. If they are to succeed, it will be by realising a radical political imaginary which centres the thought of anti-capitalist, feminist, anti-racist, queer liberation, Indigenous and anti-colonial movements.

References

Abdulhadi, Rabab, Nadine Naber, and Evelyn al-Sultany, eds., *Arab American Feminisms: Gender, Violence, and Belonging*. Syracuse: Syracuse University Press, 2011.

AFP. 'World's Richest 10% Produce Half of Global Carbon Emissions, Says Oxfam'. *Guardian*, 2 December 2015. theguardian.com.

American Studies Association Conference 2014. 'Black Radicalism, Insurgency in Israel/Palestine and the Idea of Solidarity'. youtube.com/watch?v=-WI5ePHl63Go&frags=pl%2Cwn.

Bannerji, Himani. *Thinking Through: Essays on Feminism, Marxism, and Anti-Racism*. Toronto: Women's Press, 1995.

Bell, Derrick. *And We Are Not Saved: The Elusive Quest for Racial Justice*. New York: Basic Books, 1987.

Berlant, Lauren. 'The Commons: Infrastructures for Troubling Times'. *Environment and Planning D: Society and Space* 34:3 (2016), 393–419.

Bhandar, Brenna. 'Some Reflections on BDS and Feminist Political Solidarity'. *feminists@ law* 4:1 (2014), 1–14.

Bilge, Sirma. 'Intersectionality Undone: Saving Intersectionality from Feminist Intersectionality Studies'. *Du Bois Review* 10:2 (2013), 405–24.

Brah, Avtar. 'The Scent of Memory: Strangers, Our Own, and Others'. *Feminist Review* 61:1 (1999), 4–26.

Braz, Rose, Bo Brown, Craig Gilmore et al. 'The History of Critical Resistance'. *Social Justice* 27:3 (2000), 6–10.

Browne, Simone. *Dark Matters: On the Surveillance of Blackness*. Durham: Duke University Press, 2015.

Bryan, Beverley, Stella Dadzie, and Suzanne Scafe. *Heart of the Race: Black Women's Lives in Britain*. London: Virago Press, 1985. Reprint, London and New York: Verso, 2018.

Butler, Judith. *Subjects of Desire: Hegelian Reflections in Twentieth-Century France*. New York: Columbia University Press, 1987.

Butler, Judith. *Notes Towards a Performative Theory of Assembly.* Boston, MA: Harvard University Press, 2015.

Butler, Judith. *The Force of Non-Violence: the Ethical in the Political.* London: Verso: 2020

Carmen, Gail, Shaila et al. 'Becoming Visible: Black Lesbian Discussions'. *Feminist Review* 17 (July 1984), 53–72.

Choudry, Aziz. *Learning Activism: The Intellectual Life of Contemporary Social*

Movements. Toronto: University of Toronto Press, 2015.
Collins, Patricia Hill. 'Learning from the Outsider Within: The Sociological Significance of Black Feminist Thought'. *Social Problems* 33:6 (Autumn 1986), S14–S32.
Davis, Angela Y. 'The Approaching Obsolescence of Housework: A Working-Class Perspective'. In *Women, Race and Class*, edited by Angela Y. Davis, 222–45. London: Women's Press, 1981.
Davies, Carole Boyce, ed. *Claudia Jones: Beyond Containment*. Banbury: Ayebia Clarke Publishing, 2011.
Emejulu, Akwugo, and Leah Bassel. 'Women of Colour's Anti-Austerity Activism: They Cut, We Bleed'. In *The Violence of Austerity*, edited by Vickie Cooper and David Whyte, 117–22. London: Pluto Press, 2017.
Ferguson, Roderick. *Aberrations in Black: Towards a Queer of Colour Critique*. Minneapolis: University of Minnesota Press, 2004.
Fortunati, Leopoldina. *The Arcane of Reproduction: Housework, Prostitution, Labor and Capital*. Trans. Hilary Creek. New York: Autonomedia, 1995.
Gore, David F., Jeanne Theoharis and Komozi Woodart, eds. *Want to Start a Revolution? Radical Women in the Black Freedom Struggle*. New York: New York University Press, 2009.
Hartman, Saidiya. *Wayward Lives, Beautiful Experiments: Intimate Histories of Social Upheaval*. New York: W.W. Norton & Company, 2019.
Hencke, David. '£600,000 for Shop Stewards Fired over Gate Gourmet Strike'. *Guardian*, 17 September 2006. theguardian.com.
hooks, bell. *Killing Rage: Ending Racism*. New York: Henry & Holt, 1995.
Kapoor, Nisha. *Deport, Deprive, Extradite: 21st-Century State Extremism*. London and New York: Verso, 2018.
Lloyd, David. 'It is our belief that Palestine is a Feminist Issue'. *feminists@law* 4:1 (2014).
Lowe, Lisa. *The Intimacies of Four Continents*. Durham: Duke University Press, 2015.
Mahmood, Saba. *The Politics of Piety: The Islamic Revival and the Feminist Subject*. Princeton: Princeton University Press, 2011.
Maracle, Lee. *Memory Serves: Oratories*. Edmonton: NeWest Press, 2016.
McDuffie, Erik S. *Sojourning for Freedom: Black Women, American Communism and the Making of Black Left Feminism*. Durham: Duke University Press, 2011.
Mirza, Heidi Safia. *Black British Feminism: A Reader*. London: Routledge, 1997.
Naber, Nadine. 'A Call for Consistency: Palestinian Resistance and Radical US Women of Color'. In *Color of Violence, The Incite! Anthology*, 74–9. Durham: Duke University Press, 2006.
——. *Arab America: Gender Politics and Activism*. New York: New York University Press, 2012.
Nada, Elia. 'Justice Is Indivisible: Palestine as a Feminist Issue'. *Decolonization:*

Indigeneity, Education and Society 6:1 (2017), 45–63.

Nash, Jennifer C. *Black Feminism Reimagined: After Intersectionality*. Durham: Duke University Press, 2019.

Pimlott, Daniel, and Suneal Housley. 'FT Briefing: Gate Gourmet Dispute'. *Financial Times*, 23 August 2005. ft.com.

Puwar, Nirmal. *Space Invaders: Race, Gender and Bodies Out of Place*. London: Berg Publishers, 2004.

Ransby, Barbara. *Ella Baker and the Black Freedom Movement: A Radical Democratic Vision*. Chapel Hill: University of North Carolina Press, 2003.

Razack, Sherene. *Looking White People in the Eye: Gender, Race and Culture in the Courtrooms and Classrooms*. Toronto: University of Toronto Press, 1998.

———. 'Gendered Racial Violence and Spatialized Justice: The Murder of Pamela George'. *Canadian Journal of Law and Society* 15:2 (August 2000), 91–130.

———, ed. *Race, Space and the Law: Unmapping a White Settler Society*. Toronto: Between the Lines Press, 2002.

Ritskes, Eric. 'Leanne Simpson and Glen Coulthard on Dechinta Bush University, Indigenous Land-Based Education and Embodied Resurgence'. *Decolonization: Indigeneity, Education and Society* (2014).

Roediger, David R. *The Wages of Whiteness: Race and the Making of the American Working Class*. 2nd ed. London and New York: Verso, 2007.

Shalhoub-Kevorkian, Nadera. 'Palestinian Feminist Critique and the Physics of Power: Feminists Between Thought and Practice'. *feminists@law* 4:1 (2014).

Sharif, Rana. 'Bodies, Buses and Permits: Palestinians Navigating Care'. *feminists@law* 4:1 (2014).

Sherwood, Marika, ed. *Claudia Jones: A Life in Exile*. London: Lawrence & Wishart, 1999.

Souvlis, George, and Ankica Čakardić. 'Feminism and Social Reproduction: An Interview with Silvia Federici'. *Salvage* [2017]. salvage.zone.

Striking Women. 'The Gate Gourmet Dispute'. striking-women.org.

Sudbury, Julia. *'Other Kinds of Dreams': Black Women's Organisations and the Politics of Transformation*. London: Routledge, 1998.

Swaby, Nydia. 'Disparate in Voice, Sympathetic in Direction: Gendered Political Blackness and the Politics of Solidarity'. *Feminist Review* 108 (2014), 11–25.

Tabar, Linda, and Chandni Desai. 'Decolonization Is a Global Project: From Palestine to the Americas'. *Decolonization: Indigeneity, Education and Society* 6:1 (2017), i–xix.

Thiong'o, Ngũgĩ wa. *Decolonising the Mind: The Politics of Language in African Literature*. London: East African Educational Publishers, 1986.

Tronti, Mario. *Workers and Capital*. Translated by David Broder. London and

New York: Verso, 2019.

University of Leeds. 'Gate Gourmet – Chronology of Events'. University of Leeds official website, leeds.ac.uk.

Varma, Rashmi. 'Anti-Imperialism'. In *The Bloomsbury Handbook of 21st-Century Feminist Theory*, edited by Robin Truth Goodman. London: Bloomsbury, 2019.

Ware, Vron, and Les Back. *Out of Whiteness: Color, Politics and Culture*. Chicago: University of Chicago Press, 2001.

Wildcat, Matthew, Mandee McDonald, Stephanie Irlbacher-Fox et al. 'Learning from the Land: Indigenous Land-Based Pedagogy and Decolonization'. *Decolonization: Indigeneity, Education and Society* 3:3 (2014), i–xv.

Williams, Patricia J. *The Alchemy of Race and Rights: Diary of a Law Professor*. Cambridge, MA: Harvard University Press, 1991.

Diaspora/Migration/Empire

Avtar Brah

Professor Emerita of Sociology at Birkbeck, University of London, Avtar Brah has taught at the University of Leicester and the Open University. She specialises in the study of race, gender, class, ethnicity, and diaspora, where she explores the intersections within and across these axes of power in a variety of contexts. Her work has been influential within the academy, feminist movements and diasporic communities, from organising as one of the founding members of Southall Black Sisters to roles in campaigns against racist violence. Her political activism is deeply marked by a socialist, feminist and anti-imperialist, decolonial optic. She was centrally involved in the mobilisation of solidarity politics when Asian and Afro-Caribbean groups organised jointly under the common sign of Black as a political colour. She was active within the Organisation of Women of African and Asian Descent. For a period during the early 1980s, she took up a post as Head of Resources within the Women's Committee Support Unit at the Greater London Council, which, as she recalls, was 'a left project, sometimes dubbed as an experiment in "municipal socialism"'.

Her pioneering book *Cartographies of Diaspora: Contesting Identities* (1996) helped generate new perspectives in the study of diaspora as a concept and as a practice. Together with Annie Coombes, she edited *Hybridity and Its Discontents: Politics, Science, Culture* (2000). She worked with Mary Hickman and Máirtín Mac an Ghail in coediting two volumes: *Thinking Identities: Racism, Ethnicity and Culture* (1999), and *Global Futures: Migration, Environment and Globalization* (1999). For a number of years, she served as a member of the editorial collective of *Critical Social Policy* and the editorial board of *Ethnic and Racial Studies*. She is a member of the editorial collective of *Feminist Review* and of the international editorial board of *Identities: Global Studies in Culture and Power*.

BB/RZ *Through several decades of meticulously grounded research, you have devised a methodological approach that reworks Althusser's theory of interpellation, among other Marxian theories, to account not only for the effects of capitalist social relations, but also the psychic and symbolic relations of race, migration, class and gender. Stuart Hall stated that your method, arising at a distinct historical theoretical and political conjuncture, could be termed 'the diasporic'. So the first question we want to ask is, could you tell us about this distinct conjuncture in terms of the historical moment, and the theoretical influences and the political landscape, during which you developed the diasporic as a method?*

AB The concept of diaspora, or even the term 'diaspora', came into currency during, I think, the mid-to-late eighties and nineties in Britain. If we look back, one of the major political moments that comes to mind was the 1989 crumbling of the Berlin Wall and the demise of the Soviet Union as a Communist bloc. So that had a very significant global impact. In Britain at the time, of course, we had Thatcherism. That ideology and practice had a very significant impact on people of colour. Then, in the field of research and knowledge production in academia, for instance, and outside academia too, there were a lot of intellectual contestations around postmodernity and modernity, poststructuralism and structuralism. So there was a lot of both intellectual and political ferment going on. Looking specifically at the term 'diaspora', I'll confine myself at this time to Britain, in the postwar period. Until the 1980s, really, the term used to describe people of colour was 'immigrant'.

It wasn't a straightforward descriptor; rather, it was a mode of marginalising and pathologising the communities. In fact, even British-born young people were called second-generation or third-generation immigrants. That still happens. It irritates me when I hear that. At the same time, the term 'ethnic relations', or 'ethnic', was also in currency. That was thought to be a slightly more polite way of referring to people of colour, although of course the term is not necessarily just applicable to people of colour, but any ethnic group. But in Britain that was used. Again, that particular term, although slightly more polite, still tended to pathologise minority ethnic groups. There was a tendency to talk about people of colour as a problem; the discourses were around problems.

In that kind of intellectual and political climate, people were beginning to think about ways to interrogate those terms. How could we actually talk about people whose historical trajectories touch on many continents and many countries? How could we talk about and think about those groups without pathologising them? And the term 'diaspora' emerged in that ferment. In part, it was thought to critique nationalisms or an undue focus on the nation-state. Again, we have to remember that this was a time when globalisation was a major feature of global economy and society. The concept of diaspora was intended to enable us to think beyond the nation-state and foreground communities that had links globally, so to speak. So the term emerges in that kind of political conjuncture. Paul Gilroy's *The Black Atlantic* uses the term 'diaspora', and Stuart Hall used the concept as well.[1]

1 Paul Gilroy, *The Black Atlantic: Modernity and Double Consciousness* (London: Verso, 1993); Stuart Hall, 'Cultural Identity and Diaspora', in Nicholas Mirzoeff, ed., *Diaspora and Visual Culture: Representing Africans and Jews* (London: Routledge, 1999) [essay originally published in 1996].

Then, the terms 'ethnic' and 'ethnicity' were also on the horizon; Hall coined the term 'new ethnicities', which is linked to 'diaspora' in the sense that new ethnicities were focused on generational shifts, on hybridisation, on politics of representation.[2] Hall's focus there was on the use of poststructuralist thought in relation to analysing ethnicity, again to wrench, he says, ethnicity from the older ways of pathologising communities, of marginalising communities. It is a non-essentialist concept which emphasises the place of history, language and culture. So that's the kind of context in which the term 'diaspora' emerges. For many of us, it was a more positive way of conceptualising communities, and a way to deracialise them, because they were always thought of in a racialised mode at the time. So that's the context in which the term emerges.

BB/RZ *Do you want to tell us a little bit more about Thatcherism and how that impacted people of colour in this country?*

AB Thatcherism, as you know, was linked to Powellism in the previous decade. Enoch Powell famously, or infamously, talked about young people, Black people, Asians, saying that they could be born in Britain but could never be *of* Britain. He talked about young 'piccanninies' and used all kinds of racialised language, and gave a speech focusing on 'the rivers of blood' that might flow in Britain, which expressed his predictions of the violence that might ensue. Margaret Thatcher built on and continued the same kind of discourse. She didn't always use the same language, but it was a very similar discourse. In a 1978 TV interview, she talked about the British people being scared that Britain might be 'swamped by people of a different culture'. That kind of language was creating many problems, giving respectability to racism. There was a lot of racial violence on the streets, which we tend to forget now, but there were many racial attacks; people had been murdered. I remember in Southall, for instance, Gurdip Chaggar was murdered in 1976 by young white people.[3] So there was a lot of racist violence.

But economically, as well, we were seeing not the emergence of neoliberalism (because it is much older than that), but neoliberalism becoming much more rampant, particularly in Thatcher's policies. There were attacks, which are happening again now, on the trade unions. You will remember that 1984 was when the miners were on strike and Thatcher had basically said she was totally committed to destroying the miners. There were figures given in the media about the huge sums of money the government spent on campaigning against the miners and their union, and the government did succeed in the

2 Hall, ibid.

3 Gurdip Singh Chaggar, eighteen years old, was stabbed to death by racists in Southall, London, on 3 June 1976.

end – that was one of the very sad moments in labour history. The attacks on the unions had a major impact on people of colour, partly because people of colour held jobs in places of work affected by Thatcherite policies. There were high levels of unemployment among people of colour.

All of this was happening everywhere. In 1979 in Southall, Blair Peach, a teacher, was killed by injuries sustained to the head, at the hands of the police. This happened when the racist and fascist National Front came marching through Southall to hold an election rally against which the local people had gathered to protest. The police, in the form of the notorious Special Patrol Group, came in large numbers to ensure that the National Front rally took place. In the process many protestors were injured, arrested and taken to police stations all over London. Over 700 people, mainly Asians, were arrested, and 345 were charged. Clarence Baker, the manager of the Black reggae band Misty in Roots was so badly injured on the head that he spent considerable time in hospital. So there was a lot of that kind of political ferment going on, within which there was a great deal of contestation of, and challenges to, the racism people were experiencing. At the same time, in factories there were strikes. I was in Southall in the early 1980s, and I remember there was a strike of workers at the Chix bubblegum factory in Slough.[4] We used to go and support those women – it was mostly women who were on strike. Such events were happening all the time. Mainly the term 'diaspora' itself emerged during this time to challenge racialised regimes which were connected to the very material, everyday lives of people because of unemployment and racist violence.

BB *You also draw a connection between the fall of the Berlin Wall – and the demise of the Soviet bloc, the massive impact that had on left politics – and the contemporaneous racial violence against people of colour and anti-racist resistance.*

AB Absolutely, that was a very major event of the period, globally too. We all went into depression, those of us who were involved in socialist projects. We were always critical of the Soviet Union, but nonetheless, globally there was a socialist presence, a project that we subscribed to. There was a huge amount of melancholia at the time. But also, internationally it's quite important, because the Black struggles – and I'll use the term 'Black' for the moment, including Asians – were always international struggles. The Left, particularly the Black Left, looked at imperialism always in relation to racism, whereas in other discourses they often talked about racism as if it occurred on its own. But the Black Left always looked at the links between colonialism and postcolonialism, and imperialism and new imperialisms.

---

4 The workers at the Chix factory in Slough went on strike for eight months during 1979 and 1980 and won recognition of their union.

That, of course, shifted after the demise of Soviet Communism because the ways in which global power relations had been constituted, changed. A new order, a new political order, was born now in which capitalism gained a much more pronounced ascendancy. Also, for a period, at least – although that has changed now – we found that the Soviet Union was no longer seen as a threat by the West. There was a period when the Iron Curtain was no longer seen as the Iron Curtain. So internationally, that meant the left project in Britain was affected by what happened, because it weakened the arguments for alternatives. That has changed now, of course, because Russia is again not in the good books of the West, but for a period it was not seen as a threat.

It was also the case that in, for example, the Black women's groups that we had in those days, we always explored the ways in which our life trajectories as groups had been constituted over periods of time in and through histories of imperialism. And the ways in which our presence here in Britain was connected with colonialism, in the sense that during the postwar period, Britain recruited Black people, people of colour, from its colonies to come and do the work the white workers didn't want to do, in the lowest rungs of the economy. So that was very important. Our presence here was connected with colonialism. Therefore, such issues were always crucial to emphasise. We always foregrounded those international struggles alongside our political struggles here in Britain.

BB/RZ *Do you feel that goes missing nowadays, that grounding?*

AB Yes, to some degree. Moreover, in those days we talked about capitalism. One of the biggest problems has been that there is not the same degree of focus today on the problems produced by capitalist social relations. Sometimes you find nowadays that people talk about the disadvantaged 99 per cent and all that, and it's good that it's happening, but I find it quite frustrating that people don't really talk about capitalism. There are discussions about the wars in the Middle East, and so forth, but not enough emphasis on the histories of colonialism and imperialism, which resulted in the carving out of these different countries and created these different territorial lines, new countries and new nation-states which are now having all kinds of problems. Indeed, there is insufficient problematisation of the links between capitalism and imperialism. I know we're jumping around here, but people talk about all these migrants coming from abroad, as if capitalism and imperialism has no effect in making other countries poor. In those days there was considerable discussion about the ways in which certain parts of the world became impoverished.

There was a focus on the global inequalities and inequities – people talked about them. There was a discourse around them in the media, even. But now that discourse has disappeared. There is much talk about all these so-called economic migrants coming here, but very little attention to why it is mainly people from the global South who become economic migrants to the rich global North. I find this gaping absence really problematic.

BB/RZ *It's quite common in the academy for people to take up a self-described stance as 'being critical' without considering capitalism or class in any serious fashion. What do you make of the identification of being critical, or the idea of critique, when it no longer addresses precisely the issues you were just talking about?*

AB Well, it is a big problem, even in terms of resources. Of course, you have Thomas Piketty's *Capital in the Twenty-First Century* (2013) and books like that, which are important, but they're not critiques of capitalism as such from a socialist perspective. Similarly, I was excited when I came across Ha-Joon Chang's *23 Things They Don't Tell You about Capitalism* (2010). But then he clearly states that he's not against capitalism. Whereas in the eighties and nineties, there were resources, there were books – for instance Susan George's *How the Other Half Dies* (1976), which looks at global poverty and why people in certain parts of the world are actually dying. And they were quite easily accessible kinds of books, not heavy theory, but they contained a lot of theoretical insight and you could use those with students. There used to be lots of video programmes; Channel 4 for example, did some very interesting programmes around multinational corporations, which looked at how multinationals go overseas and the ways in which they extract surplus value, particularly in special economic zones.

These were actually very accessible, excellently made programmes, which took away the mystique about how these multinationals operate globally. I remember throughout my teaching years using some of those kinds of resources with students, alongside the more strictly academic ones. I'm not teaching anymore, so you would know better than me what kinds of resources are available today, but I have a sense those kinds of resources are not that easily accessible. Am I right, or are there resources like that?

BB *There are resources like that to be used, but I think what has changed is the environment in which we are working; the landscape of higher education has changed a lot, and in some ways the space for doing that kind of teaching has shrunk.*

AB Now why is that? Is that because they find those kinds of critiques threatening? What is the reason?

BB *My view is shaped by my experience in the field that I'm in. Law is always a more conservative discipline. But there was, for a period of time, particularly in the seventies and eighties, a very left, vibrant, critical movement within legal* *studies here. That work was however, with a few very important exceptions, void of any serious engagement with issues of race, gender, colonialism, and empire. More recently, we have seen renewed engagement with law and racial capitalism, but today, academics are increasingly isolated in the academy, and scholarly work is affected by a lack of engagement with the world outside. Alternately, where engagement does take place, it is often confined by the parameters set by an audit culture and a marketised system of education.*

***BB/RZ** Going back to the concept of diaspora, you have written that diaspora can be understood in four different ways – first, by looking at diaspora as an analytical concept, which I think you explained before; second, by looking at diaspora as a genealogical concept; and third, the diasporic as focused on both 'routes' and 'roots', which we think is really compelling. Fourth, there is the fact that diaspora itself is an intersectional concept. So we just want to ask if you could tease out a few more of these different ways of thinking about those words.*

AB I think when I came to this term 'diaspora' and started using it, I was very acutely aware that we were talking about diaspora in many different ways. There are, of course, many discourses of diaspora, and James Clifford talks about this as well.[5] There are different types of *discourses* of diaspora, which need to be distinguished from the actual *lived experiences* of diaspora. Then there is the *concept* of diaspora, as distinct from lived experience and histories of diaspora. I wanted to think through the question: How can we distinguish the concept from the experience of diaspora and the discourses of diaspora? That was how I came to the notion of thinking about diaspora as a concept in terms of genealogy. I used the Foucauldian term 'genealogy' because it simultaneously foregrounds discourse and knowledge and power, which is very important when we are thinking about diasporas and how they are constituted, how they have been lived.

Then there is the notion of power, and notions of how knowledge and power are always connected, how different kinds of discourses construct diasporas in different kinds of ways. I decided that I was going to think of the concept of diaspora as a genealogy, and as a genealogy which doesn't hark back to final origins or pure essences, or present truth claims as given rather than constructed. I came up with the idea that we needed to think of diaspora as a concept in terms of an investigative technology, which looks at the historical, cultural, social and political processes in and through which diasporas are constituted. I also wanted to point to the ways in which different diasporas are positioned in relation to one another other, and not simply in relation to the dominant group in society.

Then, in terms of routes and roots – yes, that's very important, of course. I

5 James Clifford, 'Diasporas', *Cultural Anthropology* 9:3 (1994): 302–38.

think it was Paul Gilroy who in his book used this term, 'routes and roots',[6] because in a way there is a contestation between routes and roots, so to speak, in thinking about diasporas. There's movement, but there is also a sense of actually putting roots in a place to which one moves. To hold these two axes together simultaneously is critical. Diasporas are historically specific formations. Each diaspora has its own history, such that you can have diasporas which emerge out of slavery. Then there are diasporas which emerge out of labour migrations. There are diasporas which emerge out of what is happening at the moment around us, refugees coming out of wars, war-torn countries, out of poverty.

So in all those different notions of diaspora, history is critical, because not all diasporas are the same, so we have to look at the history behind each formation of the diaspora. This term 'intersectional' – actually, I didn't come to intersectionality through the work of Kimberlé Crenshaw. I was thinking about the ways in which questions of race, gender, class or sexuality constantly interact. This was during the process of writing *Cartographies of Diaspora* (1996). And I used the term 'intersectionality' in *Cartographies*. I came across Crenshaw's work later. In a sense, maybe I have a slightly different take on intersectionality. I'm told that some people think that intersectionality only applies to dominated groups; whereas I think that intersectionality is about power regimes and how they intersect, and how they position different groups differently and differentially in relation to each other. One has to look at the regimes of domination if we are to understand the ways the dominated live their lives. But we also have to look at how the dominant groups dominate. Intersectionality for me, first and foremost, is about embodiment. How do we embody social relations? And this is as much about the social, political and cultural as it is about the psychic. It's about subjectivity and it's also about identity. So I talk about intersections throughout *Cartographies*, but I'm talking about all these different levels of them. I talk about difference, which is related to intersectionality very closely, again as social relation, but also as subjectivity, as identity and as experience.

The key thing is that these different axes – class, race, gender, sexuality, disability and so on – intersect both in our physical bodies and the social body. So intersectionality operates both at the social level and at the level of the physical body and the psyche. I greatly respect the debates that came afterwards and have learnt a lot from them as well, but my own take on intersectionality may have been slightly different from the way it at times appears to have become valorised now.

BB/RZ *What do you think its valorisation has been about?*

---

6 Gilroy, *Black Atlantic.*

AB Well, intersectionality as a concept and a political practice emerges out of discussions around the experience of Black American women and working-class Black American women. And this work is really important. Yet, there are other discourses where talk about intersectionality has become a mantra now. In reality, intersectionality demands a lot of hard work – analytically, politically, in every way. It's not just about mentioning three or four words, and saying 'yes, I'm doing intersectionality' – it's really looking at grounded analysis of these different axes. We can't always do all the axes at the same time anyway. But it needs a lot of hard work.

BB *One of the effects of its valorisation has been that it has allowed, to some extent, the continued universalisation of particular women's experiences. For instance, in a given article there may be a couple of paragraphs that acknowledge, 'that this issue is different for women of colour or different for working-class women of colour'. In this cynical sense, it can almost be used as an insurance policy to guard against the criticism that one is not integrating analysis of race or class.*

RZ *Academically, that can be the case. But then there's also activist movements where it has been very much owned by people of colour. You have the Black Lives Matter movement, for example, and the insistence of the activists in BLM that this movement will be intersectional. The hard work you're speaking of is partly on the academic level, but it's required in the social movements too. When you say 'it's hard work to do', what does that mean for an activist who would be starting today? How do you think that would play out?*

AB Well, I have to go back to my roots in Southall Black Sisters.

RZ *That's what I was hoping you would do.*

AB That was hard work, when I look back on it. I was a member of the Southall Black Sisters at its inception in 1979. Then in 1982, I left London for a job in Leicester and then in Milton Keynes, so I moved away from SBS during its second phase. But I know, firstly, that it was hard work in terms of the things we've been talking about, the interconnections that we had to make between our histories – our imperial histories, colonial histories – to make sense of what was happening to us as Black women in postwar Britain, in eighties and nineties Britain. It was also hard work in terms of dealing with patriarchal issues in relation to men with whom we were working, around questions of racism, for example, or questions about socialism. That was not easy at all, you know; it was hard work to raise patriarchal issues. We would be having a political meeting about socialism or about racism. Then to raise issues of gender was seen as failing to show solidarity with brothers, so to speak.

We were planning an anti-racist and anti-fascist march from Bradford to London. The march didn't happen in the end, but we were planning one. We had a meeting with men and women in Bradford to discuss what we would do. We brought up the question of issues to do with gender, and that didn't go down very well with a number of the men – not all of them, but with some of the people who were there. There were many reasons why the march didn't happen, but some of the men tended to blame us for bringing up questions of patriarchal relations as the reason for why the march did not happen. So there was, at that level, the struggle with men on the left. There was, of course, struggle within our own communities themselves, where, as in Britain as a whole, living out patriarchal relations was an everyday experience for women.

We had to develop strategies, in a way, where we could work with people so they would listen to us and not just dismiss us as these difficult young women who were just coming up with these newfound ideas. That was quite difficult. For example, we once staged a feminist version of *Ramlila*, a play based on the Hindu epic of *Ramayana*. Some people might think, 'Why do a religious thing?' And some feminists I'm sure would say, 'Why would you do that?' But here we were in Southall, and we wanted to invite women and men, mostly women came actually, but we wanted to critique Sita's position as a woman, and we used the figure of a 'jester', who provided a humorous though pointed commentary on the proceedings. Here was a feminist stance presented through an idiom that was culturally familiar to those present. We did that. It was quite a successful event. The women could identify, because they knew what it was like when you lived the life of an 'obedient wife'. But then we were coming up with different ideas about possible alternatives. Together, we could make sense of it.

It's even more difficult now, I'm sure, with all the Islamophobia. I think you have to be able to work with people in a way where you can facilitate the emergence of a shared common project. You have to address the contradictory 'common sense' that we all live with, that Gramsci speaks of.[7] Unless you do that, then you're not going to make much headway with constructing new political agendas. To do that, you have to begin with where people are at, but not stay there, and not get sucked into that. But rather, to jointly develop new discourses and practices for the creation of new political horizons, a new common sense. Those were rather difficult things to do in relation to our communities, but also in relation to ourselves. We were Asian women, we were women of African descent.

There was once a political meeting called – not by us, but by another anti-racist group in Southall – in a hall belonging to a temple. Just as a venue,

7 Antonio Gramsci, 1891–1937. *Selections From the Prison Notebooks of Antonio Gramsci*. New York: International Publishers, 1971.

not for religious reasons. I know that some SBS members didn't want to go there because it was in a hall on the premises of a temple, a religious place, when we were secular. So there were difficult debates and issues like that. But this is what I mean. There isn't a hard and fast rule for how you would actually go about this work; you have to do hard work at the ground level, if you're an activist. It's quite hard work. It takes its toll on you psychologically, as well.

***BB/RZ** We were also wondering how your own life experiences influence your theoretical and conceptual work around diaspora?*

AB I was born in India, but I was five years old when I went to Africa. So I grew up in Uganda. I was in Uganda until I did my A levels. Then I went to America; I was in California, where I did my undergraduate degree, then Wisconsin, where I did my Master's. This was about the time when Idi Amin was coming to power. I was in Britain, on my way back to Uganda, when the Idi Amin edict was issued[8] – and even though I was a Ugandan citizen, I couldn't go back. So I was stateless for about five years in Britain, until I became a citizen. (In those days, after five years you applied for naturalisation.) Hence, I've lived in all these different countries, and diaspora is very much part and parcel of my life experience. The things we've been talking about – SBS, other politics around racism, around class and so on – all those are very much part and parcel of my life.

My analysis has always been informed by my political activism, and vice versa. I think the two have gone together. So the concept of 'diaspora space', for example, emerged out of thinking through different life experiences and how to theorise about them, how to analyse them.

***BB/RZ** We wanted to follow up with the question of belonging and your work on belonging. The Indigenous Australian scholar Aileen Moreton-Robinson draws our attention to the fact that the conjoined twin of belonging is exclusion,[9] which may sound obvious, but she points out how that often gets lost in the discourse on belonging. Lauren Berlant formulated this nicely: 'Just because we are in the room together does not mean that we belong to the room or each other: belonging is a specific genre of affect, history, and political mediation that cannot be presumed and is, indeed, a relation whose evidence and terms are always being contested.'[10] We were wondering if you could tell us a little bit about your*

---

8 On 4 August 1972, President of Uganda Idi Amin issued a decree ordering the expulsion of the 50,000 Asians who were British passport holders, forcing many to migrate to the UK, other Commonwealth nations and the United States.

9 See Aileen Moreton-Robinson, *The White Possessive: Property, Power, and Indigenous Sovereignty* (Minneapolis: University of Minnesota Press, 2015).

10 Lauren Berlant, 'The Commons: Infrastructures for Troubling Times', *Environment and Planning D: Society and Space* 34:3 (2016), 395. Berlant continues: 'Belonging is a proposition, a theory, a forensic fact, and a name for a kind of attachment. The crowded but disjointed

understanding of the discourse of belonging and how that has been useful to your thinking on migration and diaspora?

AB I think, in fact, that what these two scholars say is very important. I do find the notion of belonging compelling, because without a sense of belonging, however contested and fractured it might be, you are vulnerable as an outsider – not just physically, but psychologically and psychically, as well. If we don't feel any sense of belonging, we become quite dispersed, scattered beings. To have some sense of togetherness, of psychic coherence, means we have to have a sense of belonging – to our siblings, our families, our friends, our political allies, our 'imagined communities' as well as others that form our lifeworld. The point that Moreton-Robinson and Berlant are making is that the flip side of belonging is exclusion. Belonging only makes sense because there is exclusion. Histories of racism, class hierarchy and heteronormativity, for instance, tell us which groups, under what conditions, have belonged or been excluded.

Apart from being predicated against the socioeconomic, political and cultural landscape, belonging is also very much part of the affective domain. These different aspects need to be held together. But we always need to be aware – it's like when Stuart Hall talks about the concept of 'identity', and he says that it's a term without which he cannot do, but at the same time it's a term that he's continually interrogating. I think 'belonging' is such a term. You can't do without it, but you have to always question how it is being evoked, always remain aware how it is being used and how a sense of belonging, or a sense of alienation, is being played out. Those two may go together. If you don't feel a sense of belonging, you may become alienated. What kinds of social, political and cultural conditions favour alienation and anomie as opposed to a sense of belonging, a sense of well-being?

I would think of it that way, to be aware of those social issues alongside the sense that it gives you a feeling of being a part of something. A sense of affirmation.

BB/RZ *I think you mentioned somewhere that a feeling of being at home is one way of describing what belonging is. Because for those of us who have moved around a lot or have come from families who were also immigrant families, migrant families, refugee families, it's quite difficult to grasp what 'belonging' actually means. For many of us, the feeling of not belonging is what becomes familiar and even a primary psychic default position. What does belonging actually look like, and what does it mean?*

---

propinquity of the social calls for a proxemics, the study of sociality as proximity quite distinct from the possessive attachment languages of belonging.'

AB It is a sense of feeling at home, isn't it?

BB *Yes, I think that's why I recalled that. Because I thought, okay, that's an interesting way to think about what it means to belong – feeling at home somewhere*

RZ *From a Palestinian perspective, for example, when home is a colonised space you are not allowed to return to – the struggle is to hold on to return, but also your rights and new belonging where you have ended up.*

AB There's always a tension. I remember thinking about this when I first came here. At first, you feel you're in a new place; you don't feel at home at all. But then there comes a time when you do begin to feel at home, but you may not necessarily be seen by the dominant group as belonging. That is why affect and the psyche are implicated in all of that. It's also having that psychic strength to be able to say, 'I now feel at home, and I'm going to contest you who say I'm not at home.' To have that strength is very important. Political activism gives that collective strength, and our loved ones give us the personal strength. So it is a contest all the time. Because even now, I've been here twenty-odd years, more than that, but there are people who still think I'm an outsider. But I feel quite at home down here in London, and I challenge the processes that construct me as an outsider. But you're absolutely right – it's always contested, disputed, and how you feel does not necessarily reflect how others see you.

BB/RZ *In* Cartographies of Diaspora, *you explore how the new Europe has been constituted juridically, legally, politically, economically and culturally, through race, class and gender. You make an intervention into the discourse of new racisms by showing how the racisms that emerged in Britain in the context of debates over the EU are informed by the New Right. This relates back to our earlier discussion about how terms like 'nation' and 'people' were used by Thatcher against trade unions and the working class and so-called welfare scroungers.*

Alongside the austerity policies and politics that have saturated the UK and also the EU in the last decade, what differences do you perceive between the eighties and nineties, and this current moment? You mentioned Powellism and Thatcher and the language of the swarm, which came back, of course, in Cameron's comments on refugees. We were wondering if you could maybe talk a little bit about some of the similarities or differences you see between that earlier moment and what's happening today?

AB Well, I suppose the linguistic content can sometimes be very similar. Often, immigrant groups are represented as dirty, as inherently different, as other. There's a recursivity about ways in which certain groups are described and othered. But what changes is the broader social context, and I think that has changed hugely, if you look back at the eighties. In economic terms the situation for some groups, such as the precariat class in the gig economy, has worsened. But also the global scene has changed so much with all the wars, ever since the war in Iraq and the Gulf in 1990. We've had several other wars since. The rise of the Islamic State as well, and the ways in which the securitisation discourses and practices have come to the fore since 9/11, for instance. All of these have actually changed the world enormously. So, the racism of which we speak has never been one racism. We talk about Islamophobia or anti-Muslim racism, which is a very specific racism. Similarly, we talk about racism that is directed at asylum seekers and refugees; that is another one. And, of course, anti-Semitism, as well as the racism that is directed at the so-called economic migrants, or against people of colour; these are all distinct forms of racism.

Even the refugees are not accepted to any great degree in Britain. Turkey and Pakistan have taken millions of refugees, and here in Britain we have taken comparatively few. Indeed, we know that most of the refugees are in the Third World countries, or what we now call the global South. The global scene, in terms of these wars and what they have done to people's lives, is just horrendous. I often think, here we sit, and politicians discourse about lofty ideals while we forget how people live in dire conditions in wartime zones.

Rather than resolving issues politically, countries, particularly countries in the West, are likely to be more and more involved in situations in which military intervention is regarded as justified.

***BB** I wanted to ask you, following up on the Brexit referendum, and these different forms of racism that you're identifying, what is your diagnosis of the reemergence of the discourse around the Commonwealth?*

AB Some people who are in favour of leaving the EU argue for the importance of the Commonwealth. They seem to assume for some reason that in the post-Brexit period, Britain will suddenly allow people from Africa and the Caribbean and India and Pakistan to enter the UK, that the doors will be open wide. The Brexit campaign has made them believe, somehow, that there is a competition between the East Europeans and people from the Commonwealth. That somehow if we didn't have people from Eastern Europe, then we would get more people from the Commonwealth. That won't happen.

***BB** It seems as though people who have been denied recognition as people who truly belong in the nation are trying to reinvigorate this discourse of empire, as if to say we have a place here that precedes that of the Eastern European migrants.*

AB You are absolutely right about that – that's true. In 2015, when Greece was in a very dire economic situation, I became very anti-EU. But on the other hand, the EU has the Social Charter,[11] whereas some in Britain don't even want to retain the Human Rights Act. I felt that because of the Social Charter, we probably needed to stay in the EU and argue for a better, more democratic EU than we have now. But the Brexit group managed to convince quite a few people that the interest of the Commonwealth would be better served if we leave. It just doesn't make sense to me at all.

BB *Can we switch tack for a moment? We wanted you to address the shift in political identification with respect to the use of the term 'Black'.*

AB There has been a splintering of the sense in which we used the term 'Black' from the 1970s onwards. Even in those days, in the mid 1970s, some people didn't agree with us; they used to say, 'Asians are not Black – they don't look Black.' But at the same time, there are some women today who also want to use the term 'Black' in the sense that we used it. When we constructed the term 'Black' to refer to a political colour rather than a shade of skin, it was in a context where we were working together against shared experiences of racism. There were immigration laws, for example, against which we, as Black communities mobilised across the board. So the term had a political purchase.

But nowadays, even the term 'Asian' has itself become fractured. When you use the term 'Asian', people don't necessarily identify with that. People talk about being Muslims, or Hindus or Sikhs, so the religious identifications have become much more pronounced. The point is that unity has to be achieved through struggle and solidarity; it cannot be imposed. Because if a term doesn't have a critical purchase, then it is probably more relevant to use a term that actually does have political resonance with a new generation of people today.

I've started using the American term, 'women of colour' or 'people of colour'. Which is also problematic, because they used to use the term 'coloured' here in Britain, which was a racialised term. But people of colour has been constructed by 'nonwhite' groups in solidarity. And that is important.

RZ *It's interesting because religious affiliation has become much more common. This has taken place, like you're saying, in many situations where it is your religious affiliation, even more specifically, your sect, that people are using. What do you think of that change that has happened?*

---

11 The European Social Charter is a Council of Europe treaty that guarantees fundamental social and economic rights as a counterpart to the European Convention on Human Rights, which refers to civil and political rights. It guarantees a broad range of everyday human rights related to employment, housing, health, education, social protection and welfare. See 'The European Social Charter', Council of Europe official website, coe.int.

AB That's a very difficult one, isn't it? It's because it's so caught up with global politics as well. We can't talk about religion – we can talk about spiritualism. I've nothing against spiritualism – people can pursue their religious affiliation if they're spiritually oriented. But religion is no longer seen as separate from the geopolitical order at the moment.

BB *I think nowadays, rather than identifying people of colour by ethnicity, we are marginalised and racialised through –*

AB Being called Muslim.

RZ *Yes. There are certain types of racisms that have developed that are related to religion, and there are the tensions that come with building alliances along those lines. How do we nurture and build an anti-racist movement around these issues?*

AB I think in terms of racism, it is quite clear. One needs to fight against Islamophobia, or any other anti-religious racism that is there. That is easier to deal with, in a way, because one takes a stand against any racism that goes around. But when I and my political allies organised in the old days, we were organising as secular groups. In a sense it was easier. But nowadays, people organise around religion; I don't know what you do in universities now, because there are so many religious groups that are organising separately. So that the term 'Asian' doesn't hold much sway – that's what I meant earlier – because in the main, students don't come together as Asians in universities. Rather, they come together as Sikhs or Hindus or Muslims or Arabs or other groups, Shias and Sunnis, and so on. I think I would still say we need to come together on broader platforms, on common political concerns. I personally wouldn't organise around religion myself, unless I was oppressed on religious grounds. The key issue is one of oppression and exploitation. We know that the reality is that people *do* organise around religion. And given that there is an international onslaught on certain religious groups, it is understandable why they come together in the way they do. It is difficult to be sanctimonious. We must take politically thought-through positions. Because I don't think we can have blueprints for all situations.

BB/RZ *Do you think there is any political currency left in thinking about secularism as a basis for a feminist politics, or maybe a reconstructed secularism?*

AB I think there is a reconstructed secularism. Because some secularists are as fanatical as the religious groups can be, at times. But a reconstructed secularism, I think, is important. I'm always told by my Muslim friends, 'You don't realise what it means to be Muslim today, because of all this onslaught all the time.' My response is that there is that experiential dimension there which needs to be addressed, but it's such a tightrope – a very tight rope indeed. You have to look at everything as it happens and say, 'which way do I go?' I personally think that we need secular politics, but we have to be able to take on board the reality of, for instance, Islamophobia and anti-Muslim racism.

BB/RZ *We wanted to follow up with the concept of critical multiculturalism. Given the fragmentation of politics, that the issue of religion and religious identification has entered into the political landscape in a way that is much greater than in the eighties or nineties, does the concept of a critical multiculturalism still have relevance today?*

AB Yes. Well, one of the things that I think, given what you've just said, is that when people criticise multiculturalism, they often fail to make a distinction between multiculturalism as cultural diversity and multiculturalism as social policy. People were often critical of the latter, because in the eighties and nineties there were policies in local authorities which were informed by multiculturalism. I think some of those policies were problematic, but not all of those policies were wrong. After all, multiculturalism emerged out of struggle; it wasn't something that was just given to us by the state. It was a struggle to say, in education – the discourse of multiculturalism was most widely prevalent in education, that's where it was most strongly felt – that we didn't want an education system which pays no attention to the histories of colonialism and imperialism, which pays no attention to cultural diversity, to the ways in which people from the former colonies were concentrated in certain geographical locations where there were high rates of unemployment and poor housing and poor social services. That we wanted a different kind of education system, or different kind of social policy that actually took into account the specific needs of different groups of people.

I think at that level it was a struggle, and it was relevant to argue for multicultural education. But then there was a debate between anti-racists and multiculturalists. That was because once multiculturalism started being practised in schools and elsewhere, it became obvious that sometimes the question of racism or class was not taken very seriously. Thus, multiculturalism came to be caricatured as being about 'samosas, saris and steel drums', or something like that.

So we started talking about anti-racism in education, as opposed to multicultural education. That debate went on for a decade or so. It has now gone away, because people started attacking multiculturalism. Multiculturalism is problematic if it does not address an anti-racist critique. But what do we have instead? Monoculturalism? No! We may not call it multiculturalism; people are using different terms, currently. Instead of 'multiculturalism', they're trying to use the term 'interculturalism'. Basically, they're struggling with the same thing, which is, how do you address the hegemony of white British culture, even when we know that there is nothing called 'white British culture', in the singular, because British culture is heterogeneous.

But nonetheless, when people talk about the 'British way of life', or 'British values', which is a current discourse, they assume there is something British which is inherently different from the rest of the world, somehow unique, when often they're talking about very universal values, really. So if we don't have some kind of a politics and a discourse around cultural diversity, how do we contest the discourse of 'British way of life'? In other words, you're right that 'multiculturalism' as a term now is a problem, because it has been so discredited. But how do we deal with cultural diversity? I'm not sure what kind of term we can use, other than just 'cultural diversity'. Or 'interculturalism' – to me that sounds quite similar to 'multiculturalism' anyway. Perhaps 'anti-racist interculturalism'? And then there is that whole discourse about 'integration'. That term is a big problem, which is connected with 'multiculturalism'. 'Integration' meaning assimilation. That's what they mean. I don't want assimilation. I think we fought against assimilation.

So how do we construct a new term? I'm looking at you, as well. Can you think of something that can replace it, but without giving in to the assimilationists?

***RZ** Like you were saying, many of these things have to come out of practice. These formulations tend to come about through the struggle for something specific.*

AB It's true, it's very true.

***BB** In a way, this is related to your emphasis on practice. In thinking about intersectionality, for instance, as an approach that can only have meaning in working it through both intellectually and politically. This notion is quite distinct from the idea of grasping certain identifications in a mode of strategic essentialism, which reflects a more tactical approach.*

***RZ** Just to change course slightly – we very recently saw a film that you had directed as part of a project on the* Darkmatter *journal website.12 And it was stunningly beautiful.*

AB I'm glad you liked it.

***RZ** It was remarkable, both as a historical record but also the method that you used. How did you decide to do that, methodologically?*

---

12 Avtar Brah, *Aaj Kaal* [Yesterday, Today, Tomorrow], video, [20 mins], available at *Darkmatter* official website, darkmatter101.org.

AB Well, I was working at the Department of Extramural Studies at Birkbeck College. A large part of the courses we developed were in relation to the needs of the communities we were working with. We wanted to undertake a project in West London because I got some external funding to develop educational opportunities for people who had been out of work. We identified a range of needs and organised courses relevant to those needs. One of the things we thought we would do would be to work with older adults and look at the ways in which we could collate their life histories. Because we were interested in oral histories. We said that people are dying, literally, and our oral histories in this country are not being recorded.

We thought we would do a video project to document the lives of older people and their backgrounds, and how they had experienced life in Britain. But we also wanted to skill them; it's very easy to make a film about people and interview them, but we wanted a participatory project in which older adults would learn the skills of making a film, and that's what we did. We involved a video trainer, who actually taught older adults skills to make a video film. This was followed by the older adults making a film by themselves. A colleague and the trainer were present, but they were there to facilitate, not to direct. So that was all the work of the older adults, really.

***RZ** And did you feel the method changed the end product?*

AB I think it did, yes. In some scenes, you find, for example, that they sit very formally. And in other shots they become quite spontaneous, especially at the end, where they start dancing. That's where they really came into their own. But sometimes they were more formal, especially at the beginning, when each of them appears individually. Because traditionally, even when you had your photographs taken, you sat like that, that formal pose. I think it changed with time as the project progressed and, gradually, formality disappeared among the participants, and they loved it. They hadn't had any opportunities like that to talk about themselves on film. What was very interesting was how they were very conscious about religious diversity among themselves. There were Sikhs, Muslims, Hindus among them. But they wanted to foreground a unity. We had nothing to do with that; that is what they decided. They talked about the partition of India, and they talked about how people tried to be unified, and how people used to live together in diasporas such as East Africa. So they were also trying to construct some kind of a solidarity among themselves, working across these differences.

***BB/RZ** Has cultural production been central in your activism and research?*

AB That was the only film that we did, really. So in terms of cultural production, I haven't really been involved in making videos or films, apart from this case. But culture itself, as a concept and as a practice, has been very central in my work. Even when I was doing my PhD, I was thinking about how to conceptualise culture in non-essentialist forms. That has always been a problem – well, not a problem, a challenge. It has been a challenge.

BB/RZ *Going back to the question of the university: Can you tell us more specifically about your own experiences in the academy? How have you experienced the change in higher education from when you first started teaching to the period when you retired? It's been a time of remarkable transformation in the higher education sector.*

AB University life was challenging. I didn't actually have my permanent job until 1985. In the early years after I finished my PhD, I couldn't find a permanent job. I had a lot of temporary jobs, which come with their own problems. But politically it was a huge struggle, around knowledge production partly and these different ways of theorising. I was working around issues of race and ethnicity when I first started. In those days, you had discourses of 'race relations' and 'ethnic relations'. People like John Rex, Michael Banton – these were the big professors at the time. It was quite hard to develop a critical and radical academic practice. I think everyone who was involved in this subject at the time would probably tell you that.

It was difficult whoever you were, but if you were a person of colour then it was more of a struggle. I took some pretty unpopular positions. I didn't get much support from my immediate professors in my early years. I turned to the work of scholars such as Stuart Hall for inspiration. And later, when I got to know him at the Open University, he was very supportive. In the early years, I was employed mainly on research projects. I wasn't teaching, because they were temporary jobs. Then, of course, in the latter half, I decided I was going to leave academia, so I worked with the Greater London Council. That was a quite positive experience, I must say. I was in the Women's Support Unit and I had quite a senior position there, and we took up all kinds of issues we discussed earlier, such as intersectionality. We didn't use that term, but we were trying to involve different categories of women.

That was a positive experience, because we were doing new things. We were able to fund women's projects, and through that we were involving the women's groups themselves in telling us what they needed and what they wanted. So I enjoyed that period of my working life. Then I got this job at Birkbeck College. At the time, we weren't part of Birkbeck. It was an extramural studies department within the University of London. I found this work quite creative, actually, because for the first time I was working with a group of women that I got on very well with. There was Jane Hoy, Mary Kennedy and Nell Keddie. We had a lot of autonomy in developing courses, and we could liaise with communities, find out what they wanted, and then we could offer those educational experiences. These were courses at the certificate and diploma levels. Later on, once we merged with Birkbeck College, we developed a Master's programme as well. But initially it was the certificate- and diploma-level courses.

We developed childcare courses, we had courses around antisemitism, and we had courses about Palestine. We organised all kinds of courses that we felt were important to communities – Caribbean studies, Irish studies and Asian studies, under the rubric of 'community studies', as a generic term. So that was really very good, very creative and generative. Then John Solomos (a sociologist) and I developed the Master's programme in race and ethnicity in the politics department. That was one of the first Master's programmes on the subject.

***BB** When was that?*

AB That would have been around 1988, I think. So that too was a creative part of my experience, I must say. And it also meant we could include our own imprint. We developed a lesbian studies programme in the extramural studies department, which, again, might have been one of the first ones in Britain at the time. But on the other hand, my partner always says I was lucky that I was at extramural studies, that it might have been more difficult in other, more conventional departments. And he might be right about that. On the whole, I found academia quite difficult as a person of colour, although as I said, there were moments and stages when it was quite life-affirming as well. But it's changed so much since I've left, I think; in the last four or five years, things have changed so much. Some of the courses we were developing then might not have the same purchase today. Things have changed a great deal. The neoliberal university is now a serious problem.

Selected Writings

Brah, Avtar. '"Race" and "Culture" in the Gendering of Labour Markets: South Asian Young Muslim Women and the Labour Market'. *New Community* 19:3 (1993), 441–58.

——. 'Re-framing Europe: En-gendered Racisms, Ethnicities and Nationalisms in Contemporary Western Europe'. *Feminist Review* 45:1 (1993), 9–29.

——. *Cartographies of Diaspora: Contesting Identities* (Abingdon: Routledge, 1996).

——. 'The Scent of Memory: Strangers, Our Own, and Others'. *Feminist Review* 61:1 (1999), 4–26.

——. 'Global Mobilities, Local Predicaments: Globalization and the Critical Imagination'. *Feminist Review* 70:1 (2002), 30–45.

Brah, Avtar, and Ann Phoenix. 'Ain't I a Woman? Revisiting Intersectionality'. *Journal of International Women's Studies* 5:3 (2004), 75–86.

Gail Lewis

A psychotherapist and long-standing member of Brixton Black Women's Group and a cofounder of the Organisation of Women of African and Asian Descent, Gail Lewis has written extensively on feminism, intersectionality, the welfare state and gendered, racialised experience. She is a former faculty member of the Department of Psychosocial Studies at Birkbeck, University of London, and has taught at the Open University and Lancaster University. According to Lewis, her political subjectivity was formed in the intensities of Black feminist and anti-racist struggle and emerges from a socialist, anti-imperialist lens. Among her political and intellectual concerns, she notes, are the formation of and resistance to gendered and racialised social formation, including the lived experience of inequality within organisations, as well as bringing psychoanalytic and sociological understandings of subjectivity into creative dialogue in an effort to generate what she calls a 'practice against the grain'.

Lewis has been a member of the editorial collectives of the *European Journal of Women's Studies* and *Feminist Review*. She is the author of *Expanding the Social Policy Imaginary* (2000) and *Citizenship: Personal Lives and Social Policy* (2004), among other volumes, and has published articles in numerous journals, including *Race & Class, Cultural Studies, Feminist Review* and *Feminist Theory*.

***BB/RZ** Throughout much of your work, you explicitly draw on your own life experience as part of your theorisation of a problem. How do you articulate the relationship between one's experiences in the world and one's intellectual and political work? How do you describe this method as you've developed it in your work?*

GL You see, I don't really know the answer to that question. If I were to choose where to start this whole conversation, I would begin with something I said during analysis.

As I was explaining to my analyst, throughout my adult life, I've felt impelled to understand the world through lots of political and analytical frameworks – I've felt I really need to understand Marxism, imperialism and anti-imperialism, feminism, post-structuralism and all of these things, right across the board. But everything I've done to try and grasp this complexity, and every framework I've tried to think though – in the end, it's all because

I've been trying to understand my mum. So that's why I don't know how to begin. To say I've been trying to understand my mum means that I've been trying to understand what it means to be a gendered subject in a particular nation-state formation, through different times and in the context of transgressive cross-racial sex and yet to still inhabit whiteness at those moments when she felt intense despair, pressure, fear. What does that mean? How does one understand the structure of their household through lenses of racism, and watching, experiencing, an ebb and flow in which she moved nearer and farther away from whiteness when she'd also been, as mum was, positioned as a transgressive, bad girl?

In a way, that's what I've been trying to understand: the dynamics of a working-class household of multiraciality, living in the mid-to-late twentieth century, and why my granddad – my white granddad – was *committed* to working-class politics, an absolute socialist, but racist as fuck, excuse me, when it came to his daughter and me. And how do you understand that? What did it mean? So, I suppose, I've slowly come to more understanding across a life course; that statement to my analyst came not too long ago, when I could reflect back on my life and what shaped it. But it wasn't that I was *aware* of what I was trying to understand; it was generated by the possibilities and the pains of that kind of household formation.

It was possibilities, as well: the possibilities of what can happen when jazz is played, and how all that has a connection. I mean, what do I know about jazz as a musical form? Other than that it provided the soundscape of my childhood and adolescent life. But for me, that language seems to capture so much of what it *felt* like. On one level, carrying the exciting energy of change and possibility, bouncing out of and yet in excess of a given script, against the odds. On another level, capturing the sudden eruption of the unexpected – drawing you up short or propelling you on – that seemed to make the unarticulated, the disorienting somehow intelligible. Sort of announcing the expected/known right alongside or interwoven with the eruptive/unknown. And that's how I think it felt; it was like what happens when you walk outside and you're assaulted with racist abuse and the intimate connections just collapse. I think jazz is a sort of biography of a particular generation, in a particular space with languages of trade unionism, anti-imperialism and class politics around the household. And yet, one where all of the things that we were supposed to be opposing were being enacted. Not just in school, not just on the street, but at home in the living room, too.

Although sometimes, when I've written stuff like the 'Birthing Racial Difference' article,[1] people have said: 'Oh, you work autoethnographically, don't you?' 'You use an autoethnographic position as a kind of a case study of

1 Gail Lewis, 'Birthing Racial Difference: Conversations with My Mother and Others', *Studies in the Maternal* 1:1 (2009), 1–21.

the now, in order to apprehend wider social and cultural patterns?' I didn't know what that was – autoethnography – but I did want to capture something about a life as constituted socioculturally. Again it links to this question of the household, of its generative side and as the motor of my intellectual journey . . . And I was concerned with the lies that were being told, in the early 2000s, about where Britain was in relation to itself as a racial and racist formation. They were saying: 'Look, the fastest-growing demographic in the population are those called mixed, isn't that good? We had a bit of a tricky moment in terms of being racist, or thinking that *some* people were racist. But we're not a racist formation, and it will sort itself out – and we're certainly not the United States of America.' And it's true: Britain is not the United States, but it *is* itself, with a long colonial, imperialist history and deep implication in enslavement and indenture!

And I thought, on one register, it was just lies, absolute lies; on the other, I thought, what are these disavowals? Where do these lies come from? And, let us tell the stories of how such households are not immune from the dynamics of racism; and how, in its articulation with class, they're also totally imbricated in that racial formation – and might even be implicated in the reproduction of racism at the level of the everyday, you know, just the ordinary, 'going about life' kind of way. And it wasn't as if I was going to get Economic and Social Research Council, or other research grant money, to interview people to tell me about that kind of dynamic; I didn't believe I would get money to do that kind of research. But, I thought, I can tell my story.

So in a sense, I decided to use myself as an example, a case study. But don't forget, I was very much schooled by Ambalavaner Sivanandan in a politics of linking the individual to the collective – that brilliant phrase of his: 'making an individual/local case into an issue, turning issues into causes and causes into movements and building in the process a new political culture.'[2] But another part of me is saying: this is also lived experience; you don't just need to present this sociologically, but also psychologically – through one frame you could call affect, or through another we could call emotions and interiority, and think about the way that stuff gets 'in' us and forms, in part, our subjectivity. So I was saying, let us hold on to the ways in which this is emotional life, too, and could tell us something about the social culture.

Hence 'Birthing Racial Difference' is written in that form; it is a kind of letter from the position of a child that says: 'I don't understand – this happened and that happened, and it felt like *this*, didn't it?' And everywhere you look, the story of the reproduction of race is there, including in the music that we love so much. The music both speaks about, shows us, what racism means, and shows us its constant reproduction; of course, in the Foucauldian sense,

2 Ambalavaner Sivanandan, *Communities of Resistance: Writings on Black Struggles for Socialism* (London: Verso, 1990), 58.

we can see the idea about discourse constituting that of which it speaks in action. The music speaks of us and we identify with it. The first version of that 'Birthing Racial Difference' article was for a small conference called 'The Cultural Politics of Reproduction', organised by Imogen Tyler, a sociologist at Lancaster University. I was trying to think about the *cultural* politics of reproduction, and domestic life in that sense.

So what is it called? It has to do with the constant, iterative co-constitution of the systemic, the structural, the psychically interior, the affective, the emotional, the experiential – trying to capture something of that. This increasingly felt to me to be a really important project because sociology was, in my opinion, increasingly denuding itself of living people. Where are the people it speaks about? By then, I was gesturing towards self-analysis, psychoanalysis, but I also needed to be able to grasp something about a lived demonstration of the sociostructural culture.

BB/RZ *How were you able to identify, write and make connections between specific emotions and emotional states, and the sociocultural and the political-economic? How did you draw the connections between gender and race as social relations and forms of power, and these very strong emotional states?*

GL I don't think that's what I thought I was doing, even if that's what I deliver. In a way, I don't really *know* what I thought I was doing. I wrote *From Deepest Kilburn* in the early eighties, not too long after my mum died, and I think of that now as my 'love' piece – 'let's make it all pretty, sort of happy, in the end' kind of thing. But of course, it was in the face of an unbearable loss. My mum is this person who you think you know through the 'Birthing' piece and its narrative of her strengths, her pains, her bravery, and her retreats into whiteness. I *adored* my mum. But as I came to recall her more honestly, more fully, in what I guess we could call all her humanness, I came to understand that adoration is also a way of defending against the negative – hers and mine. And if I'm going to *really* be true to her, I need to be able to begin to dig around and see: Where does the negative develop? For me, to be angry about things she did that warrant anger and that I should be able to show my pain about is difficult. I mean I did seven years of the first analysis, and still, my analyst said at the end, 'One day you will be able to be angry with me' – in other words, one day I'll be able to acknowledge my ambivalence. But for so long, I just couldn't do it.

The analytic categories available to us (here I'm thinking about those generated by feminism) lacked the capacity to help us to understand that. We needed to try to think about what happens when we're face-to-face, knowing that the battle is around the importance, the centrality of the legacies of imperialism for the making of our lives as women in Britain at that time. But actually, what it means is asking, who are we facing? We need to know that stuff; we need to have ways of understanding that colonialism transcends, even in neocolonial times, apparently, formal independence. It ricochets down through the generations, but also down into the interactions between one constituency and another. At the Birmingham National Women's Liberation conference,[3] there was a big fight in the plenary session around imperialism. (It was also around sexuality and all sorts of other things.) We said, 'You cannot begin to move forward unless we can *grasp* Britain as a neoimperial power.' Its links with Israel and Palestine, and Ireland at the time – those old modes of imperial/colonial power – were part of the 'nowness' of empire. Women stood up in that great big hall screaming at each other. This wasn't just a battle between an ideological position that said to understand Britain now we need an anti-imperial lens, and another that said we need to form around gender; it wasn't just those ideological positions confronting each other, but groups of actual women saying, 'You are this, that, or the other' – abusing each other, in one way or another. So who is facing who then? Who have we become?

It's no longer Gail Chester and Gail Lewis on opposing sides of that ideological argument; it's a phalanx of white women facing us, and from her perspective, probably a phalanx of Black women (and I am aware of the imagery of that language!). If we're going to make an intervention to expose the limits of white feminism in whichever political frame – its limits, its *incapacity* to really grasp what it might mean to be a gendered subject in South Africa, a Black woman in Brixton, in Gaza, in Toronto – what might that mean, actually?

The feminist project did not and does not have the capacity to engage that; it needed something, and yet there we were: feminist subjects facing each other in battle. Everyone running away feeling wrecked. Everyone going home feeling like, 'Well, I'm never going to go to a feminist conference again.' With us being blamed for wrecking the conference, or the plenary at least. So in part, I want to understand how there can be such explosions, and I want to understand them psychically, affectively and emotionally, not only structurally, because I think politics needs an emotional understanding too. In that I'm totally influenced by my social, cultural *and* psychological biography, alongside theoretical approaches of people like Raymond Williams and his 'structure of feeling' concept; Wilfred Bion and his theory of thinking; Frantz Fanon and Sylvia Wynter, with the sociogenic principle; or Audre Lorde and notions about anger, the 'master's tools' and silence. These are all part of an intellectual inheritance available to me.

There is something to 'everyday racism', or what we now call everyday racism, though of course, Philomena Essed coined that term back in 1991.[4]

---

3 The Women's Liberation Movement held a series of eight national conferences beginning in 1970. In 1978 it was held in Birmingham. See 'Women's Liberation: A National Movement', British Library, Sisterhood and After, 8 March 2013, bl.uk.

4 Philomena Essed, *Understanding Everyday Racism: An Interdisciplinary Theory* (London:

To take that lead from Williams, with that acutely observant eye he had for everyday interaction, and that idea of a 'structure of feeling': not as hard as the structure, not as soft as a feeling, not the individual feeling. To ask: If we can describe moments of interaction, can we get something from it? Can we understand something beyond the parties to the interaction? I was really captivated by that concept, and that requires an attention to building your capacity to observe and to listen, but to listen to yourself in the interaction as well. And to see what can happen from paying attention. Again, I don't have funded research that somehow gives great 'authority' to my ideas, but I do have life experience, and I can bring examples from there. So, in 'Racialising Culture Is Ordinary', there are examples from observation of the everyday, and I think when you use those as ethnographic moments and then try and think about them, that's okay.[5]

But that contrasts so much with the kind of training of whichever academic disciplines we come from, where the message is that we should not use Black experience as a point of departure; we should not use an 'I', or the so-called personal, in order to get at something that's supposed to be beyond the personal. It just feels like such rubbish that I also wanted to make work intimating I think it's nonsense. And not just nonsense, but also a power play because it disauthorises experience; it means that people can't draw on a whole range of experiences and theorisation, all sorts of stuff that they might bring to the party of knowledge production, where we try to get a hold of this, these, our lives!

BB/RZ *Maybe this is a good moment for us to ask you about the genesis of the Brixton Black Women's Group, in this general context and also bearing in mind your article reflecting on twenty-five years of* Feminist Review,[6] *which assays efforts by feminist theory and politics to grapple with class alongside imperialism and race.*

GL When I joined Brixton Black Women's Group, it had been in existence for several years, but it started as a reading group in the Sabaar Bookshop.[7] I think it was women who were involved in *Race Today* who started it.[8]

For the activism I came from, reading, especially work that came out from

---

Sage, 1991).

5 Gail Lewis, 'Racialising Culture Is Ordinary', in *Contemporary Culture and Everyday Life*, ed. Elizabeth B. Silva and Tony Bennett (Durham: Sociology Press, 2004).

6 Gail Lewis, '*Feminist Review*: 25 Years and Beyond,' *Feminist Review* 81:1 (2005), 5–11.

7 Some people think that Sabaar Bookshop was the first Black bookstore in London. See Lopez de la Torre, 'Sabaar Bookshop', 27 September 2007, *Remembering Olive Collective*, rememberolivemorris.wordpress.com.

8 *Race Today* was a monthly (and later, bimonthly) magazine that was first launched in 1969 by the Institute for Race Relations. From 1973, it was published by the Race Today collective and published its last issue in 1988.

Third World scholars, was a requirement; you had to do it. Whether you understood it or not, you were supposed to read, and we'd meet together to discuss. So they got together in the Sabaar Bookshop, and at first really trying to develop frameworks for understanding, theorising I guess we'd call it, the position of Black and Third World – the term we used then – women. In BWG, we'd talk about women, but we'd always mean Black women, in the wider sense of the word; we didn't mean all women, and we weren't really including white women in that phrase.

So the point was to understand women's position and how to really take up the battle with brothers in local groups or the national liberation movements. Gerlin Bean was such an important figure for so many of us. She was also always active at the local level in terms of the attempt to develop services, resources, for Black women. So they were involved in the campaign to set up a nursery for mums to be able to put their kids in safe care. So there was also that kind of local work going on, in terms of challenging the racism of the local authority – not only in terms of the distribution of public goods, but also the lack of provision.

Then it became much more a kind of women's group – not just a reading group that took up questions, but organising around services, around the distribution of and access to services. But because the reading group had been based on issues of anti-imperialism from the beginning, the two kind of came together in BWG, where our agenda was to be in alliance with anti-imperialist struggles and take on the gendered racism of the state locally, but also to join anti-racist campaigns around the country – whether that be taking the anti-racist agenda into feminist politics more broadly, or confronting racism particularly in terms of the state, especially in immigration, women's reproductive rights and health, and policing.

BB/RZ *What is your view on intergenerational shifts in organising, the nature of the claims being made and, in particular, the demands being made of the state? How do these claims sit with ever-changing patterns of migration and mutating forms of racism?*

GL My generation is the product of postwar migration – though we absolutely need to acknowledge that we were not the first. We didn't just arrive then, you know. But in that particular moment of migration – which took place through recruitment from the Caribbean and South Asia and elsewhere, and was at the point, of course, of the formation of the welfare state – there was some structure of feeling (perhaps that is the word again), a sense of belonging to collectives. And that was organised through a state-citizen relation.

It's interesting because the notion of collective belonging that permeated the idea of a welfare state was that of 'blood', with the Blood Transfusion Service, which was and is organised on an unpaid volunteer basis, being symbolic of the welfare state. It showed that strangers were connected through something, an exchange of an intimate part of oneself, but also a symbol that carries both the idea of the universality of 'the human' – we all have and need blood – and the idea that the human is in fact divided into subunits which break up and organise 'belonging' into hierarchies of legitimate membership and claim. So there was that sense of connectivity, and therefore a kind of collective state of mind that came from the migrations and all the struggles that people had been in.

Then, there was complete disorientation that suddenly they were black and brown, whereas they had thought they were British subjects. And then they reasoned, 'Well, we'll make a demand on the state as citizens' – thus buying into this idea that the collective is the citizenry that is subject to the state, but that the state organises the connections, the connectivity. What I mean is both that the state organised the production and delivery of services (whether via a private provider or a public sector one) and benefits, and that it determined the criteria by which users were (and are) accorded legitimate entitlement. And these criteria are normative and normalising in so many ways, often linked to symbolic notions of blood as the basis of legitimate claim and belonging. At the same time, this implicates the state in fostering a sensibility of connection among 'strangers' convened under the sign of the nation/al but also, and maybe increasingly in these post-Brexit times, the sign of the regional: for instance, the 'North' versus 'London and the southern elite'. So our campaigns were aimed at advancing our citizenship rights for access to better terms with public goods – not just benefits as such, not just labour relations, but rights to the public good as members of a public, as citizens.

And some of the basis of those claims was the notion that we're owed it because of imperialism: 'You told us to come as your people; now you're telling us, "Oh, you can't live here, there or anywhere, and you can only work there."' So structuring our experiences in that way, demarcating us into particular locations, into particular employment sectors. For Caribbean people, this was into the public sector, in particular; for South Asian people, it was much more into the private sector – but in either case, it was still a gendered-racial labour market and distribution of employment opportunity.

Nevertheless, there were some legacies of that collective claim that were then carried on by my generation – the children of that first generation of post–Second World War immigrants. And I think that was informed, in part, by the legitimacy of their claims about the legacies of imperialism, so there was a continuation of the anti-imperial demand in that sense. As we've gone through these generations and the move from 'immigrants' who must be assimilated; to 'immigrants' who must be integrated and not 'flattened out';[9]

---

9 A reference to a 1966 speech by Roy Jenkins, then Labour home secretary, in which he said, 'I define integration . . . not as a flattening process of assimilation but as an equal

to 'ethnic minorities', who still bring cultural diversity but are no longer immigrants as such, but minorities. Now we have the 'settled minorities' pitched against the 'newcomers' up to post-Brexit, who were often, but by no means exclusively, European. And the settled minorities seem to have a responsibility to translate for the new ones the terms of really being here and aligning to Britain and its values. It's just staggering because, in my hearing, it says: 'You are settled; now here are the terms in which you can remain settled.' It does not so much support the English cricket team, but discipline the 'newcomers' into the correct 'values' as the basis of their, and your, subordinated inclusion.

So, the settled immigrants will have a job to do, and if you don't do it there will be problems. But even if you do – as we see so bitterly obviously with the 'Go Home' vans, the so-called hostile environment, the 'Windrush scandal' and the other daily scandals that are part of the same logics of violence and abuse, but not in the headlines – there will be trouble. And racialised people will still have to sing for their supper of belonging and still be subject to the state's patrolling of its actual and symbolic boundaries of the national, citizenship and belonging. And then we see this logic moving into and becoming part of a logic of the self-actualising neoliberal subject, who in a racialised/ethnicised structure and discourse may mobilise their 'ethnic capital' – a notion that goes all the way back to a sociology of migration and assimilation associated with the Chicago School in the 1940s (which Rod Ferguson critiques so compellingly).[10] And I think that what we see among the younger generation is that even when they do organise collectively, it's to gain a capacity to be more self-actualising in a neoliberal individual sense rather than actualising in a collective sense, where your sense of being a subject who can self-actualise, who has some degree of agency, will flow from the collective.

I think there's been a transformation across the generations – from my old age, that's what I see. And so often when I talk to the younger ones, I try to point this out a bit and say: 'You want to organise collectively, but for what? The task before you is for what purpose?' It's not that I try to lecture them too much, but to ask, for what purpose? And let's know the difference.

BB/RZ *From your vantage point, what does this generational shift look like?*

GL Well, for example, I recently attended a gathering for African women who are from the continent, but who live in Britain. And they give awards for exceptional achievement in your particular field. The reason for the gathering

---

opportunity, accompanied by cultural diversity, in an atmosphere of mutual tolerance.'

10 Roderick Ferguson, *Aberrations in Black: Towards a Queer of Colour Critique* (Minneapolis: University of Minnesota Press, 2004).

was to pay tribute to around ten women who had become successful in their field of work and had done it on their *own* – yes, against the odds, but on their own.

So, it is a collective tribute for a capacity to individually self-actualise, to advance in terms of career, absolutely. Now, in the Organisation of Women of African and Asian Descent (OWAAD), say, the idea that we would have gotten together in order to applaud the fact that someone got a job as a senior lecturer, or got a promotion, or to applaud the work that people did in the schools with changing the curriculum and all that kind of stuff – to applaud the work of one individual, say they were awarded a Member of the Order of the British Empire (MBE) or something, was not plausible. That was not the political horizon; that was not the thing to pay tribute to. The tribute was how much of the curriculum is going to be changed? Was more money going to the supplementary schools that were for all the different racialised communities in need of it? How were we getting the resources out? How was the collective going to advance, and on the back the individual?

And that shift that seems to me to be such a profound marker in relation to the racialised population – one that shows itself generationally a bit, but is such a marker of the success of the Thatcherite project, and of the success of 'integration' at one level, ideological integration, even though they're still minoritised, still othered, still deemed – what was it? Black, Asian and Minority Ethnic (BAME), as it's become known. But in terms of the indices of tribute, applaud, success, failure, they're just transformed. Maybe I'm wrong, but it seems to me that's what happens more and more.

Once, our politics was aimed at the state – the state as oppressive and the state as welfare. That's why I did the social policy work, which was about investigating the terms of inclusion or subordination, I think it became a subordinated inclusion[11] through its recognition as being in, but not of (blood again!), here – the nation. So the object of protest and claim and contestation was the state, whether that be policing or the National Health Service. Some things we needed and others we didn't; that's where you made your claim for recognition, inclusion, *transformation*. It was about trying to leverage something in the interests of making something different, *not* about trying to expand the existing state to make it more capacious, so as to include 'you'/'me'/'us' but without fundamental change – like gay marriage! Though I must say that now I think, in terms of policing and criminal justice, that it's still the state, absolutely.

But the other things seem to have fallen off the agenda. I don't know if I'm right, but let's think about it together. When people make claims about decolonising the curriculum, are they about the state organisation of education

11 See, for example, Gordon Hughes and Gail Lewis, eds., *Unsettling Welfare: The Reconstruction of Social Policy*, vol. 4 (London: Psychology Press, 1998).

that's really become private education? It's private education; students have to get a loan and pay it back, you know. It's not a grant, it's not a state-facilitated education. The state ranks the universities and all that kind of stuff, but it's really private. If mum and dad can't pay for you, you get a loan and then you pay it back for the next thirty years of your life, you know, when you're earning X amount.[12]

Is there a conception in the decolonising agenda about that move from higher education being state-provided to private? When we make a play for decolonising the curriculum, is it about an imperial state, or is it about the modules of the tutors? I don't know, I really don't, but I just feel like so much of the idea has evaporated that it is via the collective that the individual grows/develops – at the risk of being crass, the notion that it takes a village to grow a child – and not the other way round.

BB/RZ *I want to go back to this shift that you were talking about, from a collective idea of feminist politics to a more contemporary one that valorises individual accomplishment. I want to ask you how you would read that psychoanalytically. Can you tell us more about how a different subject is actually being produced through this mode of politics?*

GL Well, I suppose it would be partly in terms of the ways and contexts which organise how we live – the sociostructural, cultural formations in which we live – do have a kind of psychic life or effect in terms of how we can imagine ourselves to be – a kind of ontology of possibility of selfhood. Thinking psychoanalytically, one of the key ideas within the British object relations approach is always *the struggle*: a narcissistic one where the maintenance of yourself – your ego, the maintenance of your own individuality, protection of self and what's yours – is in constant conflict with the desire and need to have connection with others. These pulls are in constant conflict because, you must remember, psychoanalysis is a model of conflict, just as Marxism is.

Part of psychic life is this battle between a pull towards individuation and separation, on the one hand, and a pull towards connection and dependence, on the other. In the context of an attack on welfare, social relations were imagined in the welfare state as connections between strangers; of course, these were national strangers, but strangers nevertheless, and we didn't want 'outsiders'. Where that discourse of the national is rubbished as promoting a 'nanny-state' dependency, this notion so easily travels into psychic life, where it causes an increased conflict: a pull between individuation and autonomy, a fantasised omnipotence.

12 At the time of writing, the annual income threshold for the repayment of student loans taken after September 2012, for an undergraduate degree, is £25,000. For more information, see 'Repaying Your Student Loan', www.studentloanrepayment.co.uk.

So there can be a kind of mirroring between the pulls and contradictions within and between psychic structures and social structures, if you like, and the ideologies that are brought to bear and the way in which the social structures are organised. The extent to which social structures and discourses promote (or don't promote) ideas of collective responsibility for each other – not for something called British values, but for each other. So I think that's one way in which a psychoanalytic reading kind of really gives a life to that.

The push back into self-reliance, self-actualisation, on one hand can feel good, and dependency can feel like a narcissistic wound that leaves us saying: 'Yes, please, I'll have some of that fantasy of omnipotence, of independence in an era of Brexit in which we can delude ourselves about some return to greatness. Yes, I'll have some of that.' But it collapses because there *isn't* enough affordable, decent housing, and you *are* on a zero-hour contract that doesn't guarantee regular income, but is okay because it means you can balance the thousand demands you have on your time and emotional resources each week. And the banks are not going to help, because after the 2008 financial crisis, finance capital is regrouping and those guys who have actually been playing with it all, have got it all. They've been playing with your life and suddenly here again in the world beyond you, there's the collapse of the capacity to be independent; suddenly you need a welfare state that's gone, and the pressure that imposes via a sense of failure mobilises feelings of shame; and, in psychoanalytic thinking, there's a real sense of a fear of annihilation, especially in the Kleinian school, where there's a sense that's what the death drive is. (It's a bit different in the Freudian school, and in the Winnicottian, there is not a conception of the death drive.)

But you know, there is a constant fear that I'm going to be eradicated if I'm not independent, if I'm not strong enough in terms of my ego, if my sense of self is threatened or if I'm so dependent that I'm going to disappear. And that means I can start mobilising psychic defences to try and ward off those feelings that are unbearable and unintelligible. So everything can tap into that and promote feelings of hatred, the feeling of being threatened, that somebody has come and taken what's mine and gone. 'Look, there are no jobs, and even though there are no immigrants round here, the immigrants have taken the jobs and I don't fucking understand what's going on anymore.' And psychically, in unconscious fantasy, that makes sense because I can't be independent; I can't get a job; I can't do what I'm supposed to do as a proper adult, especially if I'm a man – look after my family, that kind of stuff. I think there can be a play between those kinds of psychic pulls and the dominant ideological frames that valorise narcissistic independence, a travel between psychic reality and a social world that has become unintelligible. The task of academic enquiry is, of course, to expose the conditions that support and valorise that kind of play between psychic and social processes; but often it does exactly the opposite, producing work that legitimates white – often masculine – supremacy and then claims it as and gets applauded as 'explanation'. It's outrageous!

***BB/RZ** How might this help us understand Brexit, and its race and class dynamics?*

GL In some senses what I've presented to you is the struggle between the life and the death drives. At the extreme, if and when they're really separate, it can mean that the death drive – the destructive force, the tendency that human beings have to lash out and try to psychically (or actually) annihilate others – also risks, in the process, annihilating oneself. But psychoanalytic thinking also says that they fuse, that there's a fusion of the death and life drives, and so what happens, is that there's still the struggle, but it does not, as it were, inevitably lead to destruction.

There's a struggle that allows for ordinary human ups-and-downs and aggressions, in some moments, and love and care, in another moment. But the fusion happens because of being in an environment of care, whether that be the care provided to the infant, or collective care provided to the collective through something we might call welfare – or, indeed, through activism! And that can, therefore, mediate between the more destructive and the more loving, caring aspects of relations with others. Alongside a psychic process of splitting (a complete separation in one's psyche) between the 'good' and the 'bad', the idealised and the disparaged, together with a context where the value given to collective care and the possibilities for collective care are eroded, this can produce more violence – verbal, emotional and psychic violence as well as physical – especially at the level of everyday interaction and talk. Just think about all the trolling and uninhibited hatred and violent abuse on social media.

In a context where there's much more of a capacity to care, and with that care to acknowledge there is a fear of dependency, we're frightened of being reliant, and for good reason. But when one feels that 'it's okay, I can manage it,' that collectively we can manage it, that's when it doesn't become unbearable. So psychoanalysis has a way of thinking about the stuff that mediates these two forces, and it's called fusion. This is fostered in and through relationships and structures that facilitate containment and this capacity for containment – the ability to sit with feelings that are unbearable and unintelligible, and hold them until they can be processed and made sense of, can give rise to what Wilfred Bion calls 'thinking'. And this capacity is something that we take into ourselves, so we can do it too – for ourselves and for others. It was what no one could do at that feminist conference I spoke about; the challenge is to be able to do that *and still* be able to work and think politically about minoritisation, violence and degradation of certain segments of the population here and globally. It's a real challenge in my view, but a necessary one.

BB/RZ *Through very detailed interview work, you exposed how state processes of social welfare provision are complicit in fabricating relations of power and race and gender norms when it comes to family forms, kinship, and so on. Do you believe that the social welfare state could have created the conditions for collective care that challenged racist and sexist social relations?*

GL I suppose my work itself was an intervention aimed at exposing the ways in which the welfare state produced racialised gendered subjects as subordinated, and at saying that this was not just happening at the hands of the coercive state apparatus. Changes needed to be made that were more welfare minded, if you like, by which I mean more minded to the idea of the collective care of each other – to recognise the full humanity of those different from me, even though our relationality is structured in and through hierarchy, and that we have a responsibility to pay attention to each other, without requiring people to assimilate or become normative subjects.

And to think about how to change each policy area and practice area, and how that might be done; that was the intervention. But it was also an intervention into the academic or scholarly discipline called social policy, to say, 'Look, it's no good just going with all these equal opportunities agendas or diversity; that's all irrelevant.' Something much more fundamental goes on, and we need, as scholars, to pay attention to how the inequalities of subjecthood are produced. In fact, we produce them through the very terms of welfare provision: access, quality of good provision, of service delivery and all those kinds of things.

And we can't do this kind of analysis, even if we lean to the left politically, by thinking about the welfare state only as a class state. It is a class state, but attending to the questions of the ways in which it is involved in producing a disciplined, pacified working class will not eradicate the ways in which it's also about the production of subordinated, racialised, gendered subjects. But I still get very absorbed in welfare issues in the news and keep shouting at the news. I think it is a generational thing, in a way; I am a child of the welfare state, and when I first started off, I was trying to understand why these things that are supposed to be good, like mums and households and welfare services and all that, are also not so good.

As I said, a lot of the politics – across the range, not just in terms of anti-racist politics – was about addressing the state and what it did to reproduce structures and experiences of inequality. So I was part of that moment as well. And on the other side, the question of how we might have a society that can take care of each other feels more vital now than ever. And whether we can get there – I mean, now it really feels so bad – given this dismantling that began in the 1980s. It wasn't just dismantling, it was a rearticulation that Thatcher introduced, and one that has been taken so much further since. Indeed, she started something, but both Labour under Blair and the coalition government of the Tories and Liberal Democrats have really deepened it. It's a long narrative, to do it real justice, but I guess I am thinking about the ways in which a market logic was positioned as the primary one through which to organise welfare. This was not just by privatising services and bringing in private capital, but ensuring the *logic* of private capital and the market would be privileged over a logic of meeting needs. And so this needed exactly a breakdown of the state–citizen settlement that framed the idea of collective belonging I was talking about earlier. The Thatcherite project also reorganised and devalorised modes of working within welfare organisations and attacked many of the groups of professionals within it, all in the name of 'choice'. But this was the choice of the market, rather than involvement in decisions about packages of care – it was precisely not the implementation of the idea of 'nothing about us without us' as a basis for the organisation of services. And that was followed by a sustained ideological attack on the challenges and claims that had been advanced by activists in anti-racist, disability rights and feminist campaigns – challenging the welfare state's discriminations, normativities and normalisations.

But also, the effort to resurrect and embed the idea that the state provides welfare and benefits is aimed at providing residual services and benefits for only the most needy – those who, in being 'most needy', are positioned as having failed, as a kind of welfare 'scum' who lack the capacity to be independent and provide for themselves and family, and who have been feckless and maybe even *chosen* to do so. So they become what for a while was expressly referred to as 'the underclass'. And that's where we've gotten to: meanwhile, homelessness has rocketed, kids go to school hungry, and food bank use and referrals are sky high. I don't know how we come back from that. I think the project is to begin to establish emergent formations, which must take place at local levels – that they gather in such a way that we can imagine something. And I do believe it will happen, but I'll be long, long dead.

I think the work that needs to happen is an effort to map and understand the emergent formations in their localities – in their specific sites and forms – and ask, 'What is happening?' It might be the germ of another kind of welfare state or collective organisation of welfare that might exist. And that wouldn't just be in Britain; the idea would be to understand it around the world, internationally. Part of that would also include understanding the sorts of ecological activity that go on, and I don't mean necessarily the ones that are rolled out in the developed First World or the West, or the global North (or whatever it's called). But also the local, ecological activisms that happen all across the global South – attending to the question of the environment, and land, how land is thought of differently and *lived* differently, as a relationship, not a domination. All of those things must be gathered.

This is how we look after each other, because we attend to this land which we do not 'own' or dominate, but tend, relate to and live in harmony with. I imagine that must happen. Do I know enough about it? No. But I think that's where the seeds of something different may lie. And just as the seeds of the welfare state in Britain were a result of activism, real activism on the ground. It was not led by academics; William Beveridge and John Maynard Keynes (both Liberals by the way) didn't just decide, 'Oh, okay, we'll give it to them'!

Going back to that question about changes over the decades, I suppose what Cedric Robinson told us about racial capitalism was that part of the way in which it reproduces itself is to change, not just in the sense of the drive towards ever-expanding accumulation, but beyond that, even. And that propensity to change involves the reconfiguration of 'insides' and 'outsides' and statuses of populations and their relations to one another and their capacities to move. This raises the question of mobility.

In speaking about the terminological moves from 'immigrant' status through to being considered 'settled', we're talking about reconfigurations of what's 'inside' and what's 'outside' – the relative positions within a hierarchy of subordination. I don't mean hierarchies of oppression; I mean the ways in which the subordinated inclusions work to configure a terrain of the nation/al and relations among differentiated constituencies. Women are marginalised and oppressed, of course; but white women don't occupy a position of subordinated inclusion in the way that racialised populations do.

In thinking about the way in which racial capital figures now, very much under the preeminence of finance capital and the effects of the financial crisis of 2008, we might try to map the geographical or spatial effects of finance capital on areas and regions. For example, to see how relative 'desirability', to make recourse to estate agents' talk, impacts the local economy, housing market, leisure infrastructure, transport links and so on. And then to see how that looks when overlaid by a similar mapping of the distribution and concentration of specific racialised populations and *their* relative mobilities and social value. Then, in that context, what role Brexit plays as cause and effect of the movements of racial capital.

In terms of grasping the changes that have happened in our political terrain over the past few decades, I'd be trying to think, with Robinson, about the importance of tracking how racial regimes' practices work in the context of these reconfigurations. What are they now? And how do they layer into – or what are the tensions between – an ever-increasing, strengthening and deepening neoliberal agenda and the ideological impacts of racial (and racist) discourse? For example, young Black and brown people talk about themselves as black or brown *British* without the least shiver, at least seemingly. We didn't claim Britishness in that way; we are in Britain, but we didn't really claim Britishness. It was Black feminism *in* Britain, facing the constraints and the demands and the stuff that was here, because we were here; it was our responsibility to get to work here because that links to the work that's going on there. But not because we really bought into this idea of a nation-state, to which we belonged; we didn't, and didn't want to. But we knew our job was to address it as part of anti-imperialist, international social justice politics.

BB/RZ *Finally, can you speak to your work on psychoanalysis – a field where the theory seems rooted in the experiences and worldview of the white male European subject?*

GL Oh gosh! Well I guess I can think of two ways. In terms of the theories, reading Freud, or Klein or Winnicott (I've not read enough Lacan to say anything about that approach), can be incredibly frustrating and offensive, yeah. But frankly, for me, that's certainly not been worse than reading anthropology, or specifically, social anthropology at the London School of Economics. It has not been worse than reading a lot of white feminist stuff, for sure. It's not been worse than reading a lot of Marxist stuff. So actually, I don't really buy that it's worse than any of the other disciplines that rose up out of the same formation, in which the discourse of 'the human' and 'progress' was the foundation or pivot, even for the highly sophisticated and compelling theory of Marxism.

But then, in terms of learning to be in a consulting room, it's been much more complex, actually. Because what you're learning is how to be with *that* person in the room; and you have to be informed by theory, but it's outside the door a bit. It should be evermore in your mind, really, through your own experience of being in analysis, and being able to mobilise that. What's it like to be a patient, as it were? But what you're focusing on is what the person with you brings. So in that, there's more space to allow whatever comes into the room, the psychic manifestations of the social in that person's life, because you're attending to it. And indeed, this means being attentive to and able to respond to the traces of the overspill I just talked about. And it is more difficult, because the theory doesn't give you the tools through which to analyse that difficulty as it's manifested.

So then what I do – not in an explicit way, because you talk in the terms of the language that's in the room – is to draw on all the other things that I know the world through: my own experience, but also the other theoretical resources. And when I have to write my process notes, I seem to get away with it, in terms of my supervisor; they don't say, 'Oh that was not appropriate.' I mean, they might say 'I think you missed a beat here', because there's always a moment of heat that is key to the session (usually at the very beginning), or there's a shift that you might miss.

For me, there's a paradox in that you're taught how to sit with someone – *really* sit with someone – and listen and do the work that you're there to do, which is to do something with what you feel you've heard. And at the same time, you hit the limits; that's where you hit the limits of the theoretical frame, I think. And you just have to do what you can do with it, and it can be very frustrating. It's frustrating because of how it can draw boundaries around its 'house' (to refer to the idea of scale again) and barricade itself in theoretically and in the interests of purity and what's considered to be the proper object of practice.

And that's why I say that for me, the difficulty is more when I feel I've got something – and often, for a lot of the session you think, 'I don't really know what's going on here at all.' But then you can use your own countertransference, and then you think – even if you have some sort of a sense of a theory in which you might be able to get a grasp of what's being communicated. But I guess what I'm saying is that if you have your suite of ideas and theories about conflict and emotional pain as constituted socially as well as psychically, I mean in terms of psychic conflict, then you're more equipped; and if you miss it in one session, you have other opportunities.

Selected Writings

Lewis, Gail. *Expanding the Social Policy Imaginary*. London: Sage, 2000.

———. *'Race', Gender, Social Welfare: Encounters in a Postcolonial Society*. Cambridge: Polity Press, 2000.

———. *Citizenship: Personal Lives and Social Policy*. Cambridge: Policy Press, 2004.

———.'Birthing Racial Difference: Conversations with My Mother and Others.' *Studies in the Maternal* 1:1 (2009).

———. 'Unsafe Travel: Experiencing Intersectionality and Feminist Displacements.' *Signs: Journal of Women in Culture and Society* 38:4 (2013), 869–92.

———. 'Not by Criticality Alone.' *Feminist Theory* 15:1 (2014), 31–8.

———. 'Questions of Presence'. *Feminist Review* 117 (2017), 1–19.

Lewis, Gail, in conversation with Clare Hemmings. '"Where Might We Go if We Dare"': Moving beyond the "Thick, Suffocating Fog of Whiteness" in Feminism.' *Feminist Theory* 21:4 (2019).

Vron Ware

Vron Ware began her working life as a journalist, photographer and editor at *Searchlight*, the anti-fascist magazine founded in the 1970s. Before entering academia in 1992, she worked intermittently as a freelance journalist and then as Researcher for Women's Design Service, a feminist organisation specialising in the design of the built environment. She taught cultural geography at the School of Humanities at the University of Greenwich from 1992 to 1999, and sociology and women's and gender studies at Yale University from 1999 to 2005. She was a research fellow at the Open University from 2007 to 2014, and has been a professor of sociology and gender studies at Kingston University, London, since 2014.

Ware published her first work on race and gender in a pamphlet called *Women and the National Front* (1978). Her book *Beyond the Pale: White Women, Racism and History* (1992), focused on the discursive production of 'whiteness' through a gendered reading of colonial history. After developing these ideas in a series of essays, she published *Out of Whiteness: Color, Politics and Culture* (2002), coauthored with Les Back. This was intended as an intervention into the emerging international field that has since become known as critical whiteness studies. Since then she has written numerous articles and essays on the politics of race, gender and national identity.

More recently, her research has explored the effects of the so-called War on Terror, focusing on the permanent war 'at home'. *Military Migrants: Fighting for YOUR country* (2012) addressed the relationship between racism and militarism in the contemporary postcolonial context. She writes a column on militarisation for *openDemocracy*, entitled 'Up in Arms', and has published essays on race and gender in the cultural politics of commemoration. Her latest projects include two books about the English landscape. One is a meditation on the globalisation of the countryside; the other is a collaborative study of a military base targeted for expansion under government plans to restructure the UK armed forces.

***BB/RZ** In the first chapter of* Beyond the Pale: White Women, Racism and History *(1992), you sketch out briefly your personal history and political and intellectual trajectory, including some moves between disciplinary subjects like languages and anthropology. Could you give us some idea of the kinds of things that influenced your political and intellectual formation, and critical turning points that inspired your work?*

VW I've been thinking a lot recently about the idea of generation, especially as a pedagogical tool; how does someone of my age, born in 1952, teach students who are barely out of their teens? How do you speak across those generational divides? And also, what would it mean to position yourself as a postwar child, as a way of trying to explain the different historical period you were formed in? In trying to teach about the idea of endless war in the present, I really had to think about how we account for the times in which we were born which produced this present.

Of course, at the time, as a child, you have no idea, but looking back you realise that it was very much a 'postwar' era. There was a palpable sense of 'the war' in the background: your parents had been involved in it, you didn't have to bother with any of it, and you were told you got the benefits of whatever was the outcome, if you were British.

My parents had been in the armed forces, as so many were in their generation, unwillingly, reluctantly, excitedly or whatever. In my father's case, he was in Burma towards the end, fighting the Japanese in one of the most brutal and horrifying chapters of the war. I was dimly aware of it because of the books he used to read, but he never actually wanted to talk about it.

Growing up in a village, you'd think one might have been shielded from this history of war and empire and all that. But this was the southwest of England, and as it turned out, a lot of ex-military settled there. Decolonisation was raging, although I didn't really know about this until much later. We were still under the illusion that this was peacetime. Some of my parents' friends were actually fleeing, or at least relocating, from British colonies in the 1940s and '50s. One family had gone from running a plantation in Sri Lanka to Kenya and then to South Africa (or maybe South Africa to Kenya) – obviously, they had wanted to get away from independence struggles – and they ended up farming in Hampshire. So, of course, they brought all their views and experiences with them. There was one older woman whose husband had been a headmaster at a boarding school for young rajahs. Everyone knew that she just yearned to be back in India; she would invite you to her house for curry and tried to involve everyone in her charity events to raise money for an eye hospital there.

Some of them had very obnoxious views about race, and when we started having heated arguments about immigration, for example, or apartheid, this inevitably opened up painful rifts with family friends. There was one woman who used to say: 'You don't understand if you haven't lived in South Africa. The system really works well.'

You can sometimes relate your political formation to books you read as a child, in which the sense of injustice was very strong. When I was about eleven, one of my aunts randomly gave me a children's novel, about an African American girl called Mary Jane who was bussed into a white school in the early sixties; it was told from her point of view. I still remember the story vividly. It was by Dorothy Stirling, a white American historian, who wrote a number of popular history books on African American women – one was called *Black Foremothers* (1979).

I don't know if you saw the James Baldwin documentary *I Am Not Your Negro*? Well, there's a section in it where Baldwin describes how he went with the playwright Lorraine Hansberry and a few other people to see Robert Kennedy to ask, could he not walk with one of these girls into the school? Could they not show that support together, publicly? And of course, this didn't happen and Baldwin had felt a strong sense of shame, as he explains in the film, that Hansberry had been so right to ask for this and they had let the children down, by abandoning them. Seeing the film reminded me of this experience of this girl that I had read about as a child of the same age. It's amazing what children's literature can do. There were other books that allowed you to inhabit characters from different worlds. I used to read all the time. There was a mobile library that came out to our village once a week, and we were always given books and book tokens as presents, too.

Growing up in the sixties, the whole thing around pop music had an influence as well. I didn't really know much about the Vietnam War, but I had an older sister, and we were all against it, you know? So that was the general background – and things like the pill, of course, which again, looking back, had a huge impact on our sense of freedom and possibility as young women.

This might sound strange, but when you're brought up as a Christian – and I was sent to a convent – you do actually find yourself believing in things like treating other people as you'd want to be treated, loving thy neighbour as thyself, and the importance of justice and peace, all that kind of stuff. I remember being very conscious that Christianity came from the Middle East, and I'm sure this created a sort of affinity with that part of the world.

There were other things I can recall, too: certain conversations; going to university, which was a big deal for women in those days, but really hating it when I got there. I was studying Persian and Arabic and had lived in Tehran for three months before I went to Cambridge. I won't go into details, but university was an absolute disaster for me. I was quite fluent in Farsi by that time and had learned all about the political situation in Iran from the friends I'd made, but my teachers made me start again with the ABCs and we just read the classic texts – nothing wrong with that, but there were only two of us in my class. The course in Classical Arabic was even worse, so some of us tried to change it by insisting that we did more on modern Arab societies. Then eventually, I encountered feminism there, mainly through feminist anthropologists, as it happened. After that I went to India, and I suppose it was there that I really began to understand what empire had been. I was quite disoriented for a while, but it was after going to the United States in 1977 that I really started to join things up.

The turning point, or one of them anyway, was on 13 August that year, the day of the National Front march through Lewisham. I was going to see my parents in Hampshire with a friend – we had got a lift halfway and were walking to the motorway ramp or something, and I remember thinking: 'What on earth are you doing? You should have gone to Lewisham.' The next week I went back to Birmingham, where I knew I could find somewhere to live, and a friend introduced me to Maurice Ludmer, who was editor of *Searchlight*, the anti-fascist magazine. I had never seen it, but I knew it was exactly what I wanted to do. Little did I know . . . Actually, Maurice tried to scare me off at first, as he didn't know who I was either, but it was the best thing I could have done, and I ended up staying for six years.

BB/RZ *You once said: 'I had always approached whiteness as a relational category, part of a system of meaning about race, class and gender, rather than something to be studied on its own. It was fundamentally a political project too, about taking responsibility for something that is happening in your name.'*[1] Beyond the Pale *was a groundbreaking book in its conceptualisation of whiteness in this nuanced, relational way and its intersection with gender.*

VW I'd been thinking about that for at least ten years before the book was published, even while I was still at *Searchlight*, although it took a long time to find the right ways to say it. When the British Library put *Spare Rib* online, I found a letter I wrote in 1981, which is quite funny to read now.[2] It makes you realise the difference between typing a letter and writing on a computer, as it's quite long and cumbersome. I seem to remember struggling to find the right note, although I was clearly exasperated. It starts off by pointing out that although it was great to see an interview with the poet Adrienne Rich, they missed the opportunity to ask her about her concept of 'female racism', among other things; and then it wades in about racism in the women's movement and the failure to 'open out the whole analysis of feminism to include an analysis of race' in rather a stern tone of voice. And then it ends with the convention of the time: 'in sisterhood'. I do remember constantly being irritated by what I saw as a fixation on male domination in ways that sidelined every other kind of oppression. Plus, a total blankness around racism, as though it was outside women's experience.

I first started trying to write a piece about white women and racism that same year, prompted by a Reclaim the Night march in Birmingham. At the

---

1 Bolette B. Blaagaard, 'Workings of Whiteness: Interview with Vron Ware', *Social Identities* 17:1 (2011), 156.

2 *Spare Rib*, a magazine which ran from 1972 to 1993, played an active role in the emerging feminist movement. The digitised archive can be found at: 'Spare Rib', British Library, bl.uk/spare-rib.

time, there was a panic in the media about young Black men committing street crimes – Stuart Hall and others at the Birmingham Centre for Contemporary Cultural Studies had diagnosed this in their book *Policing the Crisis* (1978) – and of course it was an issue that the National Front (NF) and other fascist groups were obsessed with. The NF papers would be plastered with big headlines like 'White Women Muggers' Main Target', which I had written about in a pamphlet for *Searchlight* in 1978. Anyway, I wrote something which drew on an episode in Papua New Guinea which I had read about in a piece by Amirah Inglis – someone whose pioneering work on white women and colonial power has been quite overlooked.[3] It was one of those moments when a white woman who's used to having boys, or young men, around as house servants, suddenly becomes aware she's being looked at in the shower, or thinks she is. So then there was a huge panic, and a new law was passed to protect white women. Literally: it was called the White Women's Protection Ordinance, and of course, it sanctioned a whole raft of new security measures directed against the 'natives'.

Something similar happened in South Africa, again focused on 'house boys', and then suddenly everyone had to have maids instead. The historian Jock McCulloch has written about this in his book *Black Peril, White Virtue* (2000). These panics happened at a moment where there was a political challenge to the whole regime. So I drew on that to question why suddenly white women were being told they were threatened by Black men. I guess within US history, that particular dynamic would have been well known, but within the British context it wasn't. So I wrote about it, and that was the beginning. Or rather, it wasn't, as I sent the article to *Spare Rib* and got into a very heated row with Linda Bellos, their first Black member. After yelling at me for my 'politics of nothingness' and putting the phone down on me, she sent me an article about a white women's anti-racist consciousness-raising group in the United States to read for my punishment. I ended up publishing my article in another magazine I was involved in at the time.

From there I started looking in bookshops, libraries and archives, and I gradually found these different historical moments under colonialism – at first having no clue how to put the book together, as it all seemed so disjointed, not just historically, but in terms of the overall argument. I was working closely with my friend Mandy Rose, who was involved in filmmaking. Thanks to her, we got money from Channel 4 to develop an idea for a film about the friendship between Catherine Impey, an anti-racist Quaker who ran her own anti-imperialist publication, and the young journalist Ida B. Wells, who were introduced to each other by Frederick Douglass. They met up in England and launched this campaign against lynching in America, and then all kinds of

3 Amirah Inglis, 'The White Women's Protection Ordinance: A Study in the History of Papua 1926–1934', Master's thesis, Australian National University, 1972.

things happened which tested their friendship. It's in the fourth chapter of *Beyond the Pale*.

We decided to make it into a drama, which was really one of the best things I've ever done, most fun anyway, but it didn't get commissioned – I think Channel 4 just thought it was too far outside their brief.

So we researched this story of Catherine Impey and her journal, *Anti-Caste*, and went to Somerset to look at archives. We even met some elderly Quakers who dimly remembered her, and it was really fascinating. One day I gave a talk about it, I think it was at East London Polytechnic, and some of the Black students in the class said, 'You're just trying to say that white women weren't that bad.' And although it wasn't actually what I was trying to do, I realised I hadn't quite been able to articulate my argument clearly. But it was mainly through trying to explain to hostile audiences that I was able to develop the ideas.

After that, Avtar Brah invited me to give a talk on race and gender, and I remember the atmosphere being quite tense – everyone was wondering what I would say. In the meantime, I had realised that this question of racialisation applied to all of us, which meant that white women were racialised too. It's totally obvious now, but at that time, whiteness was just not talked about, which compounded the idea that anything to do with race and racism was the problem of nonwhite people. But if you accept that everyone is racialised, just as they are gendered, then you can point to the relationality of all these categories in different contexts. The historical situations I had discovered could be analysed by exploring how, for example, Black masculinity and white femininity are constructed in relation to each other, as well as Black femininity, and Muslim 'oriental' femininity and white masculinity, all of which are formed in relation to each other. So that was the key, and I became more confident in explaining that I was not trying to make any claims *for* white women, but showing the power or resonance of particular constructions of white femininity that derived their power from colonial history and historical memory.

But during that time, we had also made a documentary about English women in India, although Mandy did most of it, because I think we had the production meeting on the day I gave birth to my daughter. We put out adverts in *The Times* and *Telegraph* for British women who had lived in the Raj before 1946 and we got loads of replies. People really responded – it was as though no one had ever asked them about that period of their lives, and they really wanted to talk about it – a lot of them also said things like, 'I'm sure you won't be interested in this!' After interviewing about thirty-five – and I've still got the transcripts – we narrowed it down to five women. Our criteria were: Did they play bridge? (If not, then they were likely to be a bit bolshy.) Did they know any Indians who weren't their servants? That sort of thing. The ones we chose were of all different ages and class backgrounds, and this made for a great discussion, although there was definitely an awkward argument at one point, about whether the empire was a 'good thing' or not. One of the women was of Anglo-Indian heritage. She was British, living in Hove, but of course, all the other women picked up on it – a result of having lived in a world where these things were indelibly marked, regardless of your appearance.

The idea behind the film was to puncture the stereotypical image of 'memsahibs' – that they were basically posh white women enjoying the sense of power derived from their status in colonial society. This was the standard depiction of white women in films representing the British Raj in the early eighties – like *A Passage to India* or *Heat and Dust* – and we wanted to explore the dynamics of race, class and gender in that colonial era while there was still time to ask people about their experiences. Or at least we wanted to show that it was more complicated than either being into the whole colonial power thing or dramatically rebelling against it. I think that the 1984 TV serial *The Jewel in the Crown* – based on the novels by Paul Scott – had a lot more complex stuff about white femininity and the dynamics of colonial power, but I've never got round to writing about that. One day I will. Anyway, we called the film *Hilda at Darjeeling*, after Mandy found a quote from a novel where one of the characters says: 'Hilda at Darjeeling wondered if there was any country where it was so useless and ineffective to be a woman – at any rate, an English woman.'[4]

So we did this in 1988, and it was shown on Channel 4 in early 1989. Funnily enough, I've been asked to talk about it once or twice recently, and I think that the fact that we used a lot of home movie footage from the Raj era, and oral memory too, means that it has a texture of everyday life for British people in the colonies, which is quite revealing. At the time, it was part of an effort to develop our analysis of the representational power of white femininity in film and fiction, and to relate it to the politics of racism in the present. I was also very aware, from my own life, of how near the colonial past had been – so formative to so many middle-class feminists as well, yet no one would talk about it.

Through this work it became clear that these relationships between race, class, gender and sexuality are being negotiated all the time. That was one of the reasons it was so important to stress relationality. In Birmingham in the early eighties, we often had those discussions among friends, where someone might say, about a situation where they felt slighted, or vulnerable, where they would ask themselves: 'Was it because I am Asian? Was it because I am a woman?' You could have those very frank conversations, because it wasn't quite as awkward as it became. It was still very much about double and triple oppression.[5]

---

4 Edward Thompson, *An Indian Day*, 2nd ed. (London: Penguin, 1938).

5 For discussion on triple oppression see for example, Denise Lynn, 'Socialist feminism and triple oppression: Claudia Jones and African American women in American communism', *Journal for the Study of Radicalism* 8:2 (2014), 1–20.

Those of us who wrote about gender, class and race used terms like 'overlap' and 'intersect' quite frequently, but it took a while, as you know, for that language to become orthodox. And I think, obviously, a lot of feminist theory about 'strategic essentialisms' was addressed to that issue, and 'standpoint theory' as well, which I tried to engage with at the end of *Beyond the Pale*.

***BB/RZ** In the book* Out of Whiteness: Color, Politics, and Culture *(2002), you refer to the idea of 'thinking white' as a way of understanding whiteness, and we wanted to ask, what are the implications of understanding whiteness in this way, as thinking white?*[6]

VW I can't remember exactly where we write about it, but it's the idea of just seeing the world from an unquestioning perspective, which you've been taught, and brought up with, if you happen to be white. Also, not seeing the ways in which that is itself formed by historical processes. So you don't see your relationship with other people in terms of your own racialisation as 'white'. It's like, people of colour, *they* have race, *they* are racialised as different, but we're just kind of normal. So that's what I meant by 'thinking white', basically.

***BB/RZ** You also explain that you thought it was useful to understand whiteness politically, as a political project. It was fundamentally a political project, too, about taking responsibility for something that is happening in your name.*

VW Yes. But that's not 'thinking white' ontologically; that's the opposite. I mean, it's about understanding the implications of actually not seeing whiteness as a racial construct. And maybe it's thinking *with* whiteness, or rather, it's thinking *against* it. That book was very much addressed to a transatlantic audience. I'd lived in the United States for a bit and then went back to live there again, and obviously, the conversation is always in English; you want to speak to as many people as possible. And it was obviously very influenced by American feminist writing.

But it's important to acknowledge the differences, too. It's different if you have the history of slavery and the plantation system in your country. Angela Y. Davis, bell hooks, and many other US writers – Sara Evans, Jean Fagan Yellin – were hugely influential. But there was virtually no feminist work on British colonial history in the 1970s and '80s. All that was done by activists working on their own – people like Peter Fryer, Roszina Visram and James Walvin. And in those days, they were not always thanked or acknowledged for that work, but it was incredibly important. I saw myself as following in their footsteps, as I wasn't an academic at that time either.

---

6 Vron Ware and Les Back, *Out of Whiteness: Color, Politics, and Culture* (Chicago: University of Chicago Press, 2002), 62.

It's so different in the UK, when the empire's something that happened over there and in the past, and we are pushed not to think about it anymore. And it's always been unbelievably hard to bring that up, certainly in my generation, because people really did not want to know; because again, it's like something your parents were involved in, maybe, and you didn't want to have to deal with it, because it was over. You just don't want to go back to those things, because they're nothing to do with you, although you knew they were wrong, and bad, and difficult – as though by not talking about the past, and not facing up to it, it vanishes. Then there's a problem, of course, because it comes back, because it's been there all the time.

The point about things being done in your name, obviously, has particular resonance for people in this country, because what the British government gets away with just gets worse and worse, and it goes on happening in your name. But then, it's a bit of a cliché now to say 'not in my name' – because you so easily say it, but it doesn't change anything. Les and I were really exploring the idea of being a witness, which has different ethical implications.

BB/RZ *Your work really captures the complexity of analysing whiteness without reifying race. Do you think the consolidation of critical whiteness studies as a field of enquiry has contributed to non-relational conceptions of whiteness?*

VW Yes, I suspect that in some ways it has. I think it's an inherent problem. Even if you approach whiteness as a complex and historically contingent concept, it can easily become monolithic, or, just as bad, an abstract thing that we can't ever get hold of, politically I mean. I think, again, there are significant differences between the UK and the United States, so in the States, historians like David Roediger have shown that many ethnic groups achieved their aim of 'becoming white' largely through aligning themselves with the predominant forms of racism.[7] His book *The Wages of Whiteness* (1991) came out just before *Beyond the Pale* (1992), also published by Verso, so I wrote to him, and he wrote back. It was through him that I was briefly involved in the *Race Traitor* project.[8] I really learned a lot from his approach to understanding the psychological 'wages' of whiteness identified by W.E.B. Du Bois.

In *Out of Whiteness*, Les Back and I wanted to make it clear that our analysis of whiteness was embedded in the politics of anti-racism; identifying and analysing whiteness was a strategy, a search for an ethical stance, not an

7 See David R. Roediger, *The Wages of Whiteness* (London: Verso, 1991); *Working toward Whiteness: How America's Immigrants Became White; The Strange Journey from Ellis Island to the Suburbs* (New York: Basic Books, 2005).

8 *Race Traitor* was a journal dedicated to abolishing the concept of whiteness in the United States, published in the 1990s and 2000s.

ontological state of being either white or not.[9] It's always more complicated than that. But clearly there was a growing number of people for whom the category of whiteness was something that was fixed, and there was no getting away from it; you could interrogate it, but you couldn't dismantle it. In other words, you could make people aware of what it meant, but they would still be 'white' at the end of it. So you were left with a kind of purged whiteness.

These sorts of essentialist ideas about any identity are problematic, but then, you can't just wish them away. So I think here it's important to see that you can't keep track of these things. As soon as they get into the university curriculum, they can become fixed in an academic or disciplinary context. And then people select the texts they read, and give students to read, and that often comes down to the availability of the books and journals. Of course the concept has to develop in the light of new patterns of racism – it's been fantastically important to challenge all the discourse about the white working class, and not just in the UK.

I first taught a class on whiteness at Yale in 1996, when there was comparatively little material, and I was doing it regularly until 2005, so I could keep track. Then, I didn't teach about whiteness in the UK until more recently, in 2014, and I had terrible trouble finding suitable things for the students to read – what was in the library, what was exciting in the UK context, what was current and so on. The first year, the class was pandemonium. I didn't know the students very well at that point, and, like most classes at Kingston, it was incredibly diverse. I seem to remember starting with Fanon and working my way towards the social construction of whiteness as the basis of racial ideology, and then I showed a few extracts from a website called the Whiteness Project.[10] It was based in the United States, but I thought it might be helpful if they heard other people talk about whiteness. After a very short time, some people were in tears, some were shouting, but then it turned out that it was the best thing that ever happened to them. They were still talking about the class at their graduation, a year and a half later, introducing me to their parents, saying, 'she taught me about whiteness . . . we had this amazing session on whiteness'. But honestly, I think it was as much about the mixture of people in that room – especially after I got to know some of them quite well over the next couple of years. They were a great bunch.

The second year, it was a very small, quiet class, and we sat round the table and just talked about how you think about race, how you learn about race, and all that. There were no tears, there was no nothing. And no ripples, and I had no idea how it went down. So obviously, it depends on the mix of people in the room. Stuart Hall wrote something about teaching race, about race in the

9 Ware and Back, *Out of Whiteness*.

10 Whiteness Project's first installment, *Inside the White/Caucasian Box*, is a collection of twenty-one interviews filmed in Buffalo, New York in July 2014, and released in October 2014.

classroom, arguing that it always, necessarily, has to be difficult, and that this is not a bad thing.[11]

***BB** Yes, that's right. That's a great piece.*

VW After I read it, I thought, well, I'm going to go and make it more difficult, or kind of embrace that. I mean, I learned so much from teaching.

***BB/RZ** In thinking about learning across generations, we noticed that after the horrific fire in Grenfell Tower in 2017, there wasn't much comment about the New Cross fire or the organising that happened around it.[12] As you were present and involved in documenting the Black People's Day of Action at the time, can you tell us how you are thinking through historical continuity in anti-racist organising?*

VW Perhaps I should say something about why I took those photographs, and what it meant to show them thirty-six years later. In March 1981, I went on the Black People's Day of Action demonstration out of solidarity, but also as a photographer. I wanted to be able to record the event in *Searchlight*, which I duly did. We used to monitor racist violence as well as anti-racist campaigns, so it was important to be there for that reason, too.

Over the course of the day, I took several rolls of film, starting with the gathering in New Cross and going right through to central London. I published one or two images, but the rest stayed in a box for years, along with all the other pictures I took at that time. I always knew they were historically valuable, but it was hard to know what to do with them. A few years ago, I got my own scanner and took a selection to the photographic arts nonprofit Autograph ABP, and they were able to put them in a proper archive, where at least they could be safe. Then at some point, my friend Les Back decided to put on an exhibition in Goldsmiths, which is very near to where the march assembled. He thought that it would be really important for the images to be seen and made accessible to the people within the local community who were most affected. This was the germ of the idea for the exhibition.

So in collaboration with Autograph he raised the money to curate an exhibition of twenty-two of the images in a corridor in the university, which was held in May 2017.[13] He also copied lots of documents from the George

---

11 Stuart Hall, 'Teaching Race', *Early Child Development and Care* 10:4 (1983), 259–74.

12 In the early hours of Sunday, 18 January 1981, a fire broke out on 439 New Cross Road, killing thirteen young Black Londoners. In the face of police incompetence and hostility, in a climate where racist violence was endemic, hundreds of people met on 25 January at the Moonshot Club and marched in protest. The New Cross Massacre Action Committee was set up and plans were made for the Black People's Day of Action on 2 March 1981.

13 Vron Ware, *13 Dead, Nothing Said*, exhibition announcement, Kingsway Corridor, Richard Hoggart Building, 16– 27 May 2017, gold.ac.uk/calendar/?id=10585.

Padmore Institute's archive, which has the papers of the New Cross Massacre Action Committee, and newspaper cuttings of the incredible racist outburst in the newspapers on the day after the march. At first we didn't know how to display all this amazing material, but then he had the idea to use the glass cabinets that run along the corridor. He made giant collages of the press reporting and mounted them on the wall at the back of the cabinets and then transferred quotes from Black activists and historians onto the glass doors. In this way, the racist media reporting was pushed to the background and could be read through the words of those who witnessed the Day of Action firsthand.

The responses to the exhibition were extraordinary, and thousands of people saw it. Part of what we wanted to do was create a dialogue with people from all ages, so Les put up a noticeboard with feedback cards that could be left there. By the end of the exhibition we had over 300 messages. It was very moving to read them.

I also found it extraordinarily moving to witness the reactions of people who were fifteen or sixteen years old at the time of the fire, especially when they came with younger members of their families. Older people talked about their feelings that the episode had disappeared from the culture completely, but also, the hurt and the pain of it not ever really being registered by anyone in authority. I think it was at the opening of the exhibition that somebody told me their mother, who was a community worker, not one of the bereaved, received the telegram from Margaret Thatcher six weeks later, and it said 'Please give my condolences to your people.'

That definitely resonated with what happened in the days after Grenfell. It made you think: well, that was then, more than thirty-five years ago, and how much better is it now, really?

So there is continuity, even though, as you say, not many people made the connection. It's also very important not to think you're inventing those conversations for the first time; those conversations have been going back and forth forever. So why not start from the recognition that those have been going on, and appreciate those voices, rather than just think you're the first one to come along and write about it?

***BB/RZ** There is a frustration with some of the historical amnesia around anti-racist feminist writing.*

VW Yes, I recognise the frustration and feel it too. But, at the same time, I think there's also that question of generation to keep in mind. If you think about what people are facing in their twenties now, sometimes it doesn't matter what anyone said before. Of course, if you are trying to write or summon up a history of anti-racist feminism in a book, then that's different, and you have an obligation to do the homework. That's not just true of race politics, but can be true of any sort of political stance; you need a diagnosis or a way of looking at the world that starts where you are. And that's the challenge of teaching. For example, I tried teaching my sociology students about neoliberalism and new forms of work, and it was really hard, because in a sense, we were jumping into something that seems fixed and normal for them, and I was saying, 'Look, this is relatively new' – which is quite disorienting for people. Because that's what they know; how can it be new? That's what they're born into.

But it's not necessarily easy to find out what happened before, and it needs a lot of work. When we were trying to have those conversations in the late 1970s, in the group Women against Racism and Fascism, it felt very much like a new problem. I specifically remember the discussion about what we were going to write on our leaflet. Why should women be against the National Front? There was useful work on women and fascism, but even so, we couldn't just refer to the Nazis as though things hadn't changed since then. It was much more difficult to answer the question: Why should white women be worried about racism? I mean, how were white women's lives affected by racism directed against Black people? Without a language of whiteness, or a gendered understanding of the threat posed by the Far Right – let alone the racist policies of the main political parties – it was really frustrating. And at that point, we were not reaching for historical precedents; we were totally immersed in the present, without any guidelines.

BB/RZ *We appreciate the generational issue, and see why in the immediate context of being in a movement, you are mostly dealing with the here and now. There has been a shift, due to a lot of incredible anti-racist feminist work, towards at least accepting race as an important category of analysis in feminist circles. But at times this can still be more of a mechanical addition, rather than a historically grounded, analytical one.*

VW Yes, that's true. I was reminded of that era after the attacks on New York in 2001 – I was living in the United States at the time. It opened up an area of feminist politics that was outside many people's comfort zones, so to speak. I wrote about this in the article 'Info-War and the Politics of Feminist Curiosity'.[14] It seemed to me to be really important in the aftermath of 9/11 to make connections with feminists in the 'Middle East', part of the world that had suddenly become the focus of so much pathological attention. One of the first things was to break down this idea that all women in the Middle East were manifestly the same, but it was also about being aware of forms of racism directed against Muslims nearer home, especially on the basis of gender differences. But sometimes it felt like there was a reluctance to apply those analyses

---

14 Vron Ware, 'Info-War and the Politics of Feminist Curiosity: Exploring New Frameworks for Feminist Intercultural Studies', *Cultural Studies* 20:6 (2006), 526–51.

of racism that had been developed inside the US to a more transnational context. Even though there were plenty of writers who had made similar arguments before – Marnia Lazreg, Chandra Mohanty, June Jordan spring to mind. But in the environment where I was working, I definitely sensed a fear of putting a foot wrong, or an avoidance of something that demanded a bit of homework or imagination. Meanwhile, the war in Afghanistan was being unleashed in the name of protecting veiled and subjugated women from their own culture.

This was connected to a crisis in women's studies at the time, I think; and this relates to the generational thing again. Wendy Brown had written an important piece asking, do we actually need Women's Studies?[15] And then Robyn Wiegman wrote a coherent response which broadened the conversation.[16] Yale has one of the oldest women's studies programmes, which, like many others I suspect, had inevitably lost track of the original energy and spirit, partly through being institutionalised (even though it existed on the margins at Yale). It was clear that there was another generation coming through, who were all demanding to read texts from 'third-wave feminism'. I was like, what is that? It made us question what we were doing. Students would say they didn't want Adrienne Rich; all that was old-school, second-wave stuff. Which is very precious if you've grown up with it, and it helped to change your own life.

So that was interesting. I thought, well, obviously, you can't teach feminist theory in the way in which it's developed since the late sixties, because there's too much of it, so you have to maybe start somewhere else. So we redesigned it, and that was actually very exciting intellectually and politically, to redesign the core syllabus for the Women and Gender Studies course. So the question was, how do you teach gender studies for a new generation who have grown up in a world hopefully changed by more than twenty-five years of feminism? We did this around topics, rather than the writers themselves, and this seemed to work very well at the time. It was more a case of how to think from a feminist perspective, on any topic, rather than feel you had to wade through the back catalogue of feminist theory.

So, going back to what happened in 2001 and the buildup to the Iraq War in 2003. It was also a crisis, not just of how we understand 'the Middle East' as a geopolitical term that might need dissecting, but also how we relate to places being bombed by our own countries. A lot of academics seemed really intimidated, and afraid to depart from *The New York Times* script and put their necks on the line. You would hear colleagues saying, 'I don't know anything about the Middle East; I've never been there; let's ask someone in Middle East studies.'

---

15 Wendy Brown, 'The impossibility of women's studies', (1997): 79–101.

16 Robyn Weigman, ed., *Women's Studies on Its Own* (Durham and London: Duke University Press, 2002).

Well, no – you do your own research and you think about why you might be ignorant about that part of the world.

To me this echoed the kinds of arguments from the seventies and eighties around race and the experience of Black feminists: you don't leave it to people who are experts; you have to take responsibility for knowing about it through whatever way you can that opens up those discussions. I mean, no one's ever referred to it, but I felt quite strongly about it, and I thought maybe it was just easier for me, because I speak a bit of Arabic and Farsi. So, you know, it's that thing of making conversations, and finding out, educating yourself. That as a sort of model, really, when situations come up that you don't understand, or don't feel comfortable with. You know, what are the reasons you don't feel comfortable with them? Why don't you ask: Why do you *not* know any of that history?

BB/RZ *How can we explain the resistance that some forms of feminist writing still have to addressing race or imperialism, after so much writing on those subjects?*

VW I think partly, there can be a fear. You know, there can be a fear that whatever they say is wrong. I remember older feminists, socialist feminists, saying to me, 'Oh, but they don't like it if we talk about race.' That would have been 1982, I think. Or, 'You're a person who does race.' So there is a nervousness, I think. And now it is quite policed in a different way, on social media particularly – you can get into scrapes if you say the wrong thing, as you know. I'm not making excuses. But also, I just think some people just don't get it. That's another thing.

BB/RZ *We thought it was very interesting, in* Beyond the Pale, *how you have one sentence that says, 'I just became the race person.'*

VW Yeah. It was true, actually – that happened. Maybe we don't talk enough, perhaps, about anti-racism. The focus has swung back to identity and interpersonal conflict, which can be immensely counterproductive. And you see the people at Grenfell Tower, and you see the people at Finsbury Park after the attack there in 2017; you see the people in Manchester, and all these emergencies – catastrophes – draw people out, and you see the complexity and the connectedness of people's lives.

There can be something so precious in these moments of crisis, and I think in many ways, when you see it, it is very special, and quite unusual. I mean, we were down the road last Monday, near where the attack happened at Finsbury Park, and all the world's media were there.[17] I was taking pictures

17 On 19 June 2017, during the month of Ramadan, Darren Osborne drove a van into

of them, because there was nothing else to see, really, at that point. But you could hear commentators pronouncing on what sort of place it was which was driving us mad. People who knew nothing about the area pontificating about there being a 'large Muslim community' as though it was some kind of ghetto which invited the attack. Never mind the fact that this is a really important and popular mosque that brings people from all over the place to worship there, or that it's a really historically mixed part of North London that doesn't translate into any single ethnicity or religion. Anyway someone said that Fox News was there; I thought, 'Aha, here's my chance to appear on US TV live.' I was going to go up and have a go, you know, push the reporter off his perch and get a few things off my chest to the camera. I probably wouldn't have got very far, but at least I would have felt I was doing something positive.

And then we were at the vigil in the evening, and there were a lot of white residents there, and we heard some young guy saying that this was because of 'white guilt'. That was a ridiculous thing to say, because on what grounds would you assume or project this idea that it was white guilt, as opposed to, it could be just shame, or concern that you didn't want to be thought of as someone who thought that was okay? I'm just saying it's more complicated, in terms of real life, and real emergencies. And when it comes down to it, what really matters? I'm not saying it's like that all over the country, either. I'm sure in a lot of places it's not.

***BB/RZ** But it is that more complicated space that's more and more difficult to carve out.*

VW Yes, but there's a situation in which people do live together, or they might be lumped together by the authorities in some way, or find themselves in a situation in terms of the schools or the waiting room at the National Health Service, or stuck on overcrowded and often dysfunctional transport systems.

***BB/RZ** Yes. We were meaning more in terms of the organising, and movements, because we have many smaller groups that at times operate in silos right now. How can we think about feminist praxis that has and continues to speak across different movements and issues?*

VW Well, I wouldn't want to generalise, although I think you can probably say that about so many social movements. In the early eighties, I was part of a group publishing a magazine called *Emergency*, which tried to make links between different kinds of social movements – this was a time when the Left

---

pedestrians near the Finsbury Park Mosque. In February 2018 he was found guilty on charges of terrorism-related murder and attempted murder.

was endorsing a wholescale infiltration of the Labour Party. We felt that this was misguided and that it was more productive to look at what was happening outside party politics: around race and racism, art, fiction, the environment, sex and sexuality, and often in non-British contexts as well. But there weren't many situations where gender politics and anti-racism were acknowledged as being relevant or important, and this was as true of environmental movements as anything else.

I got very interested in the road protest movement in the mid 1990s, and I went and interviewed some of the people who had occupied a whole street in Walthamstow; the developers were trying to make the M11 motorway come all the way down through East London to connect to the M25 – a horrible idea, which ultimately prevailed of course. So one of the places of resistance was in Wanstead, where there was a tree that they wanted to cut down, an old tree on the common. So some of the protestors gave it an address and started writing letters to it, which meant it couldn't be cut down legally. There were all kinds of actions: for instance, they created a republic in one street, with a flag called the Union Jill, and you had to have a passport to get in – it was very creative, and there were a lot of young women and young men who threw themselves into the campaign.

So, among other things, I tried to interview the women about what it was like for them, being part of the occupation, and at first they said it was fine, no problem. But then when they thought about it, it turned out that the men made the decisions, the women made the tea, and this was the nineties. Road protesting wasn't a feminist issue, and it attracted different people who hadn't necessarily encountered feminism before. I do think that the same can happen now. People get drawn to different causes, and sometimes with place-based campaigns, you get lots of different people with different priorities and experiences coming together.

I mean, I'm conscious now, when you get all the e-mails from different campaigns and groups that you've signed up to, of which ones you just delete without reading because they come every week – even ones that are really, really important. And you just pick the one that you want to put your energy into.

BB/RZ *In* Beyond the Pale *you discuss the practical skills that were involved in abolitionist organising among women in the UK, and in particular, the work that was involved in collecting signatures for petitions. These days, sadly, the petition, as a kind of performative online gesture, has become, or feels, rather hollow. We were wondering what your thoughts are on how social media has changed the way in which organising happens, and how that relates back to the question of practical skills involved in doing political work? Because in your own political work, you've used so many different forms of media.*

VW I think it depends on what you're doing. I don't really understand the differences between 'political work', or 'organising' or 'activism', and it just being a way of life. But I know, for example, in the 'refugee crisis', that there are lots of things going on that we don't see, and I know that in many towns all over the country, there are networks of people who have forced councils to accept families; it's all been done quietly so the families aren't identifiable. And it requires a huge amount of work, and it's all done on a volunteer basis. And I know that empirically from people who are doing it, and people who've said they're doing it, and things I've read.

So it really depends on what kind of interventions you want to do; and of course, through doing that, you might learn skills in organising and fundraising and offering solidarity. I think one of the things about technology is that you see other people organising things, and you know they're doing it, so you don't need to bother. So to what extent would that happen before? For example, the Campaign against Arms Trade. They're really fantastic at the moment, as far as I can see; they're very, very active, and they're very busy all over the place, and similarly with some of the peace groups. For example, Armed Forces Day this weekend was concentrated in Liverpool, because they choose a different place every year. So people were out in Liverpool, lots of different people. It helps amplifying the work, and showing what can be done. So passing on the message is a form of solidarity with them, but also shows that this is something which other people in your orbit might need to know about or think about.

So I wouldn't necessarily make a general argument about technology, because it also requires skills. I think there are other problems related to what extent you try and debate on social media, but I think if you're an anti-racist, you know that you can't debate anything, anyway; if someone's racist, there's no way you can prove anything with numbers or facts.

BB/RZ *So do you think there have been times – and we're wondering if the Grenfell Tower fire, maybe one of these moments – where a different confluence of factors has come together at a particular moment, that galvanises a lot of disparate groups around particular political objectives?*

VW I think that this definitely has to be the worst for a long time, in terms of not just the loss of life, but the horror of it. Sometimes surprising things sort of congeal around one terrible event, like the murder of Stephen Lawrence.[18] After all, he was one young person among many who have been killed in

18 Stephen Lawrence was born and grew up in southeast London. On 22 April 1993, at the age of eighteen, he was murdered in a racist attack. Police negligence in the investigation lead to a public inquiry into the handling of Stephen's case and the publication of the Macpherson Report which accused the Metropolitan Police of institutionalised racism.

violent racist attacks; why is that the one that students obedie
now? As though racist attacks basically started in 1993.

One thing that has been changed by the technology is tha
and choose from the past to suit your argument or cause, as it's s
to find information quickly. But at the same time, there is a real de
of thinking historically. It's like there is an absence of knowledge, when
it's so easy to look online.

One example is the history of people's inquiries in this country. There were so many inquiries, people's inquiries into different events throughout the sixties, seventies, eighties and nineties. Most of them have been largely forgotten, but it's so important to keep talking about them, and to show what's possible.

But actually, uncovering that work is part of politics, and reminding people that's what communities have done to resist. I mean, a lot of the themes we're discussing are about how there's so much work to be done, to explain that it doesn't have to be like this – that people have resisted and have done this before. This is definitely a time when you really need that information.

I was talking to someone at Inquest[19] about Grenfell, and this question of a public inquiry versus an inquest, and she said that there's no question that a public inquiry is the thing we need to do. And yet, there's so much stuff around on social media saying we don't want a public inquiry, that it'll just get swept under the carpet, that we must have an inquest. People who don't know, including myself, have gone along with it, thinking, 'That makes sense.' But staying close to the sources of those forms of resistance, I think, is really important, but very hard.

Selected Writings

Ware, Vron. 'Defining Forces: Feminism and Historical Memory of Empire'. In *The Postcolonial Question*, edited by Iain Chambers and Lidia Curti, 142–56. Basingstoke: Routledge, 1995.

———. 'Island Racism: Gender, Place and White Power'. *Feminist Review* 54 (1996), 65–86.

———. 'The Power of Recall: The Significance of Place in Writing against Racial Identity'. In *Racialization: Studies in Theory and Practice*, edited by Karim Murji and John Solomos, 123–39. Oxford: Oxford University Press, 2005.

———. 'The Space of a Movement: Writing on and against Racism'. In *Handbook of Feminist Theory*, edited by Ania Plomien, Clare Hemmings, Marsha Henry et al., 178–95. London: Sage, 2014.

---

19 Inquest is the only charity providing expertise on state-related deaths and their investigation to bereaved people, lawyers, advice and support agencies, the media and parliamentarians.

——. *Beyond the Pale: White Women, Racism and History*. 2nd ed., with new foreword by Mikki Kendall. London and New York: Verso, 2015.
———. 'A Journey through Europe's Heart of Whiteness'. In *The Intersections of Whiteness*, edited by Evangelia Kindinger and Mark Schmitt, 71–86. Basingstoke: Routledge, 2019.
———. 'All the Rage: Decolonizing the History of the British Women's Suffrage Movement'. *Cultural Studies* (2019), 1–25.
Ware, Vron, and Les Back. *Out of Whiteness: Color, Politics, and Culture*. Chicago: University of Chicago Press, 2002.

Colonialism/Capitalism/Resistance

Himani Bannerji

Himani Bannerji is a professor in the Department of Sociology (York University, Canada). Her research and writing life extends between Canada and India. Her interests encompass anti-racist feminism, Marxism, critical cultural theories and historical sociology. She has done extensive research and writing on patriarchy and class formation in colonial India as well as on different strands of nationalism, cultural identity and politics in India. She has also written extensively on Canada from an anti-racist feminist and Marxist perspective, and edited and contributed to one of the earliest volumes on anti-racist feminism, *Returning the Gaze: Essays on Gender, Race and Class by Non-white Women* (1993). Bannerji is a founder and life fellow of the School of Women's Studies at Jadavpur University, Kolkata, and an honorary visiting professor and general council member of the Institute of Development Studies, Kolkata. She has taught at Delhi University, Jadavpur University and Calcutta University, and was awarded the Tagore Memorial Prize by the Government of West Bengal's literary academy for her work on the social and cultural history of Bengal.

BB/RZ *In 1947, India won its independence from Britain. At the same time, the country was partitioned, leading to a massive loss of life, forced displacement and migration, and a legacy of communal violence. Can you please speak to us about the impact of Partition on your early political formation?*

HB I was born in 1942 and Indian independence came in 1947. My life before then was that of a little girl, but I have scattered memories of the Hindu-Muslim riots that led up to the Partition of India. My memories are based on overhearing people talk, a feeling of a strained environment and long silences. I should mention that my father was a judge in the British judiciary, a role he continued in the postindependence era.

The images of fire and smoke in the night sky, going to the district magistrate's house for protection, sandbags, locked iron gates and sentries with rifles had a great impact on my emotional and political growth. The word 'riot', which is still pervasive in Indian media, was one of my earliest nonfamilial words. I also had heard of the Indian National Congress and Mahatma Gandhi – he was revered by my parents. My mother had a soft spot for the Congress volunteers and gave them rice and vegetables for their common kitchen. This was done on the quiet, as her husband worked for the British government.

These few things I 'knew', or rather felt, are what I remember of colonialism. I overheard the word 'partition', but didn't get any of what it meant until my grandmother said that we would go to another city, in a different country – another part of Bengal, which would become East Pakistan. 'Independence' and 'freedom' (*swadhinata* in Bengali) were other important words for me. Living in a quarter of the city restricted to government officials, cut off from the rest of the city by the civil line, I had no experience of neighbours or of many visitors. The main people who visited were my three older brothers, who lived in then-Calcutta to study. My parents, my older sister and I, and eventually a brother lived in a district town called Medinipur (later part of India), in an old shady house surrounded by high walls and enclosed gardens and servants' quarters. After 14 August 1947 (Pakistan's birth), I learned another new word in English – 'option'. I did not understand what it meant, but by the speed with which our belongings were being packed, I knew that we were leaving for our *desh*, our birthland. In a vague, chaotic and powerfully experiential way, the colonial times – especially their ending – left a lifelong impression on me. I felt, even then, that while something new was beginning, something was also sad. This sadness was mainly picked up from my mother and grandmother.

At this point I should mention that we were a Hindu family and my father could have stayed on in India. In fact, this is what virtually 100 per cent of Hindu government officials did. In some way, I knew of Hindus and Muslims, and also that they were different from each other. India and Pakistan were their own free countries, but my father was 'opting' for Pakistan because his brothers and their joint families were in East Bengal (East Pakistan). My relatives were unable to 'migrate' because their asset was in landholdings and their economic situation would be dire if they came to India. Millions were 'migrating' in the wake of Partition, accompanied by riots, slaughter, violences of all kinds, including against women, and complete dispossession. These carnages were perpetrated by both Hindus and Muslims, and even Sikhs took part in them. How much of this would I have been able to articulate then? Very little, but when I feel back to the time, pieces of images, words, feelings of anxiety and fear flash like fish caught in a dark net. Children are knowledgeable in their own way. Some words and images are burnt into the mind space.

How did these memories, this 'knowing', influence me for the future that was then almost wholly ahead of me? I assume that they contribute to what I feel when I hear about other partitions, other exiles. This unconscious, I am sure, still lingers under what I feel about Palestine. It plays a role in how I feel about Hindu-Muslim communalisation, about the Hindutva (Hindu nationalist) project of the Modi government, about political classes and parties left behind by the colonial rulers as they fight over the spoils, the leftovers.

The discourse of postcolonialism was not common as I grew up. We used the discourse of independence from colonialism/imperialism, and we had immense respect for those who fought to bring it to us. This feeling still lingers in me. I learned to question nationalism – particularly for its disregard for class, caste and patriarchy, leaving us a distorted 'independence' – and I and others still think of India as an independent entity, and not solely as a 'post' phase of colonialism. By my teens, I became aware that India had given birth to a particular kind of dependent capitalism integrally connected with the worst aspects of the metropolitan capital, with Indigenous ruling classes who fetishised modernisation, a phenomenon characterised by high technology and production of scale without the social critical imperatives of 'modernity'. This drive was accompanied by the invention of cultural traditions to rein in political modernity, that is, an effective use of individual and civil rights. This invention of tradition, creating a national unity in a society of profound class inequality, began from the late nineteenth century with the Indian National Congress taking the leadership of the Indian independence movement. This contradiction, characteristic of bourgeois democracy, still continues today.

This story is the only real way in which I can approximate an answer to your questions regarding the postcolonial context and the impact of the Partition on me. Like millions, I was marked for life. If I were to be political at all, I had ample reasons to wish for a better world, one of true independence.

BB/RZ *Can you tell us about the nature of communist politics in India during these times, given the complexity of the anti-colonial struggle and independence?*

HB It should be noted that I was not a member of the Communist Party, but a dedicated sympathiser and consistent participant in its organising activities concerning the situation of women in India. My early identification with communism persists, way past the dissolution of the Soviet Union. My idea of communism was not that of an authoritarian rule and loss of individuality and personal will. I had no fear of collectivity. What communism meant to me, and in many other parts of the world, was far from the Cold War version of communism prevalent in the United States and the West. The demonisation, or an atavistic view of communism that prevail(ed/s) in the West, and that still haunts its political sphere, is even now still absent from what is called the Third World. There were attempts to hegemonise the world by cold war, especially on the part of the United States. Their attempts were, however, only partially successful. For many people in India, nothing that came from the United States was above suspicion.

It should be noted that nationalism mattered even for those who were communist, in a personal, emotional and imaginative sense. This came from a social and cultural politics which embraced everyone. When anti-colonialism is seen in sheer propertarian and economic terms, what is left out is the passion, the love and longing that people feel in their fight against colonial domination. To call it 'nationalism' in conventional political terms is to forget that anti-colonial nationalism was undergirded by a huge tide of affect. The key Bengali word for nationalism, *swadhinata*, or freedom, was saturated by the conditions and feelings of unfreedom to which colonised people were subjected. This explains the vast mobilisation power of the Indian National Congress and Gandhi's charisma. The communist movement shared the emotions of the character of anti-colonialism, and it centrally posed the concepts of class and class struggle as shaping forces for decolonisation, which is a true liberation. The struggles for the creation of the Soviet Union, as well as the cultural richness emanating from them, also provided an imaginative and affective element in communist politics in India. Soviet and Russian literary classics and children's books were much loved by people, irrespective of their political affiliations.

Communist cultures of resistance also deeply influenced our feelings about communism. The Indian People's Theatre Association, and the Anti-fascist and Progressive Writers Associations were part of the collective imaginary for struggle against capitalism and the imperialism of the Second World War. The militancy of the Tebhaga movement, a sharecroppers' insurgency in southern Bengal encompassing India and East Pakistan, was a great source of inspiration and conveyed its message of the peasant movement through rousing folk songs, plays and art. This was all organised by the Communist Party of India. I was also attracted to communism by its openness to women's participation in militant class struggle. Women's participation in Indian nationalism definitely predisposed me to this aspect of communism. Experientially speaking, I had witnessed the violence of caste patriarchy among the households of landed Bengali high-caste gentry. Women's overall unfreedom in sexual repression and in the drudgery of the household, and the torture of widows, were appalling. So it was not surprising that I admired communist militancy. By the time I was sixteen, I fully endorsed armed liberation struggles with an equal place for women.

Another source for my predisposition for feminism was my high school (an exclusive girls' school), in which debates were held regarding how girls and women should dress and behave. Sporting activities for girls were also discussed among students and teachers, particularly because of the interference by orthodox parents of some of the students. During my last two years, issues of women's rights in the context of citizenship and of choice in marriage and women in professions were much discussed and debated. The roles of women in nation building were becoming prominent in the media, as well. Another feminist intellectual influence came from our Fabian English headmistress, who was a hard-line anti-traditionalist and a dedicated suffragette. Her whole life was spent training women to go beyond marriage and domesticity and she embodied that part herself as a professional woman. She was the earliest and most important feminist example in my life up to then, and her copy of Mary Wollstonecraft's *A Vindication of the Rights of Woman* was thoroughly underlined and commented upon by me.

Looking back now, I realise that I never saw patriarchy separately from the caste/class organisation of society. This was the base from which I critiqued the separation of racialisation and heteronormativity from class. Furthermore, in the Indian context, the social mores and values of feudalism cannot be overlooked in considering the position of women. Not only economically, but in moral regulation, Bengali Hindu families were organised in semifeudal terms, especially for those whose roots lay in landholding. The same goes for the Muslim women. As my paternal family mostly depended on rent, I saw from inside the workings of the family in our own home, as well as in our village. Though well-to-do, this family (and others) had no place for women except as wives, mothers and domestic workers, and provided them with little or no educational opportunities. The peculiar feudal notion of 'honour' enjoined this oppression – the idealisation of the *grihalaxmi* (goddess of the hearth), also common among urban professionals, was accompanied by restraints on all sides, a veritable incarceration within the home (or household, in the case of a joint family).

The urban, upper-class professional families expressed their class status by educating women to some extent. This gentry sought an educated wife as a part of the companionate marriage they advocated. Women were educated enough to become good wives and mothers, and to run a home in an orderly manner, entertain colleagues and so on. Gradually, women from this background went on to become professionals, mainly schoolteachers and some doctors. The consciousness of this group also involved gendering of their personal and professional lives. All my women friends in Calcutta are daughters of these mothers. Women's political participation came from this class fraction. Not that it did fully erase the feudal Brahminical mores, but these were mutated to suit the intermediary class position between colonial and indigenous elites. The development of my feminist critique lies both in the everyday life and the intellectual tradition here described.

BB/RZ *In your book* Thinking Through, *you describe how you grew up in a postcolonial context where 'the white man finally had left us, the states were ours, but inscriptions and fossils of colonialism lay everywhere, though often unrecognisable as such because they were so effectively internalised'.*[1] *Tell us more about what you meant by 'colonial inscriptions' and their internalisation.*

HB In terms of colonial inscriptions and the supremacy of English language, I need to make some qualifications and comments, because what I wrote more than three decades ago requires some reconsideration. English-language, British property laws and laws of civil governance are of signal importance

1 Himani Bannerji, *Thinking Through: Essays on Feminism, Marxism and Anti-Racism* (Toronto: Women's Press, 1995), 55.

among the colonial inscriptions. Indian laws today are derived from them, as is the language of the judiciary, and English as the lingua franca. Even religious 'personal' laws of marriage, inheritance, adoption, and so on – compiled from Hindu and Muslim theological traditions by the East India Company, along with the common-law practices of the Whig government on other matters – continued to be present in the workings of the Indian courts. Though family laws were somewhat modified regarding age of marriage, consent, widow remarriage, polygamy and so forth, in the main, personal laws still rely on faith traditions. I would like to suggest a modification on the colonial nature of the Indian legal apparatus by pointing out that Hindu modernist traditionalists and reformers were deeply involved in shaping Indian legal philosophy and practices. This legal situation which produces the colonial hegemony is a peculiar kind of construction, because it is a combination of the wishes of both the colonisers and the resistant colonised. It is no surprise, then, that as Indians we have ceased to recognise our legal heritage as a colonial legacy.

As for English language and literature, the history is even more complicated. Initially there was no attempt by the East India Company to teach English to Indians or conduct their administration in it. In fact, it was the Bengali elite and the urban middle classes who insisted on learning English to participate in the process of governing and economic development. This had been a common practice – to learn Persian and Arabic, for example – in pre-British times. In this, both 'traditional' and reformist Hindu gentry united, and they hired Englishmen to establish private schools and tutoring. It was not until the late 1830s, with the end of the company and the rise of the Whig utilitarian state in England, that English teaching gained prominence in India. Eventually all schools taught English, though all were not English medium. As India was inserted in the British Empire, as opposed to being only a colony, by the third quarter of the nineteenth century an English-knowing middle class had developed, and English served as a device for social mobility and was a great influence in the area of culture.

In relation to learning English, we need to distinguish between English as a language which opened the world of European social and political thought and literature to Indians, and one that served as an instrument of hegemony. The British hegemonic intentions were somewhat subverted by some of the kinds of ideas that entered India, which were anti-authoritarian and anticolonial. Books by radical thinkers, such as Thomas Paine and William Godwin, were banned in India. But they arrived among other contraband from ships at their docking bays in the Calcutta ports. They sold out very quickly. This was the unintended consequence of Baron Macaulay's colonial policy of teaching English to Indians, but the intended hegemonic aspect was also very much in evidence. A large portion of the Bengali elite fulfilled Macaulay's dream by striving to be English in their cultural and political ambitions, though brown in colour. To this we need to add the Anglo and French material culture of lifestyle, interiors and architecture. Venetian mirrors, Carrara marble and oleographs from Germany crowded the houses of the semifeudal colonial bourgeoisie.

But what happened to Bengali and other Indian languages? Did they become subordinate to English? Quite the contrary. Bengali language and literature flourished as never before, to the extent that this period has been called the era of Bengal Renaissance. The meeting with European art and culture strengthened Bengali literary and other art forms. Printing presses worked overtime; theatres were full; bookshops flourished. This cultural politics brought on a severe censorship law in 1876.

Bengali gentry grew into and continued to be a Janus-faced, self-divided entity. They felt simultaneously culturally subordinate to English and Western culture, and proud of 'Indian' culture and spiritual identity. They claimed a 'universality' for their own literary values, while they looked up to Shakespeare. The poet and writer Rabindranath Tagore, among others, thought of Indian literature and philosophy as a gift to the world. Thus for people like me, Western literature and philosophy seemed 'ours'. But that was when I lived in a world where my subjectivity was not questioned, nor was I racialised.

This substantive sense of being encountered a real jolt when I entered the West, where colonialism still continued in the annexation and creation of 'others'. I speak about this in 'But Who Speaks for Us?', but also in several other essays.[2] The result was that both Shakespeare and I fell from the grace of universality to that of particularity. I became 'Indian', 'East Indian', 'South Asian' and so on as the political discourse evolved in the countries we came to. In my essay on Mary Wollstonecraft's *A Vindication of the Rights of Woman*,[3] I spoke about the three stages of change in my own perception regarding matters of politics and aesthetics. I have never regretted learning English though, because it allowed me to develop both personal communication with people and an internationalist perspective on politics, social ideas and art. Marx, for example, became accessible to me, because even now the bulk of his writings are not translated into Indian languages. As I stayed in Canada and visited numerous countries in the Western hemisphere and met people from other former colonies, the double-edged nature of learning English became vivid to me. I realised that it was not that I learned English, but the circumstances in which it arrived to us, that comprised the main problem. I was cognizant that people could, and have, expressed and transmitted the most oppressive ideas

2 Himani Bannerji, 'But Who Speaks for Us? Experience and Agency in Conventional Feminist Paradigms', in *Unsettling Relations: The University as a Site of Feminist Struggles*, ed. Bannerji, Himani, Linda Carty, Kari Dehli, Susan Heald, and Kate McKenna (Toronto: Women's Press of Canada 1992), 67.

3 Himani Bannerji, 'Mary Wollstonecraft, Feminism and Humanism: A Spectrum of Readings.' In *Mary Wollstonecraft and 200 Years of Feminisms*, edited by Eileen Yeo (New York: Rivers Oram Press, 1997), 222–42.

and practices, colonial or Indigenous, in their 'own' languages. But being pulled into the Western net felt like being recolonised. I began to understand on my body the meaning of the word 'apartheid'. In a poem I wrote, I spelt the word as 'apart – hate'.

BB/RZ *You moved to Canada in 1969 and wrote about the forms of racism you faced in this period. You explain the disjuncture you experienced between your former education in India, which inscribed a sense of 'universal culture' and superiority of English language, and the daily reality of racism you experienced in Canada, and also while visiting London. Can you tell us how you understand this disjuncture, and also, its contemporary resonances with experiences of migration?*

HB I did not come to Toronto to live there; I did not 'move' as an immigrant, but came to do a PhD on a study leave from Jadavpur University (Calcutta) after teaching there from 1965 to 1969. For six years or so, I was not a 'landed immigrant', but I sought this status when my divorce made it difficult to return. In order to qualify for part-time academic piecework at Atkinson College, York University, I applied for the 'landing' permit because this became a condition for employment.

I was not a poet or a short story writer when I arrived. I wrote a few literary critical pieces on modern Bengali literature and primarily taught in English and comparative literature departments. Being fluent in Bengali was a matter of pride for me and many others of my generation. Our communism was a combination of class struggle and anti-colonial liberation, and the Vietnam War was the single most important political event of our university years. It forged our internationalism and anti-imperialism. I became something of a poet and short story writer in Toronto, in community with feminists and emerging young Black writers (I was twenty-seven). At the time, the word 'Black' was not regionally or skin identified. I felt I had found myself among these social and cultural activists – rather than 'lost' myself in collectivity. As I say in my poem 'Doing Time': 'I became so many people.'[4] I became a political person in a way different from how I was in India. The 'denial, rejection and . . . hatred' that I experienced tested my politics. I learned that I wanted not only to express my own outrage, but also to witness and speak out together with others. Thus, 'other' cultures were not automatically 'othering' cultures for me. Dionne Brand, Makeda Silvera and Krisantha Sri Bhaggiyadatta, for example, were all writers who shared this political ground with me. Magazines and small publishing ventures, such as Sister Vision Press or *Toronto South Asian Review*, were the few publishing venues for us. The essays collected in *Returning the Gaze* (1993), edited by me, were the result of that.

---

4 Himani Bannerji, 'Doing Time', in *Doing Time: Poems* (Toronto: Sister Vision, 1986).

The devaluation of non-European cultures that I felt in the 1970s is still here today, though the former white elite confidence is somewhat shaken. The customs and immigration officers who scrutinised my papers then, making me cringe, are still looking at the documents of immigrants and refugees today. Sadly, I had to stay on in Canada. I felt miserable when I swore my oath of allegiance to the British royal family. I gave back even the problematic independence India's freedom struggle gave me when I was five years old.

***BB/RZ** You also explain that in this period, your readings of radical Black scholars helped you to grapple with this experience of racism, and also connect politically with 'others' in Canada. In what ways would you say this diasporic experience of racism impacted your thinking through 'race, gender and class in and through each other'[5]?*

HB Frantz Fanon, Aimé Césaire, Chinua Achebe, Ngũgĩ wa Thiong'o and C.L.R. James, among others, helped me to name the experiences which I and others were going through. They helped me to recognise them as experiences of the racialisation process intrinsic to capitalist colonialism. They talked about emotional and psychological consequences of slavery and indentured labour, and through them I learned how I was becoming an insider-outsider to societies and states based on genocide and settlement. These authors were exploring the historical processes of domination and resistance, and the social and cultural formations emerging from colonialism. Speaking of colonised countries integral to production for the world market, they mapped the spatialisation/geography of 'race'. Gradually I learned to understand, through them, how modern colonialism was the expansion of European capitalism founded on the violence of primitive accumulation in Europe. They all identified violence – the violation of people, their land and their cultures – as intrinsic to this process.

It is not a surprise, therefore, that in his 1961 *Wretched of the Earth*, Fanon recommends that we violate this very violence itself. His discourse on violence and support of armed struggle, equally supported by the others, has to be constructed outside of the paradigm of suicide or homicide. We must, rather, rethink violence as a mode of fundamental transformation of the status quo. They also refused to homogenise societies of the colonised, which would dehistoricise them and ignore their internal differentiations based on class, social relations and their contested cultures. They did not rob individuals of colonised societies of complex and conflicting subjectivities and agencies, advocating an identity of monolithic victimhood. Fanon points this out in the chapter on the 'pitfalls of national consciousness'. The fetishisation of indigenism, he reminds us, becomes an ideological ruse creating cultural tropes which

5 Himani Bannerji, 'But Who Speaks for Us?', in *Thinking Through*, 83.

occlude the class character and repressive intentions of the colonial bourgeoisie and their postcolonial state. The subsumption of the colonised population in the idea of total victimhood excuses the colonised people of their responsibility of making choices about the kind of decolonisation they sought. In particular, Fanon pointed out the impact of class and the corruption of the colonial elite and their complicity with the colonisers.

In my opinion, the political philosophy of anti-colonial, anti-imperialist thinkers mentioned above is as applicable to the Western politics and economies evolved on the basis of chattel slavery, indenture and wage labour of migrants and refugees. They point equally to the kinds of class formations and complicity existing among us, in terms of our ways of relating to social transformation. We must look at the internal social relations and cultures of the communities created under the exigencies of racialising neoliberal capitalism. Cultural identities cannot be made to serve outside of the context of class and capital and become alibis for creating mini-nationalisms within the larger racist, patriarchal capitalism.

The civil rights movement in the United States and the writings and practices of the Black Panthers, and George Jackson's prison letters in *Soledad Brother* (1970), enthused us in Canada as well. Instead of feeling isolated, my experiences became ever widening through these connections. It was not only 'allyship' with others, but comradeship – a loving identification that I felt. Anti-racist politics had not become so defined in terms of skin colour and geographical regions then. Studying the history of the Americas further honed my understanding of a type of capitalism based on genocidal conquest, an exponential increase of 'primitive accumulation' experienced in England and Europe from the seventeenth century onwards. Through pamphlets of the American Indian Movement, Dee Brown's *Bury My Heart at Wounded Knee* (1970), Ward Churchill's *A Little Matter of Genocide* (1997) and the poetry of Beth Brant and Chrystos, for example, I came to understand the foundational principles of white settler colonialism, but also the condition of tribal people in India. Thus, I thought of people beyond the paint box 'red', 'yellow', 'Black' and 'brown'.

You ask, in what way did the 'diasporic' experience of racism impact my thinking through race, gender and class? Personally, I felt 'exiled' rather than 'diasporic', as I was a foreign student for long and did not come with the aim of living in Canada. Circumstances prevented my permanent return to India, but I had a sense of loss even so. The hitherto privilege of being a middle-class university lecturer in India turned out to be more significant than I had thought. I was conscious of gaining and losing this as I came and went. Slowly, I developed a stereoscopic vision, and the commonalities and differences between these countries and my relations to them became clearer. I walked through a racialising looking glass. Now I live between two countries, but a sense of being in exile in Canada still persists, though to a lesser degree.

I was confused about the process of racialising that I was undergoing as both a part-time university teacher and a graduate student. Other than the types of reading I mentioned, my association with other 'nonwhite' people (I use the term intentionally), including writers, activists and friends, socialised my personal view. Our protests, solidarity work with international human rights and local labour groups clarified the social and political organisation of Canada. Interactions in streets, transit, hospital and other institutions daily added to my understanding. My life was active, engaged, and therefore happy and enriching, offsetting encounters which were humiliating, jarring and sometimes frightening. I shared these with others. Since I saw teaching as political work, I was empowered by it and felt a kinship with my students, who were also working people. Experience became a vital component of my epistemological efforts, my source for analysing and illustrating social theory.

***BB/RZ** You have developed your writing from (what you term) a 'standpoint of anti-racist feminist Marxism' that is influenced by, among many other theorists, the work of Dorothy Smith. You have insisted in your work on the salience of Marxist thought and Marxist categories – especially as they relate to understanding race, gender and class not as simplistic intersections, but internally related and co-constructed in a framework of capitalist social relations. How has a Marxian analysis helped you (or not) to understand the construction of these categories?*

HB Though I came to Canada with a grasp of some aspects of Marxist thought, its emphasis was more on political economy and a nuanced understanding of class. But coming to Canada, I discovered the feminist and anti-racist social movements. Though my reading of Engels taught me to see patriarchy as a fundamental aspect of capitalism, I was able to put my personal life in the context of patriarchy more directly in Canada. Family and male–female relations entered the arena of politics, and the 'personal' truly became 'political' for me. I joined consciousness-raising groups and regularly spent time at Women's Place, a basement in an old house, and taught feminist courses there on literature. Women's studies was not taught in the university then. There, I felt a kinship with other women, and I, at least, experienced no animosity. My marriage was breaking up, and this 'sisterhood' helped me. Feminism enriched my communism, deepening equality discourse with an understanding of the social nature of interpersonal and sexual relations. Marx and Engels' advice in *The Communist Manifesto* to 'abolish the family' was not taken really seriously in the communist tradition. Violence against women was not seen as a core aspect of class formation. I continued to recognise patriarchy as a common social condition for the containment and subjection of women, but I also see other relations of power-based difference mediating patriarchy. So racialisation or caste domination seem to me as fundamental to any mode of production articulated on relations of property and dispossession. In accordance with this, I don't see myself as a racialised woman who is incidentally implicated in class. Therefore, I am not a practitioner of sequential theorisation of gender, race and class, but rather searching for a concrete representation of a concrete existential situation of simultaneity. My writings are still fraught with this search.

I am not a believer of an abstract single strand of relations that marks our social 'otherness' and victimhood. We are both racialised and feminised within a given socioeconomic and cultural organisation, and sometimes these relations unite or conflict. In the Canadian (Western) dominant perception there is an ascription of 'class' belonging for nonwhite people, of what I ought to be doing, rather than what I actually do. I have often been mistaken as a domestic/institutional cleaner, a manual worker of some sort, but this mistake is not accidental, as it assigns us to jobs where we are found in the largest numbers. Racism is the 'common sense' of a historically racialising mode of production. This otherising gaze does not necessarily involve skin colour, hair or facial type. In other countries, other physical and cultural signs serve the same purpose. The common-sense aspect of defining social vision is less a sustaining 'gaze' than a 'glance', because common sense supplies it so quickly without disaggregating race, gender and class.

In my essay 'In the Matter of X', I unpacked a phenomenon of such a simultaneous composition of a fused identity of race, gender and class.[6] The essay is based on my work as an expert witness for a Black woman (X) who was suing an international corporation for compensation for mental injury – a type of injury not considered compensable then. I also found that of the three categories, two – race and gender – had legal standing as discrimination, but not class. But the two could not form into existential actual being unless the implicit third, class, could bind them, especially as this was a workplace-related complaint. To make this phenomenon concrete, to interpret X's 'injury' as a 'mental injury' in such a way that her being a Black woman and operating in a 'typically' male section of the industry (X had no 'physical' markers) could all become visible in characterising the injury done to her. Historicisation and 'thick' description helped me in this.

I had to constitute this 'Blackness' of X's being with being a woman and assigned a certain kind of job. But the situation was more tricky than that, because though patriarchy, racialisation and class were existentially connected in her; I saw that they signalled different valences for different kinds of legal argument. In our personal life, our struggles involve shifts in the way social relations such as gender, race and class come into play more prominently in certain situations than others. But they never entirely vanish. We have to cope

6 Himani Bannerji, 'In the Matter of "X": Building Race into Sexual Harassment', in *Thinking Through*.

with these shifts along with our own internalised patriarchy and racism, because we simultaneously exist in these situations and also resist them.

In this process of searching for a method of enquiry (not a 'theory'), for a critical epistemology, I read and taught the illuminating writings of Barbara Smith, Gloria Anzaldúa, bell hooks, Audre Lorde, June Jordan and other feminists, who were looking for an explanatory framework suited for an overall transformation of contemporary society. Some of them were critics of capitalism and imperialism, and did not separate women's liberation from socialist revolution. Before Kimberlé Crenshaw provided the idea of 'intersectionality',[7] these feminists were searching for ways to articulate gender, race and class. The idea of 'intersectionality' was one such attempt. While existentially we are aware of intricate implications of our experiences, we still need to find a way to represent this phenomenon for analytical use. This is an issue that is particularly relevant for liberal democracy itself because we are aware that the 'formal' equality it espouses always collides against actual inequality, pushes liberal citizenship against actual subjection.

In this conundrum, Crenshaw put together a framework to capture the lived reality of Black women in the United States within the legal purview of the state. She herself named it as a metaphor to describe Black women's lives at the crossroads of race and gender, and to seek legal redress on these grounds. This legal context of the idea of intersectionality must not be underestimated. In her 1989 article in the *University of Chicago Legal Forum*, Crenshaw spoke to the legally divided condition of Black women between race and gender injustices. They had to choose between the racial and gender discrimination to make their case legally actionable. But this did not correspond to lives compounded by both. Through the notion of intersectionality, Crenshaw tried to diagnose and solve the problem. In her opinion, if the Black subject were to be accorded justice, the courts would have to acknowledge the multiple power relations that intersected in each life. She assumed class as a factor, but not as a legal one, since class cannot be legislated. Instead she interpreted class in terms of status, as a category of dispossession and poverty. Her main intention was not to make class legally admissible, but rather see it as contributor to the overall oppression and excluded condition of Black women's lives.

Crenshaw sought to make the legal apparatus of the state accountable to society. The metaphor of traffic was meant to capture how different relations of power crossed through lives of individuals, and how this particularly affected the lives of Black women. Though she separates the individual from the social relations of power at the juncture of which they stand, she pointed out that the inequity of their existence compromises a citizen's right to equality in a liberal

---

7 See Kimberlé Crenshaw, 'Demarginalizing the Intersection of Race and Sex: A Black Feminist Critique of Antidiscrimination Doctrine, Feminist Theory and Antiracist Politics', *University of Chicago Legal Forum 1* (1989), 139–67.

democracy. Logically speaking, all citizens, men or women, Black or white, should have the right to pursue their own welfare and invest equally in the state's distributive apparatus. As such, the idea of intersectionality serves as a device for expanding citizens' rights. Women's, especially Black women's, present inequitable status is objectively demonstrated by their exclusion from many social and economic opportunities. Their intellectual discrimination, lack of political representation and highly disproportionate presence in prisons, and among the jobless and homeless, all point to a systemic inequality. But Crenshaw does not question the relationship between liberal democracy and capitalism, and does not ask how a system premised on inequality can deliver real justice for the lowest occupant of the social structure which has been historically developed. Instead, she seeks to bend the legal apparatus, to improve its dysfunctionality.

Crenshaw's project becomes more visible by comparing her with another legal theorist, Patricia J. Williams, author of *The Alchemy of Race and Rights* (1991). Williams also shows the connection between US property laws and the lives of Black and marginalised people. In doing so, she introduces her grandmother's bill of sale to show how deeply the violence of property in human lives, labour and commodities informs the US state and society. She contrasts the violence against socially deprived people, who receive maximum punishment for even negligible misdeeds, such as shoplifting, with how corporations are treated with extreme leniency by using every loophole that exists within the legal system. Thus, an alchemy of race and gender, she shows, is generated in the mire of slavery, wage slavery, the world market and criminalisation, making the state's framework of justice a façade. But she who exposes the injustice of the bourgeois, racialised and gendered legal framework cannot provide us with an alternative on which we can mount resistance against the entire social organisation of capital. Crenshaw, however, is more pragmatic in her approach, as 'intersectionality' has taken on national and international currency. The frequent use of this term describes the impasse that people live in and can, if legally well used, partially ameliorate some suffering. It is not meant for a challenge to capitalism, nor the vital social relations that are its constituents, and it cannot address collectively produced injustices that people suffer individually. This, for me, is a major weakness of this approach.

BB/RZ *You have written against the assertion, within liberal multicultural discourse and policy especially, of fixed, reified and fetishised cultural categories. In the meantime, there has been a right-wing backlash against even the most basic gains of liberal multiculturalism. Given this context and your well-developed critique of liberal multiculturalism, how do we understand anti-racist politics vis-à-vis the attacks on multiculturalism today?*

HB To answer your question, we need to begin from our everyday life and observe its ideological conversion into categories which serve the ruling relations of the capitalist state. This brings us to the topic of 'multiculturalism', which I treat as ideological, hegemonic discourse employed in the politics of capital and governance. Insofar as multiculturalism uses categories which are reified cultural features to create colonial bourgeois subjects, the 'others' of the central and unspoken 'self' and citizens of capitalist settler colonialism, they initiate an official identity politics. It is not multiculturalism, per se, to which I object(ed), but to this 'official' multiculturalism which constructs the ruling apparatus of the liberal state and its subjects. This ruling apparatus relies on cultural stereotypes to create 'communities' and convert individuals into fixed identities. I give this appellative device the name 'multiculturalism from above'.

My problem is not with the mixing and coexistence of many cultures within a social space. This has happened since time immemorial. (Look at language formations, aesthetics and moral values.) This process is what I call 'multiculturalism from below'. It is something historical, process oriented and forged in common experience. These cultural developments are not frozen in time and do not create fixed identities. They go way beyond blood and religious borders, and create no patronised vote banks from othered ethnicities. They are identities created in and through struggles for making a better world. They are identities of becoming rather than of being. My essays in *The Dark Side of the Nation* (2000) speak to these different identities.

The liberal state's tolerance code of multiculturalism, when it projects stereotypes of Islam as a backward religion and of Muslim youth as fanatics and terrorists, serves no positive purpose. On the contrary, identifying cultural groups as essentially patriarchal creates a rescue mentality and legitimises invasions, such as in Cherie Blair's or Hillary Clinton's enthusiasm for the Afghanistan invasion. This ideological view is so hegemonic that it becomes invisible, while the targeted population becomes visible and minoritised in the scheme of citizenship and in international relations.

Anti-racist feminists demanded a fundamental sociopolitical change, not one that could be accomplished by a designatory list of cultural categories. But they were met with official multiculturalism, which left capital's state and social relations intact. This move on the state and political society's part must also be scrutinised against the anti-capitalist political unrest fuelled by anti-imperialism waged in Europe and North America during the 1960s and '70s. Confronted with the task of controlling social unrest and crises of legitimation of the capitalist state, the Canadian bourgeois, liberal state adopted a (formal) democratic posture. It retooled its representational criteria on the basis of cultures of 'others', but to characterise these cultures through a list of sexist, racist and orientalist stereotypes. This official multiculturalism is deeply connected to the idea of 'equity' (rather than social justice) and arose at approximately the same time. A particular, officially constructed, set of cultural identities, using the most conservative, so-called traditional aspects of non-European groups living in Canada, became the ground through which a marginal representation, rephrased as equity, could be demanded. An extension of affirmative action also added to this type of representation. What we have come to call identity politics originates in this particular cultural-political formation. This is the only way that any capitalist state could meet popular demand, unless it sought its own self-extinction by helping to unravel capitalism. This, of course, could not be done. The situation left two ways open for us – one in which politics from below, class struggle understood most broadly, could be waged based on revolutionary traditions; or one which would attempt to manipulate the liberal state and institutional machinery to demand inclusion, trying to achieve an effective representation of the excluded groups. The first way is neither 'representational', nor does it demand 'recognition' from the powers that be. It does not want movement from the margin to the centre, but demolition of this structuration. But this cannot be done by individuals, operating as such, and not even by groups, state- or self-defined as communities. It calls for a huge mobilisation and *longue durée* politics of counterhegemony. It depends on the level of unrest and resistance in the larger polity.

The more doable option is the institutional, legal one, where individuals can seek redress, representation and so on in the institution's or the state's constitution and projection of itself as democratic. It draws on the ideology of citizenship resting on (formal) equality. From formal equality to equity and being represented through affirmative action is not a far cry. At a low ebb of left politics, having to live in the present, marginalised citizens, especially highly educated, professional ones, use the institutional option. Given their near-total absence from meaningful, well-paying jobs or professional training, 'equity' provided them with a weapon of struggle. It provided for a middle-class formation among ranks of the excluded and marginalised. A rank of sub-elites, an intelligentsia, emerged among them. But this situation is necessarily a double-edged one. Modelled on other capitalist institutions, universities and other highly professionalised bodies are by nature pyramidal. Competition is essential to them and is the device of exclusion. Even in white settler states, whites go through this exclusionary process – needless to say, nonwhites much more so. Failure and exclusion are the inevitable results.

This situation plays out in two ways. In one it produces cooperation by converting popular demands into devices for interpellation. But as the demands are not satisfied in real terms, people are frustrated and move towards a greater resistance. At this point, the institutions of the state's very incorporative devices are challenged. A search for legal or institutional redress is disregarded in favour of popular organisation, street marches, protest rallies and so on. In these circumstances, large social movements against globalisation, such as Occupy or Black Lives Matter, emerge. Their wrongs call for a wholesale systemic challenge.

With the multiple socioeconomic crises that followed 2008, neoliberalism created a disenfranchisement that cannot be managed by manipulation of some laws and culture. For the majority of people, appeals to representational democracy have become practically meaningless. Labelling people as anti-national, anti-patriotic or terrorist, followed by incarceration and police violence, has not been able to quell constantly bubbling social justice politics.

A real multiculturalism, one from below, cannot be provided by the state or other institutions of power. Anti-racism that existed in the United States for over a century, as exemplified by Sojourner Truth, Frederick Douglass, W.E.B. Du Bois, Martin Luther King Jr. or Malcolm X, was resisted by the ruling apparatus. Present social movements, such as Black Lives Matter, have materialised and practicalised multiculturalism from below. As politicised by them, culture is expressed by the healthy, dignified and expressive existence of all oppressed people(s). As we see in the writings of Keeanga-Yamahtta Taylor, what Black Lives Matter should aim for is a fundamental change in existing social relations and polity in the United States, such that the continuation of capitalism, and creation of new ones, is prevented.

If official multiculturalism once offered a managed, culturalised version of anti-oppression demands, today the state cannot offer that concession. Instead of 'multiculturalism', we must create anti-oppression movements which are aware of the interconstitutive nature of social relations and forms of consciousness. The ground of 'anti' will include more people and solidarity than islands of identity and equity. Of course, culture must be summoned to our cause. But it would need to create cultures of resistance of an anti-colonial and anti-imperialist nature. 'Traditional' culture must be interpreted along this line.

***BB/RZ** We see in certain modes of liberal feminist writing that capitalism itself disappears. You have also written from a perspective of an explicit anti-capitalist, anti-imperialist and anti-racist feminism and Marxism. Can you explain to us how you would view or describe this type of feminism to a younger generation of feminists coming into politics for the first time?*

HB Anti-capitalism and anti-imperialism should be by definition Marxist, feminist and anti-racist. It is the only way class struggle can be conducted. If class is an assemblage of social relations elaborated in the context of private ownership of social means of production and labour, and rooted in 'primitive accumulation' enshrined in legal apparatuses of the state, then we must aim for this ideal. There cannot be a class struggle without revolutionising commonplace, everyday ways of living and common sense, as well as social production and reproduction.

I think the younger generation today is better than we were at understanding how things work in our neoliberal capitalist times. They have grown up in a world riven with wars, which are clearly imperialist, for resource acquisition and geopolitical ambitions, especially those of the United States, but also of other former colonial powers. If the Occupy movement is something to go by – or the anti-globalisation movements of the 1990s, the environmentalist protests against devastation of human lives and nature through neoliberalism's corporate mores and demands of austerity for the poor and wealth for the rich, or protests against the surveillance state and racialised hyper-incarceration – we can see that young people today have survived much and try to resist. I think they can understand what is going on around them. It is I who have to learn how they develop social movements in ways so different from ours. After all, the high point of my political schooling was in a much less chaotic time. Then we could talk about the working class as a solid social agency – because the working class was working! Now that is not the norm.

Young people, in my opinion, have tried to make the so-called personal deeply political. That is why they have been able to develop previous feminist insights into a wider, deeper understanding of the political import of sexuality and gender. Racism, collectively and individually, expressed also through Islamophobia, is their lived experience. They have spotted the dangers and hypocrisy of official multiculturalism. We also see this consciousness in the worldwide awareness among children about environmental catastrophes, how well they connect human lives to life on the planet. In creating common struggles for the future, we, the older Left, have to learn new forms of organising. The educators, to refer to Marx, need to be educated.

The 'younger generation of feminists' that you speak about need to be specified. All of them do not have the same worldview and politics. The fear that they all subscribe to 'identity politics', a simplistic expression, seems overblown. The notion of identity itself needs to be problematised. It is a small segment of the population who are in a position to culturalise their social oppression. For most racialised and/or ethnicised people, this happens due to the cultural stereotype used for administrative and punitive purposes. As they are oppressed through them, so they are responding in these names. If access to livelihood, to some sort of social status and intellectual, critical presence in society, depends on preinscribed identities, they take recourse to them. Neglected or painfully recuperated identities are the bases for some forms of representational politics. Confronted with Western capital's systemic white privilege, they create a political atmosphere overfocused on 'whiteness', and thus, are counterproductive.

***BB/RZ** You have written about religious nationalism(s) in different contexts, including Indian politics and the rise of Narendra Modi. In your opening essay in* Demography and Democracy: Essays on Nationalism, Gender and Ideology *(2011), you explore the rise to power of the Hindu Right in India in light of Antonio Gramsci's ideas of hegemony and cultural struggle. How should we understand*

Indian politics today through Gramscian ideas? And what does it mean for our broader understanding of the rise of fascism on an international scale?

HB Gramsci's ideas on hegemony, connected to class struggle and class consciousness, and the creation of consent and legitimation, are central for us. Seeing coercion and co-optation of resistance as components of hegemony remains as essential now as it has been for decades. The rise of the Hindu Right to state power in India, and political Islam, Zionism and ultranationalism/fascism elsewhere, calls for a thorough reading of Gramsci through Marx. This means deepening and socialising Marx's ideas of class, class consciousness and class struggle beyond economism. It also means interpreting culture by implicating it in history and material life, and in social processes and formations. Unless culture and society are apprehended formatively, dialectically, neither Gramsci nor Marx will be of much use to us. To render Gramsci into a mere cultural theorist means aestheticising his politics and ideas and denying his commitment to communism in Italy and elsewhere. This move to the culturalisation of Gramsci is deeply misguided and a part of making him palatable to liberals and adapting him to bourgeois democracy. Walter Benjamin, who rejected this compromise, said in 'The Work of Art in the Age of Mechanical Reproduction' that fascists 'aestheticise politics', and communists 'politicise aesthetics'.[8] Even if this aestheticisation is done with no bad intention, it still signifies anti-revolutionary politics.

We need to deepen Marx's notion of ideology through Gramsci. Marx sees ideology as the outcome of the bourgeois intelligentsia's service for the ruling class, for their state's ruling functions and for the legitimation of the rule of capital. But we need to add to this insight Gramsci's exposition of 'hegemony' and its correlate, 'common sense', to trace the afterlife of ideology as it crumbles into the lives and minds of civil society. But that same atmosphere of common sense, we realise from Gramsci also holds ideas and worldviews arising from other social relations which are created by resistance to the ruling classes throughout history. Sociopolitical and cultural practices and ideas are born in those contexts and transmitted through memories, lore, and analytical and organisational writings. They speak of shared lives and projects of political engagements that sort out and use this antithesis within common sense into 'good sense'. This is the work of political conscientisation towards revolutionary social transformation. If the ideological (or ruling ideas) residing in the civil society are the ones which are politicised, then fascism can also emerge from the same domain. The Far Right organises those ideas into actions when capital faces crisis, such as after World War I in Italy and Germany.

In my essays 'Making India Hindu and Male' and 'Demography and Democracy', I show the process of politicisation of right-wing ideas and

8 Walter Benjamin, 'The Work of Art in the Age of Mechanical Reproduction', in *Illuminations*, trans. Harry Zohn (New York: Schocken Books, 1969 [1935].

practices by appealing to 'tradition' and 'culture'.[9] Thus tradition, largely invented, becomes the cloak for hiding or conducting the actual politics that is at work. This ideological use of culture can be found both in religious and secular fascism. The long-standing US practice of invasion to secure capitalism from rising socialism, to extract material resources and coerce abject submission from those targeted, is done under the mask of freedom, democracy and individual rights. The project of capitalist modernisation based on exponential development of productive forces carries the same intention forwards. This invasion can use a tendentious feminism with an imperialist cast to legitimise aggression, allowing countries to become rubble and slaughterhouses. Gramsci and Marx, read through each other, provide both critique and practical strategies for politics. Additional concepts from Gramsci for creating a resistance hegemony are those of 'historic bloc', 'war of position', and 'passive revolution'.[10] At the present time, when we are faced with a fracturing social polity necessitating coalitions and solidarity, we need to read Gramsci's work on state and civil society, which throws light on both right-wing and left-wing populism. It also extends critical consideration of the relationship between state and revolution. In his analysis of fascism/Caesarism, Gramsci can help us to explicate what Marx meant by an 'open' and a 'hidden' class struggle, and the political results of the 'common ruin of contending classes'.[11] With Gramsci's insights, we understand the need to rebuild the civil society as a counterhegemonic base prior to creating a socialist state. We can see how feminist anti-racist social movements, for example, can thus be counted as intrinsic to building new conceptions of class and class politics.

For a broader understanding of the rise of fascism on an international scale, we need to understand the form capital has taken in its neoliberal, globalised phase. Accompanied by militarism and various forms of violence, the monopoly finance capital of our time signals a massive crisis of overaccumulation while wreaking havoc through primitive accumulation. The thesis of class struggle still holds, and the imperialist bourgeoisie have gained a precarious and world-destroying victory for now. This has resulted in a catastrophic dispossession of people and destruction of nature, and is producing grotesque political and military phenomena globally. States, and legitimation devices which are mixtures of religious and feudal monarchic despotism and ultranationalism, are proliferating. Demographic states giving citizens carte

9 Himani Bannerji, 'Making India Hindu and Male: Cultural Nationalism and the Emergence of the Ethnic Citizen in Contemporary India', *Ethnicities* 6:3 (September 2006), 362–90; 'Demography and Democracy', in *Demography and Democracy: Essays on Nationalism, Gender and Ideology* (Toronto: Canadian Scholars' Press, 2011).

10 Antonio Gramsci, 1891–1937, *Selections From the Prison Notebooks of Antonio Gramsci* (New York: International Publishers, 1971).

11 Karl Marx, 1818–1883 and Friedrich Engels, 1820–1895, *The Communist Manifesto* (London: Penguin Classics, 2014), 219.

blanche to persecute the minoritised subjects are now normalised. Then there are the 'secular' fascisms of developed countries, in the name of democratic freedom. But the polarisation of classes and the prevalence of individualism, accompanied with the mirage of endless consumption, are present the world over.

BB/RZ *Finally, the neoliberalisation of academic institutions has been well documented, although in your work you point to the institutional racism that has existed within universities well before the latest waves of neoliberalisation. Can you reflect on the changes you have seen within academe as a space for organising?*

HB I have been teaching and researching from 1965 until now, primarily in Canada, but also in Indian universities and research institutes. This long participation in academic institutions has involved seeing many changes within them, and I have reflected on the nature of these changes, because I have had to cope with them, but also to provide a critique and organisation of resistance by taking part in union activities. Speaking broadly, when I began teaching, the institutions of higher education were based on humanist principles and possessed a degree of relative autonomy from the state and the market. Though they were largely publicly funded, both in India and Canada, this was possible; and, at least in the humanities and social sciences, they were at arm's length from the ruling apparatus. Though guided by an elite and authoritarian approach to higher learning, they were not instrumental in nature. Independent research could be pursued in the fields of classics, literature, history and so on. Research could be open-ended and non-empiricist. The administration left the faculty to their own devices, as long as they taught the canons of their disciplines. There was at least a posture of ethical commitment and the desire to arbitrate in matters of social good. Needless to say, this approach was often exaggerated and more honoured in a lazy negligence. But in the 1960s and '70s, new disciplines, such as comparative literature, were created and from the late 1970s on, social and cultural studies developed new dimensions of political critique. Areas like feminism, anti-racism, Marxism and other anti-oppression pedagogies became respectable. To accomplish this, we could fall back on the old humanist and bourgeois liberal commitment to diversity. In India this involved influences from foreign universities. An argument for an equal academic citizenship paralleled an argument for equal political citizenship. Though the institutions took some years to be modified in this direction, we didn't have to worry about producing market-oriented courses and programmes. I don't really know how things operated in business administration and the sciences. I am speaking about liberal arts.

Things also began to change because younger faculty were involved in or found attractive the social and anti-imperialist movements. Demands for creating new fields of study and research came from outside of the university as well. The world was going through intense anti-imperialist, socialist revolutionary struggles. Vietnam, Algeria, Mozambique, Angola, El Salvador and Nicaragua spread their influence. Powerful movements in the United States, such as civil rights, Black Power, Native American and student movements, drew people in. Along with these directly political movements there developed feminist movements against patriarchy. They addressed personal relations and living styles, challenged racism and homophobia. Cultural studies critiqued stereotypes and discourses involving signs and symbols of negative otherisation.

The university gained through this entry of social movements and politics. In a way it was a renewal of its older mission of humanist knowledge. Thus, the streets that we marched on came into our classrooms. But there was a paradox created by this situation. These movements were entering an institution which was a major part of the ruling apparatus of the state, serving a legitimating function to capital and its reproduction. Of course, these institutions were themselves sites of contestations – between demands for critical and insurgent knowledge and the institutions' need to 'discipline' it. The factor of professionalisation displaced the notion of vocation. The intelligentsia, as Gramsci said, leaned on either side, depending on the strength of the social and political movements. As the university was radicalised when resistance was high, so it got incorporated into the state's agenda as the movements were quelled. The defeats of the anti-imperialist struggles from the late 1980s, the decapitation and pacification of Black Power, Native American and labour militancy, and the rise of carceral and surveillance practices since 2001 disabled people's political agencies. This structured the new fields of learning, as well. As before in history, practice and critique parted ways. The 'streets' were largely 'institutionally captured' – that is, our own political subjectivities and agencies became compromised. Insurgent knowledge was academicised. We were pulled up into the ruling apparatus because the space below had shrunk. From the fall of the Soviet Union and its allied countries, socialism/communism seemed to have been consigned to what Ronald Reagan called 'the trash heap' of history – we were supposed to have reached the end of ideology. Marxism, grounded cultural critique and radical political economy took on an air of irrelevance. With this achievement of a unipolar bourgeois world, the university lost its relative autonomy and became increasingly responsive to the market and the corporate organisation of production. We were prompted to abandon any systemic attempt to overthrow the ruling relations, and larger social visions were dismissed.

This era began from an earlier time. Intellectual trends against anti-capitalism, with all its complexity and contradiction, developed the epistemological position known as 'postmodernism'. We no longer spoke of anti-colonial independence, national liberation or class struggles, but of a cultural colonialism and its afterlife in postcolonialism. What were the consequences of ignoring class and its constitutive social relations in considering colonialism as a cultural enterprise or all nationalism as a homogeneous sociopolitical formation? Critique of colonialism was thus divorced from that of capitalism and imperialism. The experiences of capitalist colonialism arising from primitive accumulation, slavery, indentured labour and super-exploitation were reduced to individual experiences. We, the intelligentsia, were caught in the institutional labyrinth in which the signposts were marked by conferences and workshops, leading us deeper into the heart of the institution. This involved no conspiracy, but engineering the institution in a certain way. The model seems to have been picked up from financial corporations, which rendered scholars (even the activists) into 'stakeholders' or 'shareholders'. As our work as labour became invisible, we were interpellated by the language of investment and its profit/return. This process is not dissimilar to how we arrived at the participation in official multiculturalism produced from above. In this context, 'the politics of representation' took on the meaning of movement from the margin to the centre, which leaves the institution intact.

The neoliberal restructuring of the universities instituted deep financial cuts in state educational budgets. Privatisation and corporatisation became the mandate of the university. Securing grants and projects became part of the requirement of holding faculty positions. The humanities, in particular, are now facing a great pressure. This atmosphere encourages competition and a corporate style of professionalism among academics. This sets off a chain reaction down the line to the graduate students. The *positive* outcome of all this is the anger that is developing in all educational communities, including that of higher education, as the situation becomes unsustainable and unbearable. So the posture of submission is gradually changing to one of contention. My hope is that competitive politics based on individualism and cultural identity will be compelled to take recourse to collective action, if we are not going to introduce the precarious work world that we find in the rest of the gig economy. We might then see the value of making common cause with workers in our own institutions, such as secretarial services and janitorial staff. The precarity that was introduced in their work situation, and which has existed for a while now in public and private sectors, has finally come to hit our relatively safe lives as academics.

My hope also lies in the fact that neoliberalism's socioeconomic mobility is showing its limits. The different cultural identities and hitherto-marginalised topics which secured an entry into the university still provide a subclass of equity-based workers and their fields. But they are rendered ineffectual in their presence and demands on the institution as a whole. Overlapping and common grounds might begin to be actively sought and politicised. Reaching out to intersectionality is a symptom of that. The illusion of radicalism is proving to be not much more than a new middle-class formation among hitherto-absent peoples, but the institution has inset barriers to mobility, as does capitalism itself. Inclusion on identity grounds is not a challenge to neoliberal institutions. Though some nonwhite women and men have reached official professional visibility, the majority of them are in a state of material and social dispossession as well as incarceration. Thus, Barack Obama's becoming president of the United States or Condoleezza Rice's rise to George W. Bush's secretary of state are exceptions, not the rule, even for Black middle-class Americans. I am hoping that if this realisation becomes common, even among nonwhite academics and other professionals, it might provide the point of departure for a really radical politics to develop outside the state and corporations. We, the workers of universities, have to return to sources of anti-capitalist politics, to social movements present outside of institutions, and not just count change of language as change in reality.

Selected Writings

Bannerji, Himani. *Unsettling Relations: The University as a Site of Feminist Struggles*. Toronto: South End Press, 1992.

———, ed. *Returning the Gaze: Essays on Racism, Feminism and Politics*. Toronto: Sister Vision, 1993.

———. *Thinking Through*. Toronto: Women's Press, 1995.

———. *The Dark Side of the Nation: Essays on Multiculturalism, Nationalism and Gender*. Toronto: Canadian Scholars' Press, 2000.

———. *Inventing Subjects: Studies in Hegemony, Patriarchy and Colonialism*. London: Anthem Press, 2002.

———. *Demography and Democracy: Essays on Nationalism, Gender and Ideology*. Toronto: Canadian Scholars' Press, 2011.

———. 'Rabindranath Tagore's Postcolonialism: A Vision of Decolonization and a Modernist Idealism'. In *History, Imperialism, Critique*, ed. Asher Ghaffar, 48–67. London: Routledge, 2018.

Gary Kinsman

A queer liberation, anti-oppression and anti-capitalist activist in solidarity with Indigenous struggles, Gary Kinsman lives much of the time in Toronto. He has organised with the AIDS Activist History Project, the No Pride in Policing Coalition and the Anti-69 Network against the mythologies of the 1969 Canadian Criminal Code reform, and was involved in the Right to Privacy Committee in opposition to the 1980s Toronto bathhouse raids. Kinsman helped found Gay Liberation against the Right Everywhere (GLARE) and the Lesbian and Gay Pride Day organising committees in Toronto and Sudbury, and was a member of the editorial collective of the gay and lesbian liberation magazine *Rites*.

Among his recent writings are essays on border policing and sexual/gender identities, and on neoliberalism and homonationalism vis-à-vis the limitations of the Canadian state's formal apology to queer communities in 2017. He is the author of *The Regulation of Desire: Homo and Hetero Sexualities* (1987), coauthor of *The Canadian War on Queers: National Security as Sexual Regulation* (2010), and a coeditor of *We Still Demand! Redefining Resistance in Sex and Gender Struggles* (2017), *Whose National Security?* (2000) and *Sociology for Changing the World* (2006). He is Professor Emeritus in Sociology at Laurentian University.

***BB/RZ** You wrote one of the foundational texts on LGBT (lesbian, gay, bisexual and trans) social history in Canada,* The Regulation of Desire. *There were key concepts in that book, like sexual regulation and rule,*[1] *but you also insisted at the same time on using a historical materialist approach. What were the intellectual and/or activist influences that led you to develop that book, in particular?*

GK You're talking about the first edition of *The Regulation of Desire*, which came out in 1987. There was another edition published in 1996, which occurred in a somewhat different context in terms of my work. But coming back to the 1987 version, the context is multiple. The first thing is that I was an activist in the gay liberation movement in Toronto from about 1972 on. I was also involved in the revolutionary Left, in particular, in groups called the

1 Sexual regulation, or the relations of sexual ruling, are the web of state, professional, corporate and cultural relations that participate in the regulation of people's erotic lives. They have a mediated gendered, raced and classed character.

Young Socialists, the Revolutionary Marxist Group (RMG) and then the Revolutionary Workers League. As an undergraduate student at York University in the 1970s, I was also involved in student activism.

I decided that after my Bachelor's I would do a Master's. So I went to the Ontario Institute for Studies in Education (OISE) (at the University of Toronto), and that overlapped with the time of the 1981 bath raids and the resistance to them.[2] At the time I worked with George Smith, a research assistant in the sociology department at OISE and a gay activist and researcher, and I took courses with feminist sociologist Dorothy Smith (no relation). I found myself in the academic world almost accidentally, at the same time I was an activist. The organising against the bath raids was going on, and I was trying to figure out how to put these different parts of my life together.

Dorothy Smith's approach, which influenced me, was elaborated and extended by George, who was active in the Right to Privacy Committee that I was involved in, which was the mass resistance organisation formed after the bath raids. Dorothy's work, for me, provided a way of bridging the divide between being in the university and being an activist. It provided me with a way of thinking through how I could produce sociological knowledge *for* oppressed people, and *for* people who were involved in the activist movements I was also involved in.

I was also involved in Gay Liberation against the Right Everywhere (GLARE). So *The Regulation of Desire* comes out of that period of time, when I was both at OISE and had this rich activist involvement. This was also combined with an increasing interest in what was then called lesbian and gay history, and a real interest in history from below. I had an interest in E.P. Thompson's work, but also how that was extended by people like Jeffrey Weeks and Sheila Rowbotham.[3]

Now, in terms of historical materialism, I was a committed Marxist of a different sort than I am now when I wrote the first edition of *The Regulation of Desire*. I was also influenced by Michel Foucault's work. That certainly shifted and transformed the work I was doing. But even at that point, I noted the limitations of approaches that focused on discourse. Discourse was sort of everything, a sort of discourse determinism that is there in Foucault, but is there even more profoundly in some people that use his work.

I felt that trying to bring some of that knowledge, some of those perspectives, together with what could be learned from historical materialism was really important. The way I would have put it at that point in time was that

2 On 5 February 1981, patrons of four bathhouses in downtown Toronto were met with a series of coordinated raids by 200 police officers.

3 See E.P. Thompson, *The Making of the English Working Class* (Harmondsworth: Penguin, 1968); Jeffrey Weeks, *Coming Out: Homosexual Politics in Britain, from the Nineteenth Century to the Present* (London: Quartet Books, 1977); Sheila Rowbotham, *Hidden from History: 300 Years of Women's Oppression and the Fight Against It*, 3rd ed. (London: Pluto Press, 1977).

Marx, given the particular conditions of his life, was able to contest the naturalism or the surface appearance of equality in the relationship between worker and capitalist. He was able to go beneath those surface relations and to unearth and analyse the social relations of exploitation on which they were based, but he was unable to actually move beyond the appearance of gender and sexual naturalism.

He was unable, given his own social location and practices and given the lack of development of social struggles, to adequately address gender, sexual and racial oppression. In some of their personal correspondence, Marx and Engels actually write about being personally threatened by movements for homosexual rights.[4] It's not like they're unaware of what's beginning to happen in Germany in particular. But they were certainly unable to apply their critical, historical materialist, dialectical method for analysing what was going on to gender and sexuality in more profound ways. Although they made more attempts around gender than sexuality.

Around sexuality, they basically accepted a form of sexual naturalism in their work. My sense was that we could actually use the same method, their same critical, historical materialist method, and apply it now in a new historical context to looking at sexual regulation and the social organisation of sexuality.

***BB/RZ** For people who are not familiar with Dorothy Smith's work, could you tell us a bit about her influential methodology and theoretical framework?*

GK Dorothy Smith is one of the most interesting feminist sociologists. In her work, she brings together three different theoretical traditions and is able to pull them together in very useful ways. One, of course, is feminism itself, and critiques of sociological knowledge produced from male-dominated standpoints, but there is also a real grounding in Marxism and an attempt to use Marxist approaches. Another is something that many people would never look at: ethnomethodology, this approach within sociology which I really love. It's sort of a bad boy or bad girl of sociological theory. It's a critical response to structural functionalism, which understood the world as being defined by structures that perform necessary and needed social functions.

Harold Garfinkel,[5] who founded ethnomethodology, basically says no, people are not cultural dopes. They're not just puppets on strings being pulled by structures; they actually engage in social practices and make sense of the world. Ethnomethodology, which is the study of people's methods, made some

---

4 Hubert Kennedy, 'Johann Baptist von Schweitzer: The Queer Marx Loved to Hate', *Journal of Homosexuality* 29:2–3 (1995), 69–96.

5 See Harold Garfinkel, *Studies in Ethnomethodology* (Cambridge, UK: Polity Press, 1984).

really important radical claims: for one, that people, through their own practices, produce the social world – not just produce the meaning of the social world, but actually produce the social world. That has produced a really interesting emphasis in Smith's work on *doing*. You actually have to recover the doing, the social practices, of people. Therefore, she's able to see there's an ontological compatibility between Marxism and ethnomethodology.

Obviously that only gets you to a certain point. There are more clarifications that need to happen. But at least it locates a particular starting place. Smith is one of the most creative and innovative feminist sociologists, and she would in some ways be seen as a feminist Marxist. I think there are limitations to her approach; initially, in developing a sociology for women, she tended to generalise from white middle-class women's experiences. But I think she was actually able to deal a lot with being challenged by Himani Bannerji and other feminists of colour, and to respond in ways that were really interesting.

Even in her early book *The Everyday World as Problematic* (1987), she reflected on social experiences of racism and colonialism. Even though there was, in her early work, a certain notion of a standpoint of women that's unitary and uniform, that tends to be coded as white and middle class, it becomes much more complicated in her work after that, which sees that there are multiple social standpoints that are much more complex. There are also other limitations that I encountered later on. There are ways, just like Foucault's work can lead people to be totally fixated on discourses of power, that her major approach, called institutional ethnography (critical ethnographic investigations of ruling relations in our society), can be really useful but can also get trapped in wonderment at the incredibly interesting ways that ruling relations operate. It is crucial for us to be able to operate within, against and, especially, beyond these ruling discourses and relations.[6]

***BB/RZ** Bringing these different influences together, which are bound by a certain transformative revolutionary project, did you feel that you had to stretch them for you book?*

GK Yes, certainly. To use Fanon's expression, Marxism needs to be stretched, to actually begin to understand the experiences of colonised people in the global South. There's a lot of that going on in *The Regulation of Desire*. I used the term 'sexual rule', which I took from Lorna Weir, who was doing her PhD at that time at York, where she examines a number of different instances of sexual regulation and develops this notion of sexual rule.

6 On 'within, against and beyond', see the work of John Holloway, *How to Change the World without Taking Power* (London: Pluto Press, 2005); and *In, Against and Beyond Capitalism: The San Francisco Lectures* (Oakland: PM Press, 2016).

But it also had a real resonance with this notion of ruling relations that Smith and people using her approach had developed. I didn't feel, in that area, that I was so much extending analysis as using what other people were doing. I used the word 'queer' then, in 1987, but in a pre–queer theory way. But in a certain sense I was engaging in a queering of Marxism, of the essentialism and naturalism within most Marxism when it came to sexualities. Not only a stretching and extension, but also a queering of what Marxism is about, and actually trying to suggest that a queering of Marxism that was still based on the crucial aspects of historical materialism could build towards a useful perspective.

BB/RZ *What is the queering of Marxism?*

GK Queering is a practice of denaturalising the taken-for-granted, from the diverse standpoints of queer people. Queering Marxism is like queering the family, queering the state. If you look at Marxism from the vantage point of the multiple social locations and standpoints of queer people, what does it look like? If you denormalise and denaturalise Marxism in relation to sexuality, what comes into view? Both in terms of its limitations and also its possibilities.

BB/RZ *Can you give us an example?*

GK One of the things I wrote about in *The Regulation of Desire*, even in the 1987 version, was sexual fetishism. The ways in which we come to understand our sexualities as being natural, essential and ahistorical. Obviously, in major ways Marx accepts that type of sexual naturalism in his work, but his fundamental method – what is really useful about Marxism as a method and theory – moves in a different direction to disclose the social character of all social practices, including gender and sexual relations. I don't accept absolute distinctions between theory and method, just to make that clear. But there was really a significance and an importance in taking that insight from Marx, one that he could not apply to the sexual terrain, and now extending it to that terrain.

It also becomes a very interesting critique of sexual essentialism that is not simply grounded in discourse. Discourse is really important – it's a social practice – but you also need to look at other aspects of the material, social world. I think one insight that can be taken from queering Marxism is this critique of essentialism that doesn't just rely on a critique of discourse, but actually looks in a much broader way at material and social practices.

BB/RZ *In the edited volume* Whose National Security? *(2000), you focus on the Canadian state and surveillance against social movements. Was that in response to a particular moment?*

GK The book came out of a conference that we held at Laurentian University. So it was from a later moment in my life when I had finished my PhD. There's a number of levels to this: first of all, I was always interested in the national security campaigns, for a number of different reasons. When I first came out in my high school, the term that was always used against me was 'commie pinko fag'. There was this left guy who I was madly, passionately desiring. I told him I was gay. He told some of his friends. After this happened, a common greeting in the hall was 'commie pinko fag'. I never really understood where the pinko part came from. But that historical association constructed between commie and fag I was really interested in.

In 1993, Dean Beeby, a journalist with the Canadian Press did a whole bunch of Access to Information requests and got information released on the national security campaigns against lesbians and gay men. Then he came out with these major stories on the purge campaigns. My colleague and friend Cynthia Wright suggested I should do research into what Beeby had uncovered. The *Whose National Security?* book comes out of all of those interests, but also from my location at Laurentian University, and working with coeditors Mercedes Steadman, who did work on the national security campaigns against the women's auxiliaries of unions, and Dieter Buse, who did historical work on national security campaigns against the Left and against unions, against Mine Mill in particular.

In my view, the importance of that book is that it illustrates a number of different sites in which national security practices have taken place, including the investigations of the Canadian Union of Postal Workers, the Housewives' Consumers Association, which Julie Guard wrote about; Christabelle Sethna on high school students and the Young Socialists, who were under Royal Canadian Mounted Police investigation in the late 1960s because they were advocating for birth control in schools, and more.

BB/RZ *There has been a rewriting of queer history that excludes the involvement of left groups within it, and vice versa.*[7] *In the 1970s and '80s, what were the key debates among people on the left in relation to queer activism?*

GK I can relay that largely through the experience in the RMG and then the Revolutionary Workers League. The first political event I ever went to was a mass meeting at Convocation Hall at the University of Toronto, organised in 1971 by the Emergency Committee to Defend Quebec Political Prisoners. This followed the declaration of the War Measures Act by the Canadian government in 1970 and its denial of civil liberties. There were about 2,000 people listening to Michel Chartrand, head of the Montreal council of the Confédération des syndicats nationaux (a Quebec

7 See Roderick Ferguson, *One Dimensional Queer* (Cambridge, UK: Polity Press, 2018).

union federation), and Robert Lemieux, one of the lawyers for the Front de libération du Québec.

I bought two newspapers at the event. One was *Mass Line*, from the Communist Party of Canada (Marxist-Leninist), and the other one was the *Young Socialist* with John Lennon and Yoko Ono on the cover. The copy of the *Young Socialist* seemed really interesting. It was part of the youth culture turn in the Young Socialists that was later overturned. But it was the interview that was done with John Lennon for one of the International Marxist Group's publications in England, when he was in his 'victory to the Irish Republican Army' political phase.[8]

Within two weeks, I called up the Young Socialists and I joined. My sexuality was still pretty undefined. When I was younger, I liked to erotically play with boys. But it wasn't something that was politically significant to me at that time. I got involved in the Young Socialists as a high school student and quickly became aware that they supported the gay liberation movement. They supported the 1971 We Demand demonstration in Ottawa.[9] I met some of the gay members of the League for Socialist Action. I ended up getting involved in sexual relationships with other men, and eventually the Young Socialists say, 'Gay pride is coming up – who wants to speak at it?'

This was gay pride when it was a really small event in late August, on the anniversary of the We Demand demonstration. So I volunteered to speak. The League for Socialist Action and the Young Socialists were initially supportive, but the American Socialist Workers Party, which was the major definer of their current, eventually decided by the end of the 1970s that the gay movement was peripheral and lacked social weight. In turning to the industrial working class and making the industrial turn, support for gay and lesbian liberation fell to the bottom. But by then I had left the Young Socialists and was in the RMG, which supported the European majority of the Fourth International and is more left-wing.

BB/RZ *You mention the book* Beyond the Fragments *as an important text that had a great influence on you in this period?*[10]

GK Yes. I was already interested in what Sheila Rowbotham wrote about in terms of socialist feminist history. The first version of *Beyond the Fragments* was not a book; it was more like a pamphlet. But it had the three central

8 John Lennon, interviewed by Tariq Ali and Robin Blackburn (March 1970), *Red Mole*, 21 January 1971.

9 This was the first demonstration for lesbian and gay rights on Parliament Hill in Ottawa. It was directed against the limitations of the 1969 criminal code reform which was along the same lines as the law reform in England and Wales in 1967.

10 Sheila Rowbotham, Lynne Segal and Hilary Wainwright, *Beyond the Fragments: Feminism and the Making of Socialism* (London: Merlin Press, 1979).

contributions that were there in the book, from Hilary Wainwright, Lynne Segal and Rowbotham. I found Rowbotham's part, in particular – which was really a critique of Leninist forms of organisation in an attempt to articulate a more prefigurative type of perspective – to be really useful.

I was also, in my own life and in my own political practice, learning a lot more from feminism and lesbian feminists at the time. It was a really important context in the late 1970s in Toronto for me, going to women's music concerts – to Holly Near, Sweet Honey in the Rock, and Womynly Way concerts. All of these were really important cultural, but also political, experiences for me, and I learned about feminism in far more profound ways, for instance, reading Marge Piercy's *Woman on the Edge of Time* (1976), which is still one of my favourite books. *Beyond the Fragments*, for me, was really important in suggesting that existing Leninism was wrong as a theory and form of organisation. The question it poses is: How do you take all of these diverse struggles, these class and social struggles, and pull them together in some overall revolutionary strategy? Unfortunately, in practice it is unable to do this since it subordinates some struggles to others and its notions of leadership reinforce top-down relations.

BB *When I think about* Beyond the Fragments *and that genre of feminist work from the 1970s, it's difficult for someone who takes a critical race, feminist lens to everything to not feel the absence of race in the analysis. I was wondering if you could comment on that absence.*

GK Yes, I think that one of the major limitations of *Beyond the Fragments*, which was not particularly visible to me at the time, in terms of my own practice and political perspectives, was almost a nonengagement with anti-racist perspectives and anti-imperialism and anti-colonial perspectives – it just wasn't there. I don't fully understand, looking back on it now, why that wasn't more central. But obviously, there were political reasons for this. I think there were some real limitations to the development of socialist feminism in England at that point in time, even in terms of the responses around lesbianism. There was really no critique of institutionalised heterosexuality that was taken up within this type of socialist feminist perspective, and lesbian feminism was often simply seen as 'separatism'.

Himani Bannerji had written about this in *En lutte*, the paper of the Maoist group from Quebec (before it dissolved). She wrote quite a critical commentary on *Beyond the Fragments* from an anti-racist perspective.

I think she was quite accurate. My real transformation by anti-racist, anti-colonial perspectives comes later. Even though one of the forms of political practice of the RMG, from which I learned a lot, was doing support work for Leonard Peltier and for Rosie Douglas, once they were trying to deport him. So it wasn't that those questions weren't part of my political consciousness, but I didn't quite see their centrality at that point in time. So I think that real transformation for me really comes later.

***BB/RZ** Can you tell us a little more about how it comes about?*

GK I continued my Master's, and also my doctoral work, at OISE. I got to know Himani Bannerji, and I learned a great deal from her on this front. The Indigenous struggles around Kanesatake/Oka in 1990, which led to conflicts between Indigenous people and the army, were also very significant for me.

I think in some ways also organising around the AIDS crisis, because I was one of the first three employees of the AIDS Committee of Toronto (ACT). Just after I finished my MA, I worked for six months for ACT. One of my tasks was to try to develop liaison work with the Haitian community in Toronto, which was significant, but tiny compared to Montreal. I learned an awful lot from that. I finally convinced this man who was the central spokesperson for the Haitian community to come to an ACT board of directors meeting. Then they treated him in a completely racist way because he didn't know the right medical language.

The big issue then was that the Red Cross was saying Haitians couldn't give blood because they were identified as a 'high-risk group', given the early reported cases of AIDS among Haitians, and this was really discriminatory. I remember getting phone calls when I was at the AIDS Committee of Toronto from people saying, 'I have a Haitian housekeeper – what should I do?' I would say you should continue to employ your housekeeper; there's no problem here. I saw quite overtly how the professional managerial strata that was emerging out of gay, and to some extent lesbian, scenes actually had this way of turning on people because they were not properly trained in medical discourse.

Another experience that influenced me took place in 1986 in Toronto. The Black Women's Collective basically came into a meeting organised by some of the white socialist feminist activists about organising International Women's Day. The Black Women's Collective said, 'Everything has to relate to struggles against racism this year.' This really freaked out a lot of the white socialist feminists. But it actually led to a profound process of transformation. I'm not saying it was a total or fully developed transformation. But I think it actually meant that after that point in time, within the framework for organising for International Women's Day, struggles against racism and colonialism were seen as part of what should be talked about. It was no longer something that was contested and challenged.

***BB/RZ** This is a good point to discuss the framework of intersectionality. You were saying how you found Bannerji's approach to critiquing intersectionality very helpful, but also realise that there is usefulness in the term itself. Could we ask you to elaborate on this?*

GK I've recently seen advertisements in Toronto for positions in social agencies that wouldn't necessarily be seen as being progressive, asking for people who are 'committed to intersectionality'; even Liberal government politicians have declared that they adopt an 'intersectional' approach. So one of the things that struck me is that somehow this word has now been incorporated into neoliberal administrative practices that are completely decontextualised from its political origins. So that's one thing that's really important to point out. What are people talking about when they talk about intersectionality? Because I think there's a number of different places it comes from. I think there were various attempts to try to bring together different social relations of exploitation and oppression; socialist feminism is, in some ways, one attempt to try to bring together gender and class.

I think it's quite an inadequate attempt, because it doesn't really centrally bring in racism, colonialism and a whole series of other relations. But there were various attempts to actually try to grapple with how to bring these relations and struggles together. We know that they're not just separate, distinct and entirely autonomous. If you're trying to develop a more overall perspective, a more radical perspective, how do you begin to bring these relations together? Intersectionality is one of those attempts. I think it's useful and it provided a vocabulary for people. So I don't want to just say it was of no use. It accomplished something, but I don't think it went far enough.

Even though it pointed in a healthy direction, it also sometimes froze the discussions. We need theoretical perspectives that relate to a social world that's constantly moving. Social practices are diverse, and relations are constantly being transformed. So how do we actually think that through?

One of the things that Bannerji suggests is the need to use the methods that Marx used, in terms of dialectical analysis. We want to put things into separate categories and boxes so we can classify them, and then they can be regulated as a different series of categories. But instead, what a dialectical analysis wants to do is show what the relationship is between all these different practices that you're trying to put into these different boxes. How does one become the other? Or, how does one influence or reshape the other? To think of it in Marxist terms, for example, how are production and consumption internally related? These are mutually-constructed processes; you can't just produce things if nobody is going to be consuming them. There has to be some relationship. So what Bannerji has done, which is really important, is to use a dialectical analysis that she refers to as a mediational approach. What it allows for us to do that's really powerful is to recognise that every single form of oppression and exploitation has its own specificity or autonomy. Sexuality is not the same as gender; gender is not the same as race; race is not the same as class.

We need to recognise that in terms of the moment of analysis that looks at their autonomy or specificity. But obviously we can't just stop there. If you stop there, you don't actually see what's going on in relationship to any of those forms of oppression, because they're all constituted and made in and through each other all of the time. So I think that leads to a concrete, historical, dynamic, moving type of analysis. We really need to be able to see that mutuality. So in that sense, sexuality is never going to be lived simply on its own. Even if it has its autonomous specific features, it's always going to be lived in relationship to class and race and gender. Now, the approach of a mediational analysis doesn't fully resolve that, and I'm not sure we always need to resolve the question of what is more important in terms of strategy.

But I think it provides us with a way of looking at class that's actually much more dynamic, much more historical and much more social. In a certain sense, I would want to say that until there's a class analysis that is able to be defined by race, gender, sexuality, ability, age and all those relations, we actually need to hold onto a perspective that at least notes the autonomy and specificity of all of these different relations. That's why if someone utters the expression 'class first', it sends shivers down my spine. Because unless they're really clear that what they're talking about as 'class' is very different, then they're really talking about this reassertion of an older model and perspective of class that doesn't actually note the specificity and autonomy of all of these social experiences and contradictions.

Bannerji develops these ideas about a mediational approach out of a much broader critique of white feminism and its limitations. One of the richest pieces of theorising that I've seen is 'But Who Speaks For Us?'[11] It lays out a set of criteria around epistemology and ontology that are actually what we need for adequate theoretical perspectives these days.

BB/RZ *Yes, and there's a really complex rendering of different positions – the way people are differently situated is quite unique in that piece.*

GK Maybe what I can add here is my commitments around 'epistemology' and 'ontology', which I've always told my students are not terms to run away from. Even though this is not the language of activists, activists actually have perspectives on these all the time. My understanding of epistemology and ontology has really drawn from Smith's and Bannerji's work. The commitment to not adopt a positivist or objectivist epistemology, but to actually adopt a reflexive epistemology, is really crucial for me.

If you're going to research to try to understand any social practice, it requires being transformed by the people and the contexts you enter yourself into, in terms of what you're investigating. This approach doesn't answer every single question, but it puts you in a certain place in which you're moving. This

11 Himani Bannerji, *Thinking Through: Essays on Feminism, Marxism and Anti-Racism* (Toronto: Women's Press, 1995).

idea of ontology, the social practices of people themselves producing the social world, leads me to be a radical anti-structuralist. 'Structure' is a word that I just want to eliminate, and to try to think of other ways of talking about. I understand why people use the word 'structure', but those structures come from somewhere, and we need to make that visible all the time. Otherwise, we just fit into that moment of people's experiences where they're dominated by these structures that they can't change.

***BB/RZ** But then how do we speak about things like capitalism, without using the language of structure?*

GK That's why, taking from Smith's work – and this is also very much there in Bannerji's work – I use the language of social relations and social practices, a focus on people's *doings* or social accomplishments, all the time. It's not necessarily an easy language to use. If you don't use the words 'social structure', you can actually still write about the world, about how social practices get coordinated and are organised. So in some ways there's this constant pressure to want to describe it that way, of capitalism as a social system; that it's out there, external to us, and that we don't actively produce it. But *we* also produce it under circumstances not chosen by ourselves.

There's another reason for this – one that I really noticed in terms of teaching students. If students begin to recognise that they are actually part of producing capitalism, patriarchy or white supremacy on a daily basis, they can get depressed, which is not really the objective. What they don't always notice is the moment of liberation that's also bound up with a focus on people's *doings*, that we have to transform the way we do things and construct different sorts of relationships. It's actually much more empowering from this perspective, since through changing our practices (our doings) we can change the social world.

***BB/RZ** Since the publication of the first version of your book, queer theory has expanded in very interesting ways. Can you tell us about what you find as interesting innovations and/or shortcomings?*

GK In terms of queer theory, it really emerged out of the academic world. It emerges simultaneously with queer nation–type activism.[12] So I think there's a certain confusion that gets created, and some of the language of queer theory gets taken up within queer nation–type activism. But I think they're actually rather distinct, even though they're using some of the same terminology. For

12 Queer nation activism emerged in response to anti-queer violence and the devastation brought about through the AIDS crisis in the late 1980s and early 1990s. It was a militant anti-homophobic form of activism that engaged in direct action politics.

me, queer theory is very academically based, and if you look at Eve Sedgwick and Judith Butler as being foundational to queer theory, though they're quite different, I think the commonality is the emphasis on discourse.

Eve Sedgwick actually says something quite remarkable in her *Epistemology of the Closet*, where she writes, 'An understanding of virtually any aspect of Western culture must be, not merely incomplete, but damaged in its central substance to the degree that it does not incorporate a critical analysis of modern homo/heterosexual definitions.'[13] Which I think is very profound. But then it's quite clear she's only talking about discourse, and again, I'm not trying to dismiss the significance of discursive practices; these are all really vital and have real material, social characteristics to them.

But I think that's the fundamental problem, and I think there's a reason why discourse becomes the central focus; it's part of this becoming an academic language, confined and institutionalised within the academic world. I think it's also part of what emerges out of post-structuralism's ruptures with structuralism, and this includes Foucault's work. As I said before, I learned an awful lot from Foucault's work, but you can actually, in *The History of Sexuality*, volume 1 (1976), read his work as saying it is as if the homosexual emerges off the pages of medical discourse. From the moment of classification, the homosexual then emerges. Well, the question I ask is: What was this medical classification developed in response to, in relationship to?

My analysis has focused on at least four mediated social processes, if you're going to look at the emergence of 'modern sexuality,' of the homosexual, the lesbian and the heterosexual. This is, first of all, with the emergence of colonialism and imperialism; the encounters led to threats from gender and erotic diversity around the world, including third- and fourth-gender groupings in Indigenous cultures, leading to the emergence of what Scott Morgensen and others describe as 'modern gender and sexuality'.[14] In this context, capitalist social relations actually alter social relations, social spaces and social possibilities, opening up some spaces for people outside the domestic family-type 'economy' – and that's not an adequate expression, but I don't want to use the word 'heterosexuality', because I think that emerges later.

But it's also very much about how people come to occupy those spaces, seize them, expand them, build cultural and erotic practices within them. And it's also how they respond to what has been described as 'the empire striking back', which is when there's the police coming down on you when there's new psychiatric and sexual classifications – how do you respond to that? The thing about Foucault's analysis is, it's one dimension of the empire

---

13 Eve Kosofsky Sedgwick, *Epistemology of the Closet* (Berkeley: University of California Press, 1990), 1.

14 Scott Lauria Morgensen, *Spaces between Us: Queer Settler Colonialism and Indigenous Decolonization* (Minneapolis: University of Minnesota Press, 2011).

striking back in terms of this discourse, the sort of stigmatising and classificatory discourse.

But it's not actually looking at those broader processes of transformation of colonial, imperialist, capitalist social relations, patriarchal social relations – at how people are actually seizing social spaces, how they're using them. All of that disappears from his analysis, and what you really focus on is this one moment – not even the criminalisation moment, not the policing moment, but this moment of forensic psychiatry and sexology and its classification of the 'homosexual'. Now, as I said, I learned a lot from Foucault, but it's that discursive dimension that then gets taken up within queer theory and played around with and reworked.

So those are some of my problems with queer theory. To clarify, I'll talk about it in terms of Butler's work and 'gender performance'.[15] I actually am much more in favour of people's 'misreadings' of *Gender Trouble* than the reading that Butler intends people to have of it. So, in *Gender Trouble*, there's a major focus on gender performance. And, I do think that's quite important: how do people actually perform their genders to try to get the gender attributions that they want to get? Because in some major ways, that's what gender is actually about; it's gender performance and gender attribution and that whole social relation. But gender as a social relation is not what Judith Butler actually intended people to get from her notion of gender performance; it really was that people have certain types of gendered discursive practices they can engage in.

And 'gender performativity', which is the term that she used, is how, when you speak gender, these ruling discourses are actually speaking through you. But they can also be located slightly differently, and every single iteration is not exactly the same, which is what opens up some possibilities for change. But really, it's a discursive practice, and it's these discourses speaking through us that she's writing about.

And I'm not trying to say there aren't forms of social power and official languages that influence how we speak, but what she's not seeing is that performative capacity of people in their everyday lives around the daily construction of gender. So, that's one of the limitations of this focus on discourse, because if you really think discourse is central, is primary, it begins to remove human social practice from the analysis. It can prevent us from seeing how gender is a social practice and relation that we can transform.

There's a problem, however, with simply rejecting queer theory – what I would describe as a 'red fundamentalist' response to queer theory and post-structuralism, which is a total rejection. The ability of queer theory to emerge is in part because Marxism was not able to respond to these questions in the academic world, in particular, but it wasn't able to respond to them in the activist world either. So there are real things that we have to

15 Judith Butler, *Gender Trouble* (New York and London: Routledge, 1990).

learn from and to take from queer theory. Some of the things that queer theory raises are really quite crucial, including the question of de-normalising and queering a whole set of naturalised 'things.' Queer theory has gone through a number of transformations, and I think there's been moments or aspects of it that have been much more useful than others. For example, Jasbir Puar's work on homonationalism.[16]

RZ *That was the next question, so go for it.*

GK I think that the moment of Jasbir Puar's development of homonationalism is really important. This is actually after 9/11; the War on Terror is in full force, and Puar provides a way of trying to think through something that was becoming very visible: that some layers of lesbians and gay men, or queer people more generally, in the West, were actually beginning to align themselves with their nation-states and to see their nation-states as the framework through which rights and liberation would be developed.

I think Puar's original articulation of homonationalism is really about orientalist homonationalism; and I think Puar now recognises there's other forms of homonationalism. And, in particular, in the so-called Canadian context, settler-homonationalism is actually the most crucial one, and orientalist forms get built on top of that. I think it's a really useful notion, and I think there was a really important political and social context in which Puar did this.

In similar ways, Lisa Duggan's popularisation of homonormativity is something that also enters into that space, as an attempt to provide some way of accounting for how it was that a radical social movement becomes, in the historical present, more into middle-class respectability, trying to reproduce itself in a much more heterosexual-type mould.[17] Also, its adoption of the neoliberal nation-state in important ways, as being central to how it's going to proceed in the future.

I think the problem with homonationalism, as it's been taken up, is that it doesn't centrally address racialised class relations as being at the centre of this development. So the historical social basis for the emergence of homonationalism is never made fully visible. I think that it's really important for us, if we're going to use homonationalism, to actually specify its class and social basis, its historical character; how does it come to emerge? And that provides, then, a grounding for beginning to challenge it, because it's not simply this ideology or discourse, it's actually a materially rooted social practice that we have to engage with.

---

16 Jasbir Puar, *Terrorist Assemblages: Homonationalism in Queer Times* (Durham and London: Duke University Press, 2007).

17 Lisa Duggan, *The Twilight of Equality?: Neoliberalism, Cultural Politics and the Attack on Democracy* (Boston: Beacon Press, 2003).

BB/RZ *Did you want to speak about the Queers against Israeli Apartheid experience in Pride? Because it does relate to struggles against Canadian homonationalism.*

GK Queers against Israeli Apartheid (QuAIA) was a group formed in Toronto in 2008. I was largely living outside Toronto throughout its history, so my major role was as a supporter. The major thing I did, aside from going on their contingents whenever I could – because I was one of the founding members of the Lesbian and Gay Pride Day organising committee in Toronto in 1981, after the bath raids – was to get together a letter from most of the organisers defending QuAIA after attempts to exclude the group from the Pride parade.

QuAIA was a really important formation; it led me to want to actually go to Pride Day again. Pride had become something that was totally different from what we were trying to do initially, with the entry of commercial and state interests, commodification, policing, the military being there – it was just a totally different type of event. So QuAIA, for me, was a breath of fresh air, a reminder of a different way of addressing queer struggles.

One of the things I experienced in QuAIA was in 2010, when there was the most intensive effort to try to kick QuAIA out of the Pride parade. There was an overreliance, I would argue, on free speech arguments, which I think grows out of this notion that queer people don't like censorship. So if you can dress this up as being anti-censorship or being about free speech, you're going to get lots of support, which was accurate. The Free Speech Coalition that was organised was pretty broad based; it had hundreds of people there during that particular Pride demonstration.

QuAIA had a fairly significant contingent – 150, maybe 200 people – so it was actually a large group of people. But, there were also debates within QuAIA about how to engage on anti-censorship and free speech terms, but *also* go beyond that to address fundamental political questions about Israel's settler colonial project and build support for the Boycott, Divestment and Sanctions campaign.

And often the latter aspect seemed to get subordinated, so my critique would be that building concrete, active support for the BDS campaign within queer and trans networks in Toronto was actually not done as significantly as it needed to be through the QuAIA experience. QuAIA also had the potential to grow to encompass more issues than Israeli apartheid, as one of the very radical spaces in Pride. But organisational and political pressures did not allow for that to happen.

BB/RZ *Moving to more recent times – on 12 June 2016, Omar Mateen, a security guard, killed forty-nine people and wounded fifty-three others in a mass shooting inside Pulse, an LGBT+ nightclub in Orlando, Florida. You spoke recently about how Islamophobia was utilised in the mainstream media in relation to this attack.*

GK I think there are actually two different levels: one is the mainstream media, and the other is the political response to the attack from mainstream queer groups. In the United States, the mainstream media portrayed the attack as one on Americans. The specificity of these being queer and trans people of colour, and a very large proportion of them being Puerto Rican, was not focused upon at all. Then there was an attempt to fit this into narratives that already exist of 'this is a terrorist attack', to try to establish it having some relationship to ISIS and to use it that way.

Within the LGBT/queer scenes, I think the mainstream response, initially, was to see this as a hate crime, as about homophobic violence, and I think that's still fundamentally the way in which people want to address it. So one fundamental problem is that this attempt to deal with it as some sort of universal attack on LGBT rights does not actually deal specifically with queer and trans people of colour.

In terms of LGBT groups, there is an attempt to say, 'Well, we really now need the police even more intently than ever before, because they're going to be the only force that can protect us.' So that's led to Black Lives Matter withdrawing from the San Francisco Pride because of the excessive policing.

In Toronto, the Black Lives Matter group has an awful lot of queer and trans people involved in it. *Xtra!* magazine actually had this really interesting article that basically said that Black Lives Matter was the most successful and interesting queer and trans organisation in Toronto today.[18] Not that it always puts itself forward as that type of organisation, but if you actually look at its central organisers, this is very accurate. In Toronto, the Pride committee asked Black Lives Matter to be the lead contingent in the Pride parade in 2016.

Since that announcement, Black Lives Matter has engaged in major confrontations with the police department over the murder of Andrew Loku, including a three-week camp-out outside police headquarters.[19] During their Pride event, it was at the police headquarters – the very same building that Black Lives Matter was camping outside of – that they announced that they now regretted the 1981 bath raids. So, Black Lives Matter, quite correctly, has critiqued this as an attempt by the police to actually use Pride against Black Lives Matter and against the very legitimate concerns within Black and other communities. Black Lives Matter stopped the Pride parade for thirty minutes with a series of community demands, including that there be no institutional

---

18 Arshy Mann, 'Why Black Lives Matter Is Toronto's Most Effective LGBT Movement', *Daily Xtra*, 28 April 2016, dailyxtra.com.

19 In July 2015, Andrew Loku, a South Sudanese man, with a history of mental illness, was fatally shot in the hallway of his apartment building in Toronto by a police officer, who alleged Loku approached him holding a hammer. Black Lives Matter (Toronto) called for greater scrutiny of police-involved shootings, including publicising the video of the shooting, issuing an apology to and financial compensation for Loku's family. This was instrumental in pushing for a coroner's inquest into Loku's death.

police presence in the parade or festival. There was a major explosion of white gay men's racism in response, but since then the Pride membership has kept an organised police presence out of the parade.

The big point here is that despite Pride's origins in a riot against police, and despite Pride in Toronto being reignited more recently in response to police repression, Pride Toronto as an institution collaborates in very integral ways with the police, and this means they don't understand that there are many people of colour who are queer and trans who are still being directly repressed and hurt by policing. So, that's a major question that now gets opened up in really interesting ways, and these are opportunities that people have to seize.

BB/RZ *Many people exist as scholar-activists within the academy, and they are trying to do work that's useful for movements, but they are doing it more and more in a neoliberal institution. How have you navigated that space?*

GK I have to say that what I learned from Dorothy Smith, and from George Smith about political activist ethnography, has provided me with a significant grounding to resist the attempts to make me accountable to the institution, to the discipline and to the department.[20] Because it's actually provided some space for me to say the work that I'm doing is producing knowledge for oppressed people or for social movements. And no, I don't have to be 'objective' in the work that I do.

One of the things that I've always felt – and this is really different for people who don't have tenured positions, and I think I was quite lucky – is that you actually have to be disloyal to the institution and disloyal to the discipline. That's actually how your radical practice has to get organised. Now, you don't say that to university officials, but I think that's actually what you have to do if you want to be able to create and build these spaces, especially in the context of the neoliberal university, when those spaces are constantly shrinking.

And it's also really important to understand that those spaces can only be maintained and extended, especially in the current context, if we have some relationship to social movements, both within universities and outside them. Without that, you can't just maintain this as an isolated academic. I guess the last thing I'd say about this is that one of the ways I navigated this was by taking early retirement, because as neoliberalism and austerity were getting more and more profound at the institution where I was teaching, that became an option that became more and more interesting. So I am actually now trying to reconstitute myself much more as a public intellectual, who continues to do

20 George Smith, 'Political Activist as Ethnographer', in *Sociology for Changing the World: Social Movements/Social Research*, ed. Caelie Frampton et al. (Halifax: Fernwood Publishing, 2006), 44–70.

scholarship and activism, but largely outside the academic world. But I have to also say that that's led to a shift in my social location, so I'm actually much less tolerant of the academic world than I would have been in the past.

I think it's useful for us to understand that universities are also workplaces and sites of struggle. There are workers there; there are power struggles going on all the time. I think there's been this notion that there's the university world and then there's the real world outside it, when the university world is part of the real world. So, it's not simply that there's struggles way over there that we need to be relating to; there's also struggles right here where we are that need to be attended to in really vital ways. I think that's crucial.

Obviously, when social struggles are at a low ebb, it makes for really difficult situations for some of us in the academic world, but I think it's really important for us to not simply retreat into 'Oh, I've got some scholarly publications to produce that will be read by the least number of people possible, so I'm just going to go into a hermit-like retreat for a period of time.' It's really important to have support networks, to recognise that this is a fundamental problem that lots of us face. Support networks that work entirely against the competitive dynamic for research funding and everything else that's going on in the academic world right now.

The other thing I've learned from Dorothy Smith, and especially from George Smith, is how activists in movements do research all the time, and how, if you're located there, this is actually an amazing political and pedagogical experience. And how the moments of rupture, or contradiction, between social movements and ruling relations are really productive spaces to be doing research, but also to produce grounded knowledge, and that this knowledge can actually then be understood and generalised much more in social movements themselves. So for me, that strand of political activist ethnography that takes us more away from the academic world is one that I'm much more interested in now.

Also, I reject the notion – this anti-intellectual, anti-academic strand – within some currents in activism that argue, 'Why would you want to have anything to do with the academic world?' I think it's still very important for those spaces to be held, and those battles can actually be important. Because there are certain skills and capacities that you can sometimes have in the academic world that you don't often get in the world of social movements outside them, so it's also important to not simply write off universities, because they are also sites of class struggle all the time. The university world is one area (but just one area) of continuous struggle and transformation.

Selected Writings

Kinsman, Gary. *The Regulation of Desire, Homo and Hetero Sexualities* 2nd ed. (Montreal: Black Rose, 1996).

———. 'The Politics of Revolution: Learning from Autonomist Marxism'. *Upping the Anti: A Journal of Theory and Action* 1 (2005), 44–53.

———. 'Within, Against and Beyond: Urgency and Patience in Queer and Anti-Capitalist Struggles'. In *What Moves Us: The Lives and Times of the Radical Imagination*, edited by Alex Khasnabish and Max Haiven, 131–52. Halifax and Winnipeg: Fernwood, 2017.

———. 'Queer Resistance and Regulation in the 1970s: From Liberation to Rights'. In *We Still Demand! Redefining Resistance in Sex and Gender Struggles*, edited by Patrizia Gentile, Gary Kinsman and L. Pauline Rankin, 137–82. Vancouver: University of British Columbia Press, 2017.

———. 'Policing Borders and Sexual/Gender Identities: Queer Refugees in the Years of Canadian Neoliberalism and Homonationalism'. In *Envisioning Global LGBT Human Rights: (Neo) Colonialism, Neoliberalism and Hope*, edited by Nancy Nicol, Adrian Jjuuko, Richard Lusimbo et al., 97–129. London: Human Rights Consortium, School of Advanced Study, University of London, 2018.

———. 'Forgetting National Security in "Canada", Towards Pedagogies of Resistance'. In *Activists and the Surveillance State, Learning From Repression*, edited by Aziz Choudry. London: Pluto Press and BTL, 2019.

Kinsman, Gary, Dieter K. Buse and Mercedes Steedman, eds. *Whose National Security?: Canadian State Surveillance and the Creation of Enemies*. Toronto: Between the Lines, 2000.

Kinsman, Gary, and Patrizia Gentile. *The Canadian War on Queers: National Security as Sexual Regulation*. Vancouver: University of British Columbia Press, 2010.

———. 'National Security and Homonationalism: The QuAIA Wars and the Making of the Neoliberal Queer'. In *Disrupting Queer Inclusion: Canadian Homonationalism and the Politics of Belonging*, edited by OmiSoore H. Dryden and Suzanne Lenon, 133–49. Vancouver: University of British Columbia Press, 2015.

Leanne Betasamosake Simpson

An Indigenous (Michi Saagiig Nishnaabeg) artist, writer and scholar, Leanne Betasamosake Simpson has worked for over a decade as an independent scholar using Nishnaabeg intellectual practices. She has lectured and taught extensively at universities across Canada and has extensive experience with Indigenous land-based education. She holds a PhD from the University of Manitoba and teaches at the Dechinta Centre for Research and Learning in Denendeh.

Leanne is the author of five previous books, including *This Accident of Being Lost*, which won the MacEwan University Book of the Year; was a finalist for the Rogers Writers' Trust Fiction Prize and the Trillium Book Award; was long listed for CBC Canada Reads; and was named a best book of the year by the *Globe and Mail*, the *National Post*, and *Quill & Quire*. Her latest book, *As We Have Always Done: Indigenous Freedom Through Radical Resistance* was published by the University of Minnesota Press in 2017, and was awarded Best Subsequent Book by the Native American and Indigenous Studies Association. Her new novel *Noopiming: The Cure for White Ladies* is forthcoming from House of Anansi Press in the autumn of 2020. As a musician, she also combines poetry, storytelling, songwriting and performance to create unique spoken songs and soundscapes.

***BB/RZ** Can you tell us about your early political and intellectual formation? What were some of the major influences on your scholarly writing, your work as an educator, and as a poet?*

LBS I often say that witnessing the so-called Oka Crisis during the summer of 1990 was my political education. The resistance at Kanehsatà:ke and Kahnawake, the leadership of Ellen Gabriel acting as spokesperson for the People of the Longhouse, the response from white Canada, and observing the beautiful, grounded solidarity of Indigenous nations across the country certainly set me on a trajectory and was most definitely my political awakening, as is true for many of my generation. Coming of age during the 1990s, I learned from the organising and mobilisation of the James Bay Cree over hydroelectric development, was involved with anti-racist organising on campus and was in proximity, at least geographically, to the organising of the Black community in Toronto. The 1990s, as Idil Abdillahi and Rinaldo Walcott write in their 2019 book *Black Life: Post-BLM and the Struggle for Freedom*, was the decade where

Black cultural production in places like Toronto had fully emerged. Writers like Dionne Brand gave me language to name things I hadn't been able to before.

It was during this time that I was first exposed to the writings of Indigenous peoples like Vine Deloria Jr, Patricia Monture-Angus and Lee Maracle. I first encountered the writings of bell hooks, Audre Lorde, Angela Y. Davis, James Baldwin and Frantz Fanon. And, as I write about in *As We Have Always Done*, I also spent a lot of time on the land with Nishnaabeg elders, and this facilitated a very deep love and connection to land, story, language and Nishnaabeg life. That love is perhaps what has propelled my career for the past two decades.

BB/RZ *You have emphasised the importance of children in networks of learning and community building. You set out a powerful critique of the way the Canadian state has targeted Indigenous children (through the residential school system, for instance) as a core aspect of colonisation. Your work also very powerfully counters the way the care of children has become commoditised and sorely devalued in many (if not most) places. Can you tell us more about how you see the care of children as central to feminist, anti-colonial, anti-capitalist struggles?*

LBS This is a Nishnaabeg practice as I understand it; people of all ages were and are to be included and engaged in all aspects of life, and those engagements were and are predicated on consent, nonauthoritarianism, self-determination, noninterference, kindness, gentleness and a very deep form of caring. So, one would create and maintain an extended family life that embodies the sort of political and ethical life we want to create collectively. Our children were present during most of our economic, political, religious and daily activities, so they learned by doing, from observing and from being a part of things. Education took place on the land, and in the context of family and community. It was not institutionalised. While every person needed a foundation of life skills, young people were supported in finding and developing their gifts, their loves and their interests. This also meant that the way we did things accommodated the needs of children – for movement, joy, engagement and belonging. We can't just bring children along to a boring three-day conference taking place inside a building and expect that this will bring out their best selves, nor can we expect all children to thrive in childcare settings at conferences where they are in an unfamiliar environment, with people they have never met. We certainly *can* bring children along to a three-day gathering taking place outside in the bush, with snowmobiles, food, fire, fishing, laughter and fun people to keep them entertained when the adults get into serious conversations.

In my work at the Dechinta Centre for Research and Learning, we have identified the biggest barrier to postsecondary education for Indigenous women in the north as childcare, so we provide a land-based programme for kids to learn alongside their parents. This has been a very necessary and difficult part of this work, because the presence of children and their needs has a beautiful and significant impact on our programme. It simply doesn't work to use a day care sort of model, so rather, we view children as full participants and teachers and accept their influence as part of our learning. We recently hosted a solidarity gathering for BIPOC (Black, Indigenous and People of Colour) community organisers. Rather than hosting this in the city, we hosted it on an island in the lake, during the early part of spring. Participants brought their children. We snowmobiled out to the site, sat around a fire, set and fished nets together and shared food. The group of children had a blast, and although no one presented papers, we shared informally about our work and began to deepen our relationships to each other. Solidarity became very clear to each of us, as a responsibility. It sounds very simple, and in some ways it is. But this is a very old way of Indigenous organising, predicated on relationships and taking care. It is also a profoundly different way of interacting with people from other anti-colonial movements.

BB/RZ *As a member of the Nishnaabeg First Nation, the concept of freedom that you have been developing and practicing is one rooted in Nishnaabeg intelligence, which incorporates emotional intelligence, land-based associative forms of knowledge (to draw on the words of Glen Coulthard), and is kinetic, that is, involves movement. It is a 'whole body intelligence', as you have written. Can you tell us more about your concept of freedom, particularly as it relates to feminist, anti-colonial struggle?*

LBS It is a sort of relational or grounded freedom, meaning that it takes place in the context of a complex relationality with all of the other beings, communities and nations with whom we share time and space – one that is designed to propel life. It's a freedom to individually and collectively determine the world in which we live. I've learned about this sort of freedom on the land and by practicing it. Think back to the solidarity gathering I described earlier. The children were running around playing, laughing, interacting with each other and the rest of the group in the context of sharing, kindness, gentleness and care. Procedurally, the group was making decisions using consensus and care, fully aware that not everyone feels comfortable on the land and outside of their home environments. To me, this is a glimpse of grounded freedom – a sort of freedom that Indigenous peoples under occupation have almost no experience of feeling and being immersed in. A sort of freedom that is an individual and collective practice, designed to promote the well-being and self-determination of both the individual and the communal as interlocking projects. It does not therefore mean one can do whatever they want without hindrance, because causing harm to oneself or to other living beings is not ethically acceptable. But it does mean that one can be self-determining in the context of shared values and practices. In this context, colonial impositions like heteropatriarchy and anti-Blackness, and the internal replication of these systems of harm, are an attack on grounded freedom.

***BB/RZ** In the context of writing about the Radical Resurgence Project, you develop the idea of 'generative refusal'. What is 'generative refusal' and why is it important to anti-colonial and anti-capitalist struggles?*

LBS In its simplest form, for Indigenous peoples it means not just rejecting, critiquing and dismantling colonialism and its adjacent projects (although this is crucial), but generating, building, making, organising and struggling to create and actualise alternatives, even if those iterations are failures. It means continually engaging in the process of making something better, because every time we do that, we unlock theory and knowledge about how to do that. This doesn't mean organising in a haphazard fashion; to me, it means being fully aware and articulate about how those who have gone before us have organised and struggled, how other anti-colonial movements adjacent to us are organising and struggling.

There are and have been many, many sites of generative refusals over the past four centuries of colonialism, and really, it is the generative refusal of my ancestors that ensured that I exist and can function as Nishnaabeg. Each generation inherits this struggle and a particularly temporal iteration of this struggle, and it is our collective responsibility to contribute to the making of Indigenous life, in spite of whatever eliminatory forces are working against us. Generative refusal, then, is a presencing – it is concerned with using all of the individual and collective tools available to us to make a different present, which inevitably gives birth to the future. There are so many sites of this in our communities, whether it is families passing along language, songs and stories; moments of urban organising that create (often temporary) spaces of decolonial potential where we live out our theories and ethics; spaces of Indigenous resistance and life created by blockades, and the networks of care that we build to support those actions; collectives of artists intervening with visions of possibility; and solidarities with anti-colonial movements generating affirmation, shared experience and respect for differences.

***BB/RZ** First Nations have long been 'internationalist' in outlook. This has two very different meanings. On the one hand, as you set out in your work, there are the complex relationships of diplomacy between First Nations, and then also, with plant worlds, animal worlds, and nonhuman life forms. On the other hand, there is the history of First Nations political activism in broader, internationalist anti-colonial coalitions. Can you tell us about the significance of these different aspects of First Nations' internationalism?*

LBS There is a tendency to view Indigenous peoples and Indigenous knowledge as *only* locally generated and oriented systems that come from an intimate, land-based existence – which is, of course, true, but it demonstrates a limited understanding of Indigenous thought. Indigenous politics and ethics frame this differently. We are peoples with reciprocal relationships of life, through which we have always ethically shared land, time and space with plants, animals and other humans, stretching back to the past and reaching forward to coming generations. Our peoples have always been philosophically and materially interested in the nations of life that make up our universe, our universe as a life-generating system, both inside our spheres of influence and outside those circles. Our deep relationality exists in both intra- and interdependent ways across scales, and so these different aspects of internationalism are intrinsically associated; one gives birth to another. For instance, I believe Nishnaabeg ethics requires me to act and live in solidarity with movements for Black life in Toronto, the Zapatistas in Chiapas, and Palestinian struggles for freedom in Palestine. Many Indigenous nations have long histories of connecting to, sharing with and learning from and standing beside these movements as co-resistors. Indigenous societies were never insular – we have always practiced complex diplomatic relations with other forms of life.

BB/RZ *Relatedly, can you tell us about how you see the concept of the nation, and how it differs from the Westphalian nation-state system and its nationalisms that are rooted in imperialism, racism and exclusion?*

LBS Indigenous nationhoods are not built upon enclosure, borders, authoritarian power, violence or even exclusive use. Indigenous nationhoods are not a replication of the nation-state and the violence required to maintain statehood; in the context of colonialism, they are a generative refusal of the Westphalian nation-state system. Indigenous nationhoods are a different way of organising life, structuring the ways we live and relate to the worlds around us, and this should be done in a manner that not only refuses and dismantles anti-Blackness, white supremacy, capitalism and heteropatriarchy, but generates alternatives based on deep relationality, grounded solidarities, the self-determination and freedom of our co-resistors and, of course, a bringing forth of more life. Thought of in this way, Indigenous nationhood cannot fully exist alongside capitalism. It *can* most certainly share land and space with those communities and nations interested in living with the sanctity of the land, and with a plurality of other nations and collectives already doing so.

BB/RZ *Indigenous feminisms in Canada (and the Americas more broadly) are distinctive from other radical feminist traditions such as Black feminism and Third World feminisms, but also grapple with the effects of colonialism on racialised women and sexual minorities. Could you tell us about some of the differences* *and contact points between Indigenous feminisms and other feminist traditions that you have found exhilarating, or challenging, or both?*

LBS For me, I understand heteropatriarchy as something that was injected into my nation and our people by the colonisers as a mechanism to control, manipulate and eliminate our bodies, minds and spirits, our solidarities and our connection to our lands. This was done strategically, because heteropatriarchy in its most violent forms removes people from the land very quickly and efficiently. It destroys the intimacy that connects people to each other, and it attacks our ability to effectively organise against it. Although certain target segments of society – Two Spirit and queer people, women and children – experience the violence in an asymmetrical fashion, it impacts all families and all genders and the entire nation. Engaging in the replication of heteropatriarchy, to me, is a betrayal of our most cherished values and ethics.

As I write in *As We Have Always Done*, Nishnaabeg society has a plurality of genders and sexual orientations that wasn't exceptional, because it was normal to respect diversity and live in a manner that supported individuals, both in being self-sufficient and in being self-actualising, becoming their best selves. This was visible to the colonisers and read as both a threat and a barrier to the exploitation of land and natural resources; and so, it was queer Indigenous peoples that were first violently targeted for elimination. The state, working in cohort with the church, infused our communities with a heteropatriarchy designed to replicate Victorian gender roles reinforced by both intimate and structural violence. Generations of Indigenous children were indoctrinated into this heteropatriarchy at residential schools, at the same time that our communities were faced with forced relocation, waves of epidemics, dispossession of land and economic means, and Christianisation, while the 1876 Indian Act rendered our political systems inert and encoded homophobia, transphobia and sexism into daily life. Physical, sexual and emotional violence was inflicted on all genders as part of the colonial project by the state, until they had created a system where we simply replicated the trauma, violence and harm in our own communities. White women were often accomplices and working in cohort with the state to advance this harm, and white mainstream feminism and second-wave feminism haven't been particularly useful tools in addressing these issues in our communities. Issues of gender in Indigenous communities, therefore, are complex, and many kinds of feminism, particularly white mainstream feminist analyses, are too simplistic and racist to be of use in our world-building projects. We can only start where our communities and where our peoples are, and with their immediate needs. Our ethics demand that we do this with care.

I am exceedingly grateful to Black feminists – radical, world-building Black people who are providing incisive analysis on white supremacy, capitalism and heteropatriarchy, while also responding to the needs of the Black community – for their writing and example in navigating similar, but not identical, issues in their own projects for Black life and Black freedom. For decades now, they have challenged me to think, rethink, think otherwise, to ask questions of myself and my people, to refuse whiteness. To organise, continuously, tirelessly, from a place of strength, against the eliminatory practices of the state, and to do this with a profound love for community.

***BB/RZ** You write that Nishnaabeg ethical practices require you to 'engage not just with their theories but with the people and peoples that embody and enact these theories'. Solidarity, in other words, requires you to develop 'relationships of reciprocity and co-resistance' with revolutionary movements emanating from the global South, with radical Black thinkers and activists, abolitionists and so on. Can you tell us more about what this looks like? Are there any examples you can draw on to tell us about the meaning of relationships of reciprocity?*

LBS Indigenous peoples have a long history of this, although this history doesn't appear in the literature very often, as of yet. My colleague Glen Coulthard is doing a lot of this work in his own nation, the Dene. In his book *Red Skin, White Masks* (2014), he demonstrates how Dene thought intervenes theoretically in Marxism, and his more recent work concerns the Dene's engagement with anti-colonial thought in the 1960s and '70s, and their connections to places like Tanzania. He is also documenting some of the Native organising at this time on the west coast of Canada and its connection to the Black Panthers and Maoism. This work has translated into relationship building at the Dechinta Centre for Research and Learning, where we both work, with organisers from the Black Lives Matter Freedom School in Toronto, and interlocutors from various movements in Canada and the United States. In my own territory, Black activists in Toronto stood in solidarity with us during Idle No More. We have more work to do in terms of coming to terms with anti-Blackness, but I am encouraged by folks in both movements supporting each other materially, and beginning to build relationships. Black Lives Matter, in its various forms and manifestations, provided me personally with an incredibly well-organised, well-executed response to white violence.

***BB/RZ** Idle No More seemed to mark the beginning of a resurgence of First Nations radical political action in a very public way. Chief Theresa Spence's hunger strike, which she began as a protest over the unacceptable conditions on her reserve (the Attawapiskat, in northern Ontario) was also a part of these actions. Can you tell us what your view is of those remarkable months of action, and their effects on the political landscape in Canada and beyond?*

LBS Idle No More was the most recent visible national mobilisation of Indigenous peoples, but it occurred in the context of four centuries of resistance and struggle. And although in many ways it was unsuccessful in bringing about the structural changes segments of the movement were demanding, I think we collectively unlocked a lot knowledge about how to organise. I learned how important face-to-face relationships are in the building and maintenance of movements. I learned how powerful the Internet, at least in its earlier days, could be in terms of mobilisation, but also how it commodifies our identities and selfhood, and causes, amplifies and maintains a sort of internal harm. I learned how easy it is for states to incite internal divisions and conflict, and how if that conflict is not resolved, it will destroy the good work of movements. Witnessing Black Lives Matter, I learned how important it is in our movements to be meeting the material needs of our people, to be strategic and organised, to build care into our mobilisations. Watching the 2016–17 mobilisation at Standing Rock unfold, I was reminded of the power of putting Indigenous bodies between colonisers and the resources they want, while also building a communal life under the direct threat of state violence. I am reminded that I was born into 400 years of struggle, that I have gifts and privileges my ancestors didn't have and that I have a responsibility to use those effectively to make life better for the coming generations.

BB/RZ *There have been many criticisms of truth and reconciliation commissions (TRCs) that have operated in many parts of the world, to deal with state violence and atrocity. The criticisms cover a whole spectrum of issues, from the notion that justice is often illusory in such processes, to the idea that the truth of systemic injustices can never really be apprehended in such fora. What is your view of the TRC in Canada – how it operated, and its conclusions?*

LBS Indigenous peoples and the Canadian state have very different ideas about the word 'reconciliation'. The TRC in Canada was a state-run affair fuelled by the commodification of Indigenous suffering and grief, designed to placate Indigenous resistance and to satisfy white Canada's guilt, while avoiding any structural changes in the colonial relationship. That's what I will always remember. These fora are designed by the state to maintain colonialism under the guise of justice. The mandate of the TRC also focused on individual suffering associated with residential schools, and erased the collective impact of residential schools, dispossession and the wider colonial project on Indigenous communities and nations. These processes are a performance, and justice is an illusion.

It was interesting, then, that the Indigenous community pushed for a national inquiry into our missing and murdered Indigenous women, girls and Two Spirit queer relations, given our experience with state reconciliation. Like the TRC, this inquiry came about because of decades of Indigenous organising, this time by Indigenous women and families of the missing women.

Although I think, mechanically, the inquiry played out in a similar way to the TRC, I think the movement that created it is still intact, primarily because families and women organised through the inquiry. The desire to hold the state accountable for violence, suffering and atrocity is strong in our communities, and I'm not sure any of us thought an inquiry and a report would substantively change Indigenous state relations in Canada. We will use every tool presented to us to try.

BB/RZ *In addition to your scholarly writing, you are a poet and an artist. Can you tell us about the place of your artistic practice in your political life? How does it connect with other traditions of radical knowledge production through art?*

LBS The spine of my practice is Nishnaabeg life and a love of our land, thought, culture, languages and the Nishnaabeg processes that make up that life. I spend a lot of time on Nishnaabeg and Dene lands. I spend a lot of time thinking, writing and making music. Everything I make comes from the same place; I just refuse the disciplinary and genre boundaries of Western thought. My intellectual, artistic and political life are the same.

In *As We Have Always Done*, I write about and provide evidence to back up my writing regarding, for instance, queer normativity in Nishnaabeg contexts. In the short film *Biidaaban* (2018), based on three of my short stories and poetry, we show queer normativity in a contemporary and urban Nishnaabeg context. This affirms queer Indigenous peoples to and for heterosexual and cisgendered audiences – so that they see queer Indigeneity as normal. In *As We Have Always Done*, I tell about queer normativity, in *Biidaaban*, we built a Nishnaabeg world where it is normal – we show it.

My work with my band and in performance is also an extension of these ideas. I was performing at the National Arts Centre in Ottawa, Canada, when the Colton Bushie verdict came down. (Bushie was a beautiful Cree young man who was fatally shot by a white farmer in Saskatchewan, who was found not guilty of murder.) Rosanna Deerchild, a Cree poet and writer, was the host of the evening, in honour of an elder Indigenous musician, and my band was there to honour him. Rosanna went out to introduce me, seconds after learning the verdict. She was upset and angry, and she communicated the verdict and her feelings to the audience – who fell silent. As I walked across the stage to take the mic, I was thinking only of the heartbroken, sad, furious, devastated Indigenous people in the audience, and I was asking myself: in this brutal moment, what do we need? Gentleness, kindness, decolonial love, affirmation, peace, feelings of freedom. And so for ten minutes, I did everything I could do with my voice, my body and my heart to give that to us.

Knowledge production in artistic spaces is somewhat of a refuge for me. These are spaces in which I can say things and do things I can't say or do in the academy because the literature or the evidence doesn't exist or isn't in an acceptable form. Aesthetically, I like the idea of opacity and speaking in a coded, and therefore protected, way to different audiences. Opacity isn't exactly embraced by the academy; the academy demands white legibility, although I certainly try by writing my work for Indigenous audiences first. And I simply love the idea of making new worlds, rather than just talking about them. That's how one unlocks Indigenous theory, brilliance and inspiration.

Selected Writings

Simpson, Leanne Betasamosake. *Dancing on Our Turtles' Back: Stories of Nishnaabeg Re-creation, Resurgence, and a New Emergence*. New York: Arbeiter, 2012.

———. *Islands of Decolonial Love: Stories and Songs*. Winnipeg: Arp Books, 2013.

———. *This Accident of Being Lost: Stories and Songs*. Toronto: Astoria, 2017.

———. *As We Have Always Done: Indigenous Freedom through Radical Resistance*. Minneapolis: University of Minnesota Press, 2017.

Silvia Federici

Silvia Federici is Professor Emerita at Hofstra University in Hempstead, New York, and a scholar, teacher and activist from the radical autonomist feminist Marxist tradition. In the 1970s, she was a cofounder of the International Feminist Collective, and an organiser of the International Wages for Housework Campaign. In the 1990s, after a period of teaching at the University of Port Harcourt in Nigeria, she was a cofounder of the Committee for Academic Freedom in Africa, as well as the Anti–Death Penalty project of the US-based Radical Philosophy Association.

Federici has written several influential works, including *Caliban and the Witch: Women, the Body and Primitive Accumulation* (2004) and *Revolution at Point Zero: Housework, Reproduction and Feminist Struggles* (2012). She is the editor of the essay collections *A Thousand Flowers: Social Struggles against Structural Adjustment in African Universities* (2000; with George Caffentzis and Ousseina Alidou) and *Enduring Western Civilization: The Construction of the Concept of Western Civilization and Its 'Others'* (1995).

BB/RZ *How would you describe your political and intellectual formation?*

SF I think my political and intellectual formation began with the war. The war, I think, politicised us, the generation of '68, from the time we had use of reason. I spoke of it in the introduction to *Revolution at Point Zero* (2012). We knew very early in our lives that we had entered a world that was unjust, because our parents never stopped talking about it – unjust and dangerous. Very early, we learned to distrust the state. Very young, with my class, we went to see the photos of the concentration camps. And my mother always reminded me of what it was like to be a mother under the bombs, waking up every night, seeing a red sky and knowing that very soon the bombs would be dropping. That was a process of politicisation. Until the age of thirteen, I grew up in a small village, where my parents had gone to escape the continuous bombing of my town. Later we returned to Parma, which was a communist town. So, politics was in the air. On the first of May, there were speeches and songs and red carnations. I grew up in an environment that was full of history and politics, and, like many of my generation, I believed that the worse was behind us and democracy had won. But there were many contradictory elements in that landscape; so joining a student demonstration or becoming a feminist were very natural steps for me. The fascist culture was totally misogynist. It was full of contempt of women, who were just the producers of soldiers, the mothers for the fatherland. I grew up in a cultural context that was political, but also patriarchal. By the time I was eleven, I was in revolt against being a girl. The summer that I developed breasts, I wore a large wool sweater to hide it. I felt trapped. When the feminist movement began, I knew I was a feminist.

BB/RZ *Was your family a supportive environment for your rebellion, or was it difficult?*

SF My family was the perfect place to become political because it was full of contradictions. I saw in my family everything that unfolded in Italy at that time. My father was anti-fascist, though not a communist, and he was an intellectual. He gave me political and historical knowledge. When I went to church with my mother, as a child, he would ask me, 'What did the priest say?' and proceed to criticise it or give me some of the historical background. So I learned a lot from him. My mother was a full-time housewife, and for a long time I saw her as less interesting. But she would complain that she worked and worked, and at times would say that she did not understand why she was not paid. At that point my father would explain that it was because her work was not productive. I heard that first in my family. At the time, I didn't know what that meant, but my mother always replied that it was nonsense. So the family dynamics were very conducive to my developing a feminist consciousness.

BB/RZ *Can you tell us about the double character of reproductive work that you talk about in* Revolution at Point Zero? *You say in the preface that now, when you reflect back on your childhood and the years in your family home, you see that it was not only a place of exploitation, but also a place of security and nurturing. You refer to the work of bell hooks, who pointed out that for women of colour, the domestic space of the home often provides security and protection from a racist environment outside of it.*[1]

SF When she says that the home is a place that is safe, where people value each other, she speaks of a reality that goes beyond the Black community. That side of the family has not been recognised by the women's movement, myself included when I was younger. Now that I am older, thinking back, images come back from that life that tell me that my mother made our home a space where we felt valorised. Through my engagement in the women's movement, I regained my mother. Wages for Housework helped me reconnect with her. She also started confiding in me, telling me how upsetting it was for her to have to ask my father for the money she needed, not only for the family but for

1 See bell hooks, 'Homeplace (A Site of Resistance)', in *Yearning: Race, Gender and Cultural Politics* (Boston: South End Press, 1990), 41–9.

herself. And she started giving me some money, because I was very poor when I was a student. I would come back from the States with no money and she would say: 'This I put to the side.' I began to see her own struggle. She didn't say anything, but slowly she readjusted her relation with my father.

BB/RZ *I think this takes us into the question of Wages for Housework (WFH). Can you tell us about the specific historical context in which this campaign developed?*

SF The historical context was, on one side, the women's movement that was looking for strategies, with left feminists telling us to get a waged job and join the unions, join the class struggle. Then there was the struggle of women on welfare who were being attacked and vilified, in a very racist way, as welfare was wrongly identified as a Black women's issue. As Dorothy Roberts writes in her book *Killing the Black Body* (1999), the attack on women, on welfare, was functional to the building of the image of the dysfunctional Black family that later served to justify the policy of mass incarceration. Women on welfare were saying that raising children is work and that every mother is a working woman. Provocatively, they would say that if child-rearing is recognised as work only when we raise the children of other women, then we should swap our children. Then, in England, there was the struggle over the Family Allowance, which was money that went directly to women.[2] In the early seventies, there was an attempt to take it away, which brought dozens of women's groups into the streets. So the question was also, how should we position ourselves towards these movements? And there was, of course, the question of all the unpaid labour generations of women have done.

BB/RZ *Our next question is about domestic work and migrant domestic labour, which are overlapping spheres of paid and unpaid work for many women. Can you tell us more about how the relation between the two figured in the WFH campaign?*

SF For us, the question of domestic work was primarily the question of women's unpaid labour, because by the 1970s paid domestic work seemed on the way out as a female occupation. More and more, women preferred taking jobs in factories or in the service sector, rather than working in a relationship where they had so little bargaining power. It was, for us, a miscalculation,

2 In 1970, with the election of a Conservative government in the UK, the Family Allowance, which had first been introduced in 1946 to provide a non-contributory allowance funded through taxation, was impacted by the introduction of the Family Income Supplement, a means-tested benefit intended to cap any rises in the Family Allowance. The introduction of this measure was also accompanied by the very unpopular withdrawal of subsidised milk for children.

because by the 1980s that began to change. As we know, with the restructuring of the global economy, as women in the United States and many countries of Europe entered the waged workforce, their work in the home, at least in middle-class families, was replaced by that of immigrant women, coming from countries impoverished by the austerity programmes imposed on them by the International Monetary Fund, in the name of debt repayment and structural adjustment. This global restructuring of reproductive work was a very calculated policy, facilitated by various organisations like the World Bank, Caritas, and, of course, the governments of the countries from which women migrated, like the Philippines, who benefited from the remittances the women sent back home. But as we know, migrant women have paid a high price for their quest for some economic security, having to leave their families behind, and often their children, for many years. There is now a broad literature documenting also the abuses to which these workers – mostly women of colour, coming from countries formerly colonised – have been exposed to, including sexual assaults, especially when living in the homes where they work. This, too, challenges the assumption that it's only in the street that we have to worry about sexual violence.

***BB/RZ** If you were going to think about a WFH campaign now, what would that look like, with the benefit of hindsight?*

SF We would ask not only for money, though money would still be important, but for other material resources – housing, for instance – and then struggle more openly for a reorganisation of reproductive work, organised not by the state but from below. Demanding Wages for Housework was crucial to make visible the nature of this work and its true beneficiaries. It was a refusal of unpaid labour and a strategy of reappropriation. But we also need to reorganise reproductive work in a way that takes us beyond the nuclear family.

***BB/RZ** Domestic work has become a part of the globalised economy, as you just discussed, in which the service sector exploded after the 1970s. Women, mainly from the global South, migrate to the North to perform this work. Of course, you have a much longer history in the Americas and elsewhere of Black women performing unfree and unpaid domestic labour during slavery and in the post-slavery era, paid as well as unpaid domestic labour. The nature of domestic work is still feminised and racialised, and remains among the worst-paid and most undervalued work. So this is our situation, where child-rearing, let's say, is an activity that's still highly commodified, and we haven't succeeded in decommodifying this work and making it into something else. We continue to live with this contradictory terrain, where racialised and feminised domestic work is both invisible and unpaid, and also commercialised and marketised. What are your thoughts about how to navigate these contradictions?*

SF We need to change the conditions of work, both on the domestic front and in the areas where reproductive work is done on a market basis. The two are closely connected in more than one way. For instance, it is no accident that when women go to work outside the home, most of the time the jobs they get are extensions of housework. Moreover, it is because domestic work is so devalued that the wages women can earn when they perform it outside the home are so low. Ideally, then, we would have a movement in which all women unite, struggling over the question of reproductive work, collectively deciding how we want to change it, how we want to reorganise this work. We need a reduction of waged work time and better services; above all, we need services we control. But we will never obtain this as long as it is considered natural for women to do housework, and for millions of us do it for no remuneration. So a struggle for the remuneration of reproductive work is still important. It is important to assert that reproductive work is the reproduction of labour power, and not a personal service – that it is work that contributes to the wealth the capitalist class accumulates. This is not to glorify work or to imply that only those who work have a right to live. Rather, it is to refuse providing more unpaid labour, and having to spend our lives working, working, working, in the home, outside the home – to have some economic security and not depend on men. Keep also in mind that today unpaid labour is expanding. Now, students are doing unpaid labour, even in the high schools, and there are many people who work for free, hoping to obtain a permanent job.

***BB/RZ** Are there any movements you see today that are capturing these issues, this mode of organising or this way of thinking about things?*

SF Yes. There is the struggle of migrant domestic workers that has been growing in the United States, forcing many states to recognise them as workers, entitled to certain benefits, which all previous labour laws had denied. In Canada, in Quebec, there is also a movement of students against unpaid labour, which always makes the connection between the exploitation of students through the system of internships and the exploitation of houseworkers. In the feminist movement, there is also a greater concern today for care work. But I do not see any movement addressing the question of domestic work in its totality. As I have said, I see the struggle for the recognition of the productive character of domestic work as a question of reappropriation, as a refusal of unpaid labour, a refusal of a double job, a double workweek, and a struggle for the broadening of our options. And of course, I see it as means to denaturalise and defeminise reproductive work. We can discuss how this should be organised, under what label. What we can demand, what we can obtain, would depend on the level of power we have. The important thing is that what we ask should be such that it cannot be used to create division among us, and instead give us all more social power. If I understand it correctly, the Family Allowance in England did that, whereas Social Security in the United States benefitted only certain workers. Many jobs done by Black workers did not qualify for Social Security; domestic workers did not qualify. Let me add that sharing the housework with men, as feminists always propose, is necessary but not enough. It is still unpaid labour that we give to capital. Moreover, many families are headed by women, with no men with whom to share the work.

BB/RZ *So, the point is that it's not necessarily a contradiction to make a claim for the value of reproductive work – for instance, child-rearing – through demanding a recognition of its economic value in the form of a wage, and at the same time, working towards the decommodification of this activity?*

SF That's right, because capitalism has built its power appropriating our unpaid labour, not only in factories and offices, but in the home as well.

BB/RZ *We just wanted to go back to the point about fragmentation, because you're right, in most spaces we're talking about one thing or the other as if they're unrelated –*

SF But it's the same woman's life.

BB/RZ *It's not like the theory is not there. Feminists have written about it. Yet somehow, when it comes to action, there is still a lot of fragmentation on these issues.*

SF I worry, above all, about the divisions within the feminist movement with regard to sex work, and also with regard to maternity. I think some younger feminists look at reproduction work as a lower form of activity; they accept that having children is necessarily drudgery. I understand it, because in this society domestic work is organised in a way that makes it oppressive. But we need to see that it could be different if we have the space, time and resources necessary, and if we organised this work in a collective way. I understand not wanting to have children, especially under the present conditions. This is what I decided, and I never regretted it. But we should not devalue maternity and make 'sterility' a strategy of liberation, as some feminists did in the 1970s, arguing that women will not be completely free until procreation occurs outside the womb. I'm also concerned because I see a tendency to devalue women as a political subjects. 'Woman', for me, stands for a whole history of struggle that has had a transformative power; it has transformed what it means to be a woman, so that there is nothing frozen or static about it.

***BB/RZ** Let's turn to the work you are currently doing on children and the elderly, and care work.*

SF Both children and the elderly are under attack today, as they belong to the population of 'nonproductive' individuals. So the time and the resources dedicated to them are being constantly reduced. Proletarian families have little time for them; schools are cutting programmes that could interest children, and now teach them mostly to pass tests. Children are clearly suffering in this situation. There are now approximately 8 million children who, from a very early age, are given a variety of pills for hyperactivity, attention deficit or depression. It is a social problem having to do with lack of care, lack of attention, but it is being medicalised. The conditions of the elderly are even more worrisome. Many senior centres have been closed. Home care has been reduced. In the working class, many live a life of poverty and isolation, which is reflected in the increase in the number of suicides.

As for children, another concern is the trend towards gender reassignment at a very early age. How do girls or boys know, at five or six, what it is like to be the opposite sex? What can a boy mean when he says, 'I know I am a girl'? Is 'woman' an essence? Something that is clearly identifiable, independently of any specific experience? When I was a child, I didn't want to be a woman, because I didn't like the way women were treated, and I was always reminded of what I could not do because I was a girl. This is why I became a feminist and have spent a good part of my life fighting to change what it means to be a woman, and above all, making something open-ended. I am concerned about children making crucial decisions about their lives so young, without really knowing their implications and what they may desire and need when they age.

***BB/RZ** Some feminists believe that it has become increasingly difficult to make the argument that the category 'woman' relates to a particular kind of life experience, that of being categorised as 'female' from birth and then being gendered as a woman. On the other hand, there is the problem of transphobia amongst some feminists, who insist that transgender women cannot be defined as women.*

SF My concern is that there is a tendency to forget that it was the feminist movement that destabilised what it meant to be a woman and initiated a critique of femininity, of heterosexual family relations, that facilitated the emergence of other movements like the sex worker movement and the lesbian movement. The critique of biological conceptions of social identities did not begin with the trans movement.

Women's liberation has transformed what it means to be a woman, created women as political subjects. We have fought against being defined as bodies, vaginas. We were the first to say that what we call sex, gender and nature are socially constructed realities, not because material differences do not exist, but because they are always apprehended and acted upon through social and cultural value systems, and above all, through class systems.

BB/RZ *Can you tell us a bit about the Midnight Notes Collective, and how that came into being?*

SF *Midnight Notes* began after the Three Mile Island accident in 1979.[3] In response to it, an anti-nuclear movement developed. However, it had no class analysis; it was all about the threat of nuclear power, the danger of extermination by nuclear explosions. But some of us objected that for many people, particularly Black people, the apocalypse was already happening, now. We were also critical of the tactics of the movement, like civil disobedience, going limp into the arms of the police. This is how *Midnight Notes* began, mostly by the initiative of American philosopher George Caffentzis and, in an early phase, the Swiss anti-capitalist Hans Widmer. I wrote many articles for it over the years but was never a full member of the collective. Over time, the journal was influenced by struggles in Latin America; then, there was an influence from the Italian movement and from Wages for Housework. Theoretically, *Midnight Notes* represented a different reading of capitalist development and anti-capitalist struggle than that proposed by the Marxist autonomist tradition. It was very inspired, for instance, by struggles in Mexico and Guatemala, struggles in Africa, and by the feminist movement as well.

BB/RZ *We want to go back to your relationship to Marx, Marxism and communist politics. Earlier, you spoke about Italy and the general political environment in the postwar era, and the specific dynamics of your family life. Could you elaborate on your engagements with Marxist categories like 'primitive accumulation', or your critique of 'immaterial labour'? Could you elaborate on how your conceptualisations of these categories fit with, or are antagonistic to, different Marxist traditions?*

SF Through my work with Italian feminists like Mariarosa Dalla Costa, and even prior to that, I came into contact with the Italian Marxist tradition of *operaismo* (workerism), which recuperated the active side of Marxism, arguing that capitalist society develops not out of an inner dynamic, but always in response to struggle. Operaismo, with the work of Mario Tronti,[4] also rejected the Leninist separation of economic and political struggle, introducing the

3 On 28 March 1979, a reactor partially melted down at Three Mile Island Nuclear Generating Station near Middletown, Pennsylvania.

4 See Mario Tronti, *Workers and Capital*, trans. David Broder (London and New York: Verso, 2019), originally published as *Operai e capitale* (Torino: Einaudi, 1966).

concept of the 'social factory' – that is the idea, already in Marx, that with capitalist development, 'society' is subsumed to the factory (i.e., to the production of value).

But Tronti never saw women as the central subjects of the social factory; he only saw students. Another critique I have of Tronti's work is that he always argued that the struggle against capitalism has to take place at the highest levels of capitalist development; for instance, he was never interested in the struggles that were taking place in the so-called Third World. But by the time I read Tronti, I was already living in the United States and was aware of the struggle against slavery, for civil rights and Black Power, and the anti-colonial struggle, as for example the struggle of the Vietnamese people.

For similar reasons, I do not accept the concepts of 'cognitive capitalism' and 'immaterial labour', which again privilege a particular sect of workers as the revolutionary subjects. It is a Eurocentric concept, which forgets what it takes to produce computers and other forms of digital technology.

Also, the category of 'immaterial labour' is too Cartesian for me, and the distinction between immaterial and affective labour, which Marxist autonomists make, is artificial and reproduces the sexual division of labour. It presumes (among other things) that there is no cognitive content in emotional/affective labour. I read the introduction of 'affective work' as a gesture made to the women's movement. But it is taken from Spinoza and has a different meaning than 'emotional work.' Most importantly, you cannot separate material and immaterial labour. Care work, raising a child, is that material or immaterial? Sex work, is that material or immaterial?

BB/RZ *Finally, can you tell us what your view is of the recent resurgence of academic work on social reproduction theory?*

SF Some of the recent work on social reproduction, by connecting social reproduction to a wide range of activities performed outside of the home, is useful. It expands the concept of reproductive work, demonstrating that it is no longer only domestic work. It never was completely, in reality. Reproductive work always also took place outside the home, in schools, hospitals. The problem is that there is also a tendency to forget the work that is done in the home, and now all attention is on commercialised reproduction.

I think that any theory of social reproduction should also be concerned with the ecological struggle and the struggles of Indigenous people. These are powerful social movements that cannot be ignored, and that demand we rethink Marx's work in some important respects. For instance, his optimistic view of the effects of the spread of industrialisation worldwide. First of all, the global expansion of capitalist development has never been a factor of unification among proletarians worldwide. It has only created new divisions, new stratifications, new areas of unlimited exploitation. Moreover, how can we reconcile this expansion with the preservation of the environment? Industrialisation was already destroying the environment in Marx's time; now we can see how destructive it is. This, I would argue, must be a key issue for any theory of social reproduction.

Last, I want to mention that I have published a book that collects, archives most of the materials produced by the New York Wages for Housework campaign in the period between 1972 and 1977.[5] It demonstrates how much work we did, not only theoretically, but also through our participation in specific struggles, and how, in the late seventies, we also began a critique of the new forms of capitalist development produced by the rise of economic and cultural neoliberalism.

Selected Writings

Federici, Silvia. 'Wages against Housework'. Bristol: Falling Wall Press, 1975.

———. *Caliban and the Witch: Women, The Body and Primitive Accumulation*. New York: Autonomedia, 2004.

———. 'Precarious Labor: A Feminist Viewpoint'. *Variant* 37 (2008). variant.org.uk.

———. *Revolution at Point Zero: Housework, Reproduction and Feminist Struggle*. Oakland: PM Press, 2012.

———. *Re-enchanting the World: Feminism and the Politics of Commons*. Oakland: PM Press, 2018.

———. *Witch-Hunting, Witches and Women*. Oakland: PM Press, 2018.

Federici, Silvia, and Arlen Austin, eds. *Wages for Housework: The New York Committee 1972–1977: History, Theory, Documents*. New York: Autonomedia, 2018.

Federici, Silvia, Constantine George Caffentzis and Ousseina Alidou, eds. *A Thousand Flowers: Social Struggles against Structural Adjustment in African Universities*. Asmara: Africa World Press, 2000.

5 *Wages for Housework: The New York Committee 1972–1977; History, Theory, Documents*, ed. Silvia Federici and Arlen Austin (New York: Autonomedia, 2017).

Abolition Feminism

Ruth Wilson Gilmore

Ruth Wilson Gilmore is Professor of Earth and Environmental Sciences, and American Studies at the Graduate Center of the City University of New York, where she is also director of the Center for Place, Culture and Politics. She writes about abolition, racial capitalism, organised violence, organised abandonment, changing state structure, the aesthetics and politics of seeing, and labour and social movements. Gilmore is the author of *Golden Gulag: Prisons, Surplus, Crisis, and Opposition in Globalizing California* (2007) and has published articles in the journals *Race & Class*, *The Professional Geographer* and *Social Justice*, among others. Her essays appear in several edited volumes, including *Policing the Planet* (2016, with Craig Gilmore; edited by Jordan T. Camp and Christina Heatherton) and *Futures of Black Radicalism* (2017, edited by Gaye Theresa Johnson and Alex Lubin).

Gilmore is a cofounder of many grassroots organisations, including the California Prison Moratorium Project, Critical Resistance, and the Central California Environmental Justice Network. She has lectured in Africa, Asia, Europe and North America, and is working on a number of inter- and transnational projects. Among her honours are the American Studies Association Angela Y. Davis Award for Public Scholarship and the Association of American Geographers' Harold Rose Award for Anti-racist Research and Practice.

BB/RZ *You once said, in an interview with Michael Preston, 'I've had many lives Michael . . . many, many lives.' Can you tell us about these many lives, particularly in regard to your early political formation?*

RWG Yeah, I'd be happy to. It cracked me up when I saw Michael Preston's name here, of all people in the world. Very kind person. Left liberal, Black political scientist who was one of my protectors when I worked at the University of California, Santa Cruz, so I don't even remember doing an interview with him.

I grew up in a family of organisers and activists. One way to describe them was using the old-fashioned term 'race people'. We were Black people for Black people, or before that we were negroes for negroes, or coloured people for coloured people. My father and his father were labour organisers; my grandfather was a janitor and was one of the organisers of the first union at Yale – the blue-collar union, Local 35, which organised during World War II. And then, my father was a machinist, and he organised the Tool and Die Makers at

Winchester Repeating Firearm Factory – the guns that won the West – in the 1950s. There was a lot of organising, as well, in New Haven around housing, access to education. New Haven was a city that had a very small Black population when my parents grew up there, but after World War II a lot of Black people, mostly (but not exclusively) from North Carolina, moved into New Haven to take jobs in the then-expanding military industrial complex.

New Haven's principal products, as I've written about, in those days were weapons and students.[1] Guns and graduates, if you want to put it that way. So I grew up in a household in which organising was part of everyday life. I was sent out to desegregate a school when I was ten years old, and so that was part of my project, to get through this girl's prep school intact, which actually was kind of a struggle. But it never occurred to me not to do it. After the fact, people would ask me all the time, 'Didn't your parents know you would be miserable?' And it's like, what part does that play in the world of liberation struggle? Parents deciding that something shouldn't happen because it might be hard for their kids to do it – that was never even a concern. They never asked me if I was happy and I never told them I was unhappy. I just did it. And I kind of loved it for four years because I'm a nerd; and then I hated it for four years because I was a teenager.

Then I did a lot of political work doing all kinds of things – anti-war work, work in solidarity with the Black Panther Party. I wasn't a member of the Party, but in solidarity with it. Very close family members were members of the Black Panthers.

BB/RZ *Why did you decide not to join the Black Panther Party?*

RWG I had already joined a communist tendency that seemed satisfactory to me at the time. I wasn't against the Party, I just had my formation that was sensible to me, so that's what I did. I'm actually a little embarrassed about it now, not because it was communist, but just that particular one. In California, I spent many years doing work that tended more and more to revolve around access to universities. School curriculum, that kind of thing. And it wasn't a plan of mine, it was just a world I knew really well, and I figure people should organise what they know, and in doing so will learn what they don't know. And then they can extend and expand their work.

So by the time I was forty-three, I had been out of school for seventeen years, and I had decided that as much as I had been really thrilled to study dramatic literature and criticism as a student, I was never going to make my living either in the professional theatre or in academia teaching that stuff. Because, although I could see the connections between the sort of world

1 Ruth Wilson Gilmore, 'Race, Prisons and War: Scenes from the History of US Violence', *Socialist Register* 45 (March 2009).

making that characterises drama or theatre, and the world making that characterises our everyday experiences, I wasn't all that interested in pounding into people's heads that there was a continuum that was worth paying attention to. Rather, I thought that what I should do was go back to school, study political economy in a really systematic way, so that I could do something else with my energy and brainpower.

So I went back to school when I was forty-three and did a PhD in geography. I hadn't done a geography course between age thirteen and forty-three and I still have my geography book from age thirteen, which was actually pretty splendid. It was a book that laid out, very carefully, different modes of production.

Fast forward to 1993. I went back to school at Rutgers, where I worked with Neil Smith, who is a geographer; Dorothy Sue Cobble, who is a labour historian; Bob Lake, who does work on urban planning and policy; and Ann Markeson, who is really quite a fine economist. We eventually separated paths because we had different ways of thinking, but I learned an enormous amount from her. And from my own reading that I'd done in study groups and on my own that preceded my return to school, to graduate school; this meant that I was already a student of Stuart Hall, Cedric Robinson, Stephen London, Hazel Carby – all of these people whose work I had read and reread, and, indeed, as an adjunct I'd taught. So all that shaped what I did in geography school, doing the PhD, and it shaped my approach to the work that I've done on mass incarceration, criminalisation and the other topics that I've been writing, organising and thinking about.

***BB/RZ** What do you think geography added to your way of understanding the world?*

RWG Geography added a rigorously material imperative to anything I thought about; that would not necessarily have been the case if I had done a PhD in, say, American studies or cultural studies. It doesn't mean that in those interdisciplines I couldn't have done what I did in geography. But in geography, you have to have the real, all the time, and since geography is the study of how we write the world, the real, then, is never static anyway. It has everything to do with human–environment interactions, it has to do with the social, it has to do with the scale and organisation of capitalist and anti-capitalist space. So all of that enabled me to keep my focus on what mattered to me and to learn to think about those things in ways that I hadn't ever thought before.

***BB/RZ** Could you tell us a little bit more about taking your background in radical Black thought into the field of geography, and what that was like? You didn't really have any models to follow in bringing that work into the field of Marxist geography.*

RWG That's a really great question, and I didn't have models to follow, which is to say this: because of the experience I had desegregating that school, it never occurred to me that I couldn't do what I wanted to do and needed to do, no matter the context. And I knew it would be a struggle, but it never occurred to me that I couldn't do that. And I realise now that when I went off to geography school, I wasn't thinking, 'Oh, this is going to be like the Day Prospect Hill School for Girls,' but obviously that experience had shaped me in so many ways, some of which I'm still probably not aware of.

So there was that. But the other thing is that once I started geography school, and I went off to my first geography conference, the American Association of Geographers (AAG) annual meeting, I looked around and I found some other Black people, and some other people of colour and white people, who were talking about interesting stuff, and we hung out. And we never stopped hanging out. And we spent time together. We talked a lot, we fought a lot. We went through all kinds of intellectual and social development together.

The most senior person in the group that I hung out with was this incredible guy called Bobby M. Wilson, who taught his whole career at the University of Alabama. He's since retired. We're around the same age. He might be a couple of years older than I am, but he'd gone and done his PhD straight out of college, so he'd been a professor since he was in his twenties. And his work is phenomenal. His greatest work, which everybody in the world should read, is called *America's Johannesburg*,[2] and it's about Birmingham. It's an astonishing book. It's a book that asks the question: How did it happen that so much of the most radical expression of the Black liberation movement emerged in Birmingham? What was it about Birmingham?

He laid out the shifts in Birmingham from its founding as a post–Civil War city. It's about the same age as Johannesburg; its extractive industry is like Johannesburg; it's apartheid, like Johannesburg. And he laid out the development and consolidation of that city's economy and racial order over time. It's just an amazing piece of work. He's a Marxist, and he writes about race in everything that he does.

Another one of our little coterie was the late Clyde Woods.[3] Clyde, who had been a student of Edward Soja at the University of California, Los Angeles, had been, as it were, educated in a certain kind of Marxist geography tradition, and himself had realised the limits of a certain core of Marxist thought – in

2 Bobby M. Wilson, *America's Johannesburg: Industrialisation and Racial Transformation in Birmingham* (New York: Rowman & Littlefield, 2000).

3 Clyde Woods (1957–2011) authored *Development Arrested: The Blues and Plantation Power in the Mississippi Delta,* introd. Ruth Wilson Gilmore (London and New York: Verso, 2017); and *Development Drowned and Reborn: The Blues and Bourbon Restorations in Post-Katrina New Orleans,* ed. Jordan T. Camp and Laura Pulido (Athens: University of Georgia Press, 2017).

part, because Ed himself had been an Africanist by training, and he knew that a lot of the stuff that he was encountering in the work of white geographers, guys, his comrades, was not attentive to the contradictory dynamics of race and class and gender. And Ed wanted to understand that, so Ed started reading bell hooks, and he was Clyde's mentor.

I mean, this was actually the world. There was a world that was changing, there was a lot of scepticism, I will say, on the part of some people who, in the US context, looked at a certain kind of American cultural studies that made claims about political commitments to be kind of more noise than anything else. Some left social scientists were trying to work up useful theories for engaging the problems that capitalism and racism and sexism create and reproduce; some wanted to reject cultural studies outright. Others, including me, said: 'Wait a second – you're making a really varied intellectual landscape into this flat plane. Let's actually look more at what Stuart Hall and so on have said and done and written.' So we brought that cultural studies, the Birmingham school, as it were, into the AAG.

Another person who became a dear friend and close colleague is the Chicana geographer Laura Pulido, who's written about race, organising, and rural and urban struggles. So we formed this coterie, and we spent a lot of time together. As I said, we argued a lot; we fought a lot to try to figure out what we should do and how we should do it.

And I'll say that one of the legacies of that effort that really characterised the mid 1990s in geography in the United States has bloomed now in the twenty-first century in the general field of Black geographies. That field wouldn't exist if we hadn't done what we did, and I know that Katherine McKittrick, who is one of the central people in it, would attest to this. When she was a graduate student, I met her when I was junior faculty, and we had a very long, intense engagement about her work that became *Demonic Grounds*.[4] And so, those were some of the things that happened to geography over time.

So, did I enter geography thinking, 'I'm going to change this discipline'? No, I entered geography so I could learn how to do some things. That was my purpose. I needed some tools. I got the tools, but in getting the tools, acquiring the tools, I brought to them other tools that I had, and so they do work that's somewhat different, perhaps, than if I hadn't had the other tools to start with.

***BB/RZ** Something that you refer to in your work, and that you're quite adamant about, is that you're a historical materialist, and that formulation has been used in some absurd ways and some very interesting ways. Can you tell us a bit about how you're using it and why it's so important to you?*

4 Katherine McKittrick, *Demonic Grounds: Black Women and the Cartographies of Struggle* (Minneapolis: University of Minnesota Press, 2006).

RWG That formulation is important to me because, in the struggles that I've engaged with over time, and in things that I've thought about and studies that haven't been firsthand engagements, what's always apparent is that people make what's new out of something that's already there. And the something that's already there might not be adequate to the task, just as I was talking about earlier with the tools that I had and then the tools that I acquired, but there's a there-ness that matters. It matters in how we figure out how to change the conditions of life, how we improve our conditions of existence, and I did think for a long time that experience is what mattered in some way. That it was really about experience. And one of the formulations in Marx that I always found very beautiful is where he talks about how we mix our labour with the earth, and in so doing we change the external world and change our own nature. I think that's a really beautiful thing. I also think it's true.[5]

However, one of my mentors, the late, great Cedric Robinson, thwacked me on the arm one day and said: 'I've been trying to tell you as long as I've known you – it's not just experience, it's *consciousness*.' So, because of the influence that Cedric and others have had on my work, I shifted. I haven't disavowed historical materialism, and I can't imagine I ever would, but I realised that consciousness has to play a bigger role in my analytical work if I want to get beyond the notion that experience is all that matters. Because if it's all that matters, then that would also mean that a certain kind of extremely flat and categorised – or, to use a word that you used, abstracted – view of identity is enough to change the world. And it's not, and I know better than to think that.

BB/RZ *There are many theories of consciousness that exist within Marxist and Marxist-Hegelian traditions. Can you tell us how you are thinking about political consciousness specifically?*

RWG I'm thinking about consciousness these days in the terms developed by, for example, Amílcar Cabral and the PAIGC (African Party for the Independence of Guinea and Cape Verde), and popularised by people like Paolo Freire. So consciousness, and conscience-isation, which is to say, to translate that word from Portuguese to English: awareness is not just a matter of information; it's not a matter of facts, but one of developing and pursuing things through a sensibility that shows a different possibility can emerge.

To go back to Cedric's work, probably one of the most quoted phrases from all of his work is 'ontological totality'. And while many people repeat this, I don't think most of them have actually sat and thought about what this might mean. And that ontology has to do with what, for example, Clyde Woods writes about with his formulation of blues epistemology, which is to say, an

5 Karl Marx, *Capital: A Critique of Political Economy*; Volume I, trans. Ben Fowkes (London: Penguin, 1976), 284.

already elaborated, but not fixed, sense of how 'small d' development might proceed. Of how, as Cedric writes, having a commitment to what he calls the survival of the community, means that one's pursuit of liberation is different from having a commitment to, say, the restoration of land to the landed bourgeoisie in Palestine from before 1948, to take another example. Or what Frantz Fanon talks about when he talks about the pitfalls of national consciousness. Part of how I put that into operation is through asking questions that have more stretch and resonance than other questions. So there's an example that I use in something that I wrote, about how in organising in rural California against prison expansion, I learned pretty soon – not soon enough, but pretty soon – to ask not 'Why do you want a prison?', but instead, 'What do you want?'

And even that opened up my consciousness to understanding, as well as provoked a kind of consciousness-shaping, even among two or three or four people, that could then become the foundation for further organising. So again, consciousness isn't a matter of having adequate information, although information is not unimportant. And consciousness is not an effect of experience, although experience matters.

BB/RZ *You've written that you were influenced by the work of the Wages for Housework campaign and the activism of Margaret Prescod and Selma James. Could you tell us how your work on prisons with Mothers Reclaiming Our Children presented a different reality or understanding of social reproduction and how it's related to struggles that go beyond an understanding of social reproduction as solely focused on care work in the domestic sphere?*

RWG I spent two or three years in Los Angeles organising with Margaret Prescod, and I met Selma off and on over time. Selma is a fierce and cantankerous person but also a really good teacher, and what mostly impressed me, which is to say shaped how I went about doing things with respect to the Wages for Housework campaign, was not so much the call – 'Raising a child is a job,' 'Pay women, not the military' (although that was fine, I thought it was a terrific slogan) – but rather how they went about particularising their work in terms of campaigns of immediate need.

In South Central Los Angeles, people were struggling over the fact that there were fewer and fewer places that they could pay their electric bill, and so that meant that people's lives were stretched because they would have to take the time to take public transportation to somewhere way out of their community to pay it. So that was one of the organising campaigns. This all made a lot of sense to me. It was that kind of organising and the proliferation of the various little formations that Wages for Housework sparked – Time Off for Prostitutes and so forth – that I thought was really strong. So that was my connection with the Wages for Housework campaign.

And they also did some important intervention on me in the early years that we knew each other. In the late eighties and early nineties, as I said earlier, I had been involved in a lot of study groups and reading a lot of difficult stuff, and I was a little proud of the fact that I had mastered a rather enormous specialised vocabulary – one we started calling theory then and still passes for theory today. And some of it was useful, and some of it was not, and I sometimes would speak that language when it was absolutely unnecessary and Ann Margaret would always call me out. The stern tutelage for which I thank them in the acknowledgements to *Golden Gulag* has to do with them helping me to understand how my understanding could be more useful if I could do more fluid code switching. And I was grateful for that.

In relation to the question of social reproduction – well, reproduction *and* social reproduction – it seems like nowadays more and more people are raising the standard of social reproduction as a fundamental category of thinking, organising and theorising in writing, and people seem to mean a pretty wide variety of things. Some people are talking, more or less, about what happens at the scale of the household – which is not unimportant, but it's not enough. Other people are trying to look at the multi-scalar, or inter-scalar, relations to which social reproduction emerges.

To go back to the Wages for Housework thinking, and the thinking that Selma James and Mariarosa Dalla Costa formulated decades ago: if we do agree that the source of all value is labour and that the source of all labour is reproduction, including daily as well as intergenerational reproduction, then that line has to move. It has to move. And that's exciting, because it opens up so many possibilities for organising.

BB/RZ *This leads nicely to the question on method and the question of scale. You've developed a method of analysis that uses the concept of scale to connect the body to territory and to connect the individual to the communities in which individuals exist, and to histories and economies and material forces that are global in scale and their operation. Can you tell us more about this method and your conceptualisation of scale?*

RWG The notion of scale that I'm working from actually was developed by my adviser and mentor Neil Smith, I don't know, twenty-eight, thirty years ago. He started thinking about how we might more forcefully consider the kinds of places in which we do political organising for the purpose of what he called 'jumping scale'.[6] So, 'jumping scale' is something we could read off, although this isn't quite adequate, as say, internationalism, right?

6 See Neil Smith, 'Geography, Difference and the Politics of Scale', in *Postmodernism and the Social Sciences*, ed. Joe Doherty, Elspeth Graham and Mo Malek (London: Macmillan, 1992), 57–79.

In the late eighties and early nineties, Neil laid out this typology of what he called the 'organisation of capitalist space.'[7] And at the time, it was a typology, so it's just ideal types; there's nothing absolutely fixed. But he proposed this nested hierarchy of scales, from the body to the global; then, in his elaboration of what kinds of social processes dominated each scale, he gave us some insights into thinking about how to stretch political work, or to lead political work over certain kinds of barriers and join forces to achieve whatever. And one of the questions, actually, that came up in the nineties – not one I raised but other people raised –was whether the organisation of capitalist space that Neil proposed was changing in the context of what we came to call globalisation. And it seems like it actually has, and one of the big shifts has been the fall in the specific importance of the region and the rise of the urban. And that if, once upon a time, for a very long time, the region was more or less the scale of production, that that has been overtaken by the expansion of the urban, if we think about the manufacturing platforms in eastern China or Vietnam or Bangladesh, in northern Mexico, you name it. And that has happened, in part, because of the drop in the cost of transportation, especially ocean transportation, ship transportation, so that the factories of production can move around more easily when they're in their capital form – and, of course, with greater difficulty when they're in their labour form.

So, to go back to my own work, what I've done is try to think about scale in order to think about the sites of struggles. Neil used the word 'territory' to mean a jurisdiction or juridically defined area. But how, in thinking about political struggles, can we identify antagonists in such a way that the possibility for people to join forces across differentiated places becomes stronger? In order to think about that, I did a lot of work – I mean both the research and writing in *Golden Gulag*, but also the research in organising to try to convert California from a very prison-building-friendly state to a somewhat abolitionist state. Not that you go door to door and people say, 'Yes, I'm an abolitionist,' but if you look, you see that California has not managed to build a prison each year, the way it had been doing. And that happened because people joined forces across different kinds of places, which is to say different regions and communities and so forth, to make it difficult, if not impossible, for the state to continue doing what it was doing.

Neil intended for his typology to be a way for us to think about, as he wrote, the organisation of capitalist space, but also to think about how geographies are partitioned and repartitioned. This thinking of partitioned-ness is very close to my heart, including partitions that seem to actually go through the scale of the body. So then I got to thinking that people *live kinds of places that are not organised by capitalism.*

7 See Neil Smith, *Uneven Development: Nature, Capital and the Production of Space*, 2nd ed. (Oxford: Basil Blackwell, 1990).

So, I spent some time trying to think through a concept that I learned from a number of scholars of Southeast Asia, and a Malay word, *desakota*, which means 'neither urban nor rural'. And this got me excited because I thought: so many people who are long-distance migrants, whether voluntary or not, who are constantly on the move, live these multiple places at once. So sometimes serially, but also in a trajectory that seems to have no return, and sometimes in long-term circular, waving migrations, those migrations matter, and so does people's consciousness of the possibility of the kinds of places they live – which involves crossing borders, quietly or openly. And I thought, well, how can we think those kinds of spaces to enliven our ability to imagine fighting racial capitalism in a way that doesn't enclose them in a single system of juridical logics, racial formations and so forth?

I said something about anarchist withdrawal communities – I mean, I'm all for anybody who can figure out a way to live the way they want to live. I'm all for that, so don't get me wrong. But that's not going to save us. Not enough people of the 7 billion of us on this planet can step aside and say, 'Okay, we're going to grow our own squash and everything's going to be cool.' Not enough people can do it, not enough people should have to do it, and yet we still have to change things.

So thinking desakota, and thinking about changing places, got me interested in trying to develop an idea that arose in the 1990s in the radical anti-prison community, which was the idea of abolition, or unfinished abolition. For some people, unfinished abolition means simply ending slavery, or whatever its afterlives are. And to me, abolition is not the absence of something; it's the presence of something. That's what abolition actually is, and I arrived at this through a number of different challenges and experiences.

So the obvious one is that in the nineties, when we got up and revived the notion of prison abolition, people would say, 'If you're going to abolish prisons, what are you going to do instead?' So for them, everything else was to remain the same, except the building with the bars. We had to explain we don't mean just the building with the bars; we mean all of the kinds of relationships that lead to our enabled problems, which then people come to understand as solvable only by buildings with bars. So they go: 'Okay, okay. What about the rapists and the child molesters and the murderers?' Then we have to answer those questions. Those questions don't come up the way they used to. At every public presentation I did in the nineties, that was the first set of questions, and those questions have gone down, which is really exciting, and means that people's consciousness is shifting about what it is we're talking about, anyway. Which is to say, they're hearing something different from, 'Open the gate, let everybody go!'

BB/RZ *Has prison abolition been a specific form of an anti-capitalist revolutionary politics?*

RWG Yeah. Prison abolition is a specific form of anti-capitalism, which is to say, prison abolition is a specific form of anti–*all* capitalism, all of which is racial capitalism, so it's specific to that. That is to say that the presence that's necessary to – forget imagine – *live* in a world without prisons has to be a presence in which all kinds of relations, all kinds of exclusions and all kinds of opportunities, have to change. Everything has to change.

For example, in *Black Reconstruction in America*,[8] Du Bois talks about the kinds of things that people did during radical reconstruction in the US South. They started public schools, they did all kinds of things. That was abolition. The abolition wasn't the end of slavery; the abolition was what they did. And what they did, they did because they already had ideas of things to do, consciousness and also practices that might be invisible to we who don't have any deep sense of the social life of slaves – and I said 'slaves', not 'enslaved people'. Slaves. But that doesn't mean all of this work and thinking and practice and so forth wasn't there. And it came to the surface and configured and became extremely lively for the time that it lasted.

A fantastic writer and scholar called Thulani Davis, a librettist who was a journalist for many years, did an amazing PhD at New York University quite recently. She traces the movements of blueswomen in the South, and she was trying to figure out why they performed where they performed. And what she learned in her research was that the patterns or the pathways that blueswomen took throughout the South kind of overlaid where the most robust communities during radical reconstruction grew up. So even though those central places, as central places, were no longer there, there was enough remnant that a generation or two later, the kind of place where blueswomen who were singing a critique – which is to say, singing the blues epistemology, as Clyde would put it – would show up to perform. And people in the audience might or might not be aware of what the history of their locality was. And actually, that didn't matter; what matters is that the work had been done, and that work like that can be done and is done.

I'll give another example, and this is an example of things that are gone but probably not forgotten. In 1990, I was in Palestine and it was a time of great hope – it wasn't even, but it was really intense, and people were doing projects everywhere I went. They were projects that were about the day after. The projects were the projects that I am often talking to people about in terms of having a plan to win, meaning: What do you do the day after you win? What will already be here? And the day after that, and the day after that? So we went around and we toured. People were doing these amazing things and also had a critique, the persistent critique of 'Okay, we've managed to do this, but

8 W.E.B. Du Bois, *Black Reconstruction in America: An Essay Toward a History of the Part Which Black Folk Played in the Attempt to Reconstruct Democracy in America, 1860–1880* (1935, repr., New York: Free Press, 1998).

these problems still exist, so we're continually doing everything, and if the occupation ended tomorrow we wouldn't be done.' The revolution doesn't end when the occupation ends; the revolution actually begins its next phase. So those are two examples of, probably, many.

BB/RZ *We would like to jump to a question about the concepts of the anti-state state and organised abandonment.*

RWG I'll start with 'anti-state state'. So, when I set out to ask, and answer, the question of how California embarked on what one state contractor-researcher called the biggest prison building project in the history of the world, I was, of course, thinking very hard about the kinds of protections from calamity and opportunities for advancement that were fast crumbling in California in the context of, or hand in hand with, prison expansion.

The fight over free postsecondary education for all California residents, whether you went to a public school or a private school, was about to hit the skids. The expansion of certain kinds of health and welfare benefits were starting to tighten; welfare for people with dependent children, most of whom were women, most of whom were mothers, became workfare. All in the early 1980s, all of these things were happening.

The retraction of the weak but real welfare state in California – of course, that, plus the polemics, as it were, the rhetoric about how that state was really a culture of dependency, that we couldn't afford it – made it seem like the state itself was just going to crumble and somebody would bring out the broom, and then it would be in the dustbin of history.

Then one day, when I was at Rutgers, I was sitting in a class with a fantastic political scientist called Susan Fainstein and she just said offhand, 'States don't go away.' This goes back to the question of historical materialism. They don't just go away, they don't just disappear. She's right. What's happening here? And so that sent me down the path of thinking about and studying and trying to elaborate a different concept related to 'anti-state state', which was this concept of surplus state capacity, which I studied to shreds, thanks especially to the work of a rural sociologist called Greg Hooks, whose work *Forging the Military Industrial Complex* (1991) showed me how to think about how certain kinds of fiscal and bureaucratic capacities developed for one thing can become something else.

So, thinking with hooks's work and thinking with Susan's rather offhand comment, I realised that the people who had seized, or who had persisted as appointed or career employees in, state power at the California level weren't ever going to undo the state; they were just going to change it. And that the rhetoric that the government is what's bad, and the government is what's on our backs, is the one that got them elected, would get them re-elected. But when I counted the money, I saw the state is getting bigger and bigger.

I decided to start calling this formation the anti-state state. So these are people who achieve or retain political power by condemning all aspects of the state while building it. And the foundation of the anti-state state in my view, at least in the US context, is prisons. And I think actually, now, it's prisons and police, and probably always was, but they're second seat. I thought it might be useful for people to have this concept, anti-state state, so that they can think about, to the degree they're interested in thinking about it, that the state isn't this one unchanging, inflexible, unified thing. That it's complex, it's contradictory; that there's struggle between institutions of the state, and sometimes they absorb each other's missions, sometimes they imitate each other's missions. All of this I've written about in the chapter I cowrote with Craig Gilmore in *Policing The Planet.*[9]

So this form is a form that we should understand rather than thinking there's just, in general, this objectionable thing, a cudgel in the corner coming to get us, called the state. I am not an anarchist. I haven't yet come to the conclusion that something we call the state has got to be more against us than for us. I might get there, but I'm not there. I'm not there by a long shot.

Why? Because I think having clean water that will come every day is a good thing, and the kind of institution that can deliver that would be an institution that I would call a state institution. I think free public education, universal healthcare, all of that, is too – how would that happen? It's not volunteerism. So what do we call it? It would be the state that's *not* the anti-state state. But I don't know exactly what it is.

So that concept actually ties with the other concept you asked about, which is organised abandonment.

When I was working on the piece I just mentioned, 'Beyond Bratton', I wanted to make this whole long argument about organised abandonment so people could understand that it's not *only* the state, it *is* the state; it's not *only* capital, it *is* capital. And it's not only the large scale, like the factory; it's all these different scales. I wanted people to be able to think about it in this multi-scalar way.

BB/RZ *What is the temporality around this idea of organised abandonment? Is there a relationship between the idea of organised abandonment and crisis?*

RWG When I talk about organised abandonment, I'm talking about the various forces, institutional forces, that are able to withdraw, and do. The ones that just dump you, whatever. And that have all kinds of dimensions that we could talk about for hours and hours.

---

9 Ruth Wilson Gilmore and Craig Gilmore, 'Beyond Bratton', in *Policing the Planet: Why the Policing Crisis Led to Black Lives Matter*, ed. Jordan T. Camp and Christina Heatherton (London and New York: Verso, 2016), 173–201.

Capitalist crisis generally is a crisis in profit, and that crisis in profit has a bunch of different features; so in some cases it might not, to the untrained eye, look like a crisis at all. How many industries throughout the overdeveloped world hit 'normal' profit level and were coasting along after having enjoyed 'normal-plus' profits for whatever reason, let's say the long rebuild after World War II being a big reason that normal-plus profits then dropped to normal. So normal could go on, but not in a form in which capitalism remains capitalism, because the imperative is 'Grow or die.' And crisis then throws everybody and everything into motion, and then the question is what happens as a result of that motion. So the motion is withdrawal of capital; the motion is the stepping back of the state or the stepping in of the state in the form of criminalisation; the motion is families being dispersed for the focus of finding wages; the motion is housing becoming Airbnb. There are just so many things that crisis can provoke.

And then, going back to what we were talking about earlier, the way that I have tried to become a thinker attuned to detail while having a huge ambition for revolutionary change means that in every problem that I look at, or I think we should look at, we all have to be able to see the details and then think about how those connect or articulate with other things, and then figure out how to organise. And I think there's always a possibility for organising.

BB/RZ *How do you think through the work of theorising and finding spaces for organising? How do we actually build a community of scholars who are interested in engaging with the real world and want to change it? The neoliberalisation of academia goes completely in the other direction, emphasising individual career advancement over collective activity.*

RWG This is a great question. For a very long time, I called myself, and people called me and all of us, scholar-activists. We all tried to inhabit that hyphen in any way we could. And actually, I'm tired of that phrase, for one because it's like everything else, like 'racial capitalism', 'blues epistemology', 'social reproduction'. All of these key terms that can have so much depth and meaning stop, and they become a label or a flag that people display to show that they're on the right team. So even though the words I'm about to propose are not impervious to that kind of obliteration: "militant scholars" captures what I mean well. There are militant scholars everywhere. And they're ready to do things, and all we have to do is figure them out and do them.

I already do some work in contexts which are not without their own weirdnesses and contradictions; for example, I teach in Barcelona in the Dialogo Decolonial programme. I am fine with what I do there. I always meet really exciting people from around the world who are doing stuff, and then there are all these poseurs, and you can't escape the poseurs, so it's just a matter of focusing on the people who are there to learn and share and so forth. There are always organisers; there are always some high school teachers. It's very cool, again, even though there are the holier-than-thou, 'I'm more decolonial than you', 'I'm more Indigenous than you' – and the North Americans are always the biggest problem.

The Liberation Schools were established throughout Guinea-Bissau during the thirteen-year war. They would liberate an area, and build a school that had already been designed. Teachers were also soldiers, so they stayed behind; they'd learn to be teachers, and they had books that had been written in Paris and printed in Sweden. It's an amazing thing, to do the work of consciousness as well as literacy.

Anyway, I gave this whole talk about Guinea-Bissau, and in the Q and A somebody said: 'See, this school is really rotten because you think race is only about being Black. Indigenous people in North America are struggling for land, and you haven't said anything about it.' And I said, 'I just talked about an Indigenous struggle for land. You're the one who thinks race is Black, not me. Do you realise there are Indigenous people with woolly hair, as well as with straight hair?' I mean, *really*? It was deep, man, it was really, really deep.

BB/RZ *Going back to your experience at the Barcelona decolonial theory programme, we want to pick up on the comment made about the sensitivity that people have that stops them from listening, and often it's around identity or an identity formed through an injury. That when it comes to organising and political solidarity, to be in solidarity with other people across difference, to actually find spaces for joy and support and conviviality, are really important.*

There is some relationship here between the anger and rage and hurt experienced because of racism, sexism, transphobia, economic oppression and so on, and the expression of these emotions in the online virtual world. The implications of political and personal rage being contained within online media are proving to be problematic and possibly quite toxic.

RWG I don't know if my response will be very satisfactory about the online and virtual world. But it seems to me that people have capitulated to a level of defeat that I've not experienced before in my life. But the way people explain it to themselves is not that we have capitulated to defeat, but rather that everything is bad. That this is the description, and then they insist on being able to specify the badness for themselves in terms of a group category that's as small as possible, as specific as possible, that then allows a certain authenticity of expression about the particularities of the badness. But I really think this is all defeatism.

I see that a whole lot of work seems to be dedicated to reproducing the terms of every inner injury, rather than saying, as your book does:[10] 'Here's

10 Brenna Bhandar, *Colonial Lives of Property: Law, Land and Racial Regimes of Ownership*

how the injury happened, but look – there's nothing inevitable, there's nothing undoable, as hard as undoing it would be.' You can see how it works, and if that isn't the purpose of theory, I don't know what is. To explain how things work. To be a guide for action.

But, back to the categories of injury in this great defeat, this great vanquishment. People are expressing, 'I am defeated, too.' 'I am defeated as a Black woman who is middle aged.' 'I am defeated as a young trans man of colour.' It's all of this defeat, and to me that fracturing into these particular categories is not just like, 'Oh well, that's where identity politics is going anyway'; rather, it's a particular expression of a particularly flat identity politics that, to me, is shaped by the devolutionary forces that have pushed the anti-state state to relinquish, over and over again, any kind of large centralisation. Again, to relinquish capacities to provide protections from calamity, or opportunities for advancement, and instead delegate to more local jurisdictions – let's say councils – that responsibility. And the responsibility then becomes one that can be enacted by deepening inequality, rather than remedying it. So, the locality, the intimacy, produces exactly the opposite of what the rhetoric says.

I think all of that is true, but the devolutionary force – and in a certain way, that political culture that imagines itself to be oppositional, that is adopting or imitating the form of the anti-state state – is the problem. So there is defeatism, on the one hand, but also, the fragmentation is a kind of imitation or an adoption or a shaping (I don't even know a good word for it) of the anti-state state. And the way that people talk not about solidarity but about allyship – that's just so military. And I say to people, so at the end of our allyship, are you going to go back to white people land, and you're going back to trans people land, I'm going to go back to middle-aged Black woman land (actually, I'm elderly now)? Is that what it is?

That brings me back to militant scholarship, and I went down this whole path of talking about the PAIGC and the Liberation Schools. Some of my comrades in Lisbon live or grew up in Cova da Moura, which is mostly a community of immigrants and their children and grandchildren, but the original immigrants who established this community were actually long-distance migrants from rural Portugal. Under the fascist state, they were not allowed to move to the city, so they lived off the radar, up on this hill, and built their own houses, and then various waves of long-distance migrants came through and settled there.

So now it's mostly, but not exclusively, a community of people, or the descendants of people, from Cabo Verde, Angola, and some from Mozambique and São Tomé and Principe. But there are still the children or grandchildren or great grandchildren of rural Portuguese who, if they had to check a box, would probably check 'light', up there as well, on that hill. And in the context

(Durham: Duke University Press, 2018).

of struggle up there, on the part of the community, to keep the municipality (which is not Lisbon but Amadora) from condemning all their houses because they were not built to code, the people organised, the community organised, and they had a very lively organising over time.

People learned a lot, to figure out how they could forestall the destruction. Then meanwhile, a group of young people, in the context of an already-existing youth programme, said: 'Well, what about us here? How did this happen? How come we're here?' So they developed study groups, because in this country language instruction starts very young, formal language instruction in the public schools. Even people who don't finish school – and all these people did, and they're doing Master's and doctorates – but people who don't finish school have two or three languages, plus whatever they learned at home. So English is actually really strong here. It wasn't a generation ago; no one spoke English.

They started study groups and would read stuff in English, for example, bell hooks, and translate a chapter and share it around the community, and read somebody else and translate it, share around the community, and have these debates. It's a really lively and long-standing political intellectual community, many of whom embrace communism, not as members of the Communist Party of Portugal, but communism as a way to shape or theorise how the world should be. They do pop-up universities that are just occasional; they'll last for three or four days. People come, debate, and there are various, as it were, political tendencies within the formation. And the age range has spread over time, so there are people who are interested in a certain kind of Marxist political economy, which they didn't learn from me, but they get excited when I talk with them. Then there are people who have come out of Steve Biko's Black Consciousness, and they have these debates about ontology, materiality. These are young people, and they come back for more. This is where to be.

So these are some of the possibilities. And then the MST (Landless Workers' Movement) in Brazil has this big multi-league summer school, which I've been invited to teach in, but it just hasn't been the right time for me to go. And we did a conference at the CUNY Graduate Center on consciousness and revolution, with a focus on education for liberation, and people came from #FeesMustFall, and from the MST and elsewhere so we could talk about these different ways to do this.

Selected Writings

Gilmore, Ruth Wilson. 'You Have Dislodged a Boulder: Mothers and Prisoners in the Post-Keynesian California Landscape'. *Transforming Anthropology* 8:1–2 (1999), 12–38.

———. 'Globalisation and US Prison Growth: From Military Keynesianism to Post-Keynesian militarism'. *Race & Class* 40:2–3 (1999), 171–88.

———. 'Fatal Couplings of Power and Difference: Notes on Racism and Geography'. *Professional Geographer* 54:1 (2002), 15–24.

———. *Golden Gulag: Prisons, Surplus, Crisis, and Opposition in Globalizing California*. Berkeley: University of California Press, 2007.

———. 'Forgotten Places and the Seeds of Grassroots Planning'. *Engaging Contradictions: Theory, Politics and Methods of Activist Scholarship*, edited by Charles R. Hale.

———. 'Race, Prisons and War: Scenes from the History of US Violence'. *Socialist Register* 45 (2009), 73–87.

Gilmore, Ruth Wilson, and Craig Gilmore, 'Beyond Bratton'. In *Policing the Planet: Why the Policing Crisis Led to Black Lives Matter*, edited by Jordan T. Camp and Christina Heatherton, 173–201. London and New York: Verso, 2016.

———. 'Abolition Geographies and the Problem of Innocence'. In *Futures of Black Radicalism*, edited by Gaye Theresa Johnson and Alex Lubin, 225–41. London and New York: Verso, 2017.

Avery F. Gordon

Avery F. Gordon is a professor of sociology at the University of California, Santa Barbara, and a visiting professor at Birkbeck School of Law, University of London. Her work focuses on radical thought and practice, and she writes about captivity, enslavement, war and other forms of dispossession and how to eliminate them.

She serves on the editorial committee of the journal *Race & Class* and is the cohost of *No Alibis*, a weekly public affairs radio programme on KCSB-FM Santa Barbara. She is the author of *The Hawthorn Archive: Letters from the Utopian Margins* (2017), *The Workhouse: The Breitenau Room* (with Ines Schaber, 2014), *Ghostly Matters: Haunting and the Sociological Imagination* (2008) and *Keeping Good Time: Reflections on Knowledge, Power and People* (2004). In addition to routinely collaborating with artists, she is the former keeper of the Hawthorn Archive.

BB/RZ *Can you speak to us about both the context of your early political formation, as well as any particular intellectual influences that informed your theoretical and activist practice?*

AFG Owing to the difficult and unhappy situation in my early home life, I ran away from the house, and also into books, which provided alternative and better worlds, and the idea of being a writer. I was already an experienced runaway (and truant) by the age of thirteen, and by fourteen, with all the annoying precociousness you could imagine, I had decided that I would be an existential philosopher, write poetry and short stories, and 'change the world', all of which at the time seemed reasonable occupations for an angry, smart and desperately miserable young woman, and were encouraged by well-meaning teachers and public librarians ('Read Camus's *The Stranger*,' I was advised on several occasions!). Thankfully, the United Farm Workers (UFW) launched a national grape boycott starting in 1967 and by 1970 they were organising high school students in Florida, where I lived. It was from them that I received my first real education in political campaigns and grassroots organising. We sat outside the local supermarkets trying to persuade our mothers and the other women shoppers not to buy nonunion grapes and iceberg lettuce. There was also a surge of activity in 1972 when the UFW were heavily lobbying the Democratic Party at the 1972 convention in Miami.

I grew up in a Florida that was very much a Southern Confederate state. My maternal family is from rural Georgia, a small town not too far from

Macon, many of whom eventually moved to Savannah, and my mother was raised in coastal South Carolina. I spent a good deal of time in Georgia and South Carolina as a child and grew up in an intensely and openly racist family and social environment, in the context of powerful anti-racist agitation and national mobilisation. My early political formation was thus heavily influenced both by the civil rights and Black Power movements, as these took shape in Florida, and my experience with the UFW union organisers, to whom I remain grateful today for having profoundly raised my consciousness and for having taught me to always ask who gathered, grew and built, and under what conditions, all the things we need and use.

My primary intellectual influences were whatever novels I could get my hands on in the secondhand shop, and American history, in school, until I went to university, where I began to study political theory and Marxism. For complicated reasons having to do with how someone not destined for university gets a place in a very good private one (in my case, with the help of the Jesuits, who, in light of my Spanish proficiency, answered the question of my life's ambition with 'Live in another country!') I ended up in Georgetown University's School of Foreign Service. I was ill-suited for the school, which prepared elites for diplomatic service, but, in addition to four years of economics taught according to the rote method and surviving the required course on 'the problem of God,' I was able to rigorously study Marxist theory, the Russian Revolution, and the history of communism. More importantly, I encountered the distinguished Palestinian historian and philosopher Hisham Sharabi, who made survival at Georgetown possible, and who had a profound influence on me. For me, he brought alive not the world of the diplomatic corps, but a vibrant non-aligned world of radical anti-capitalist anti-colonialism, in which intellectual life and culture more generally were central, not peripheral. This was a cultural lesson confirmed later by Raymond Williams, E.P. Thompson, and Stuart Hall, whose writings I first encountered during this same period, when I studied history at Warwick (1977–78), and who were also important influences on me. Remember, too, that this was a remarkable moment to be in England: widespread mobilisation against the National Front, the emergence of Rock against Racism, the lead up to the so-called Winter of Discontent and the rise of Thatcher. That first time in England was formative not just for the experience of selling newspapers for the Socialist Workers Party at the Coventry car factory gates at dawn, but because there was a left public culture then; and though it was highly sectarian, it was also a revelation to me.

I was helped along in life by a few people who took an interest in me, and who not only assisted with practical matters but also reoriented my way of thinking. Professor Sharabi was one of them; Phyllis Palmer was another, and it was she who both got me a better job than being a secretary, when I finished university, and introduced me to an anti-racist Marxist feminism I'd never encountered before. These were the main intellectual foundations I took with me to graduate school in 1980, where I continued to pursue them, as well as revise and redirect them with further study and in conversation with others. South Africa, Palestine, Central and South America, Northern Ireland, the United States – these were the points on the then-current geopolitical scene that organised my thinking and political engagements.

BB/RZ *Your 2008* Ghostly Matters: Haunting and the Sociological Imagination *is an incredibly rich and textured book. Can you unpack some of the concepts you use there, especially around the framing of 'societal ghosts', which frame our ways of thinking and acting?*

AFG The ambitious problem that preoccupied me in *Ghostly Matters* – and still does to a large extent – was how to understand and write evocatively about some of the ways that modern forms of dispossession, exploitation and repression concretely impact the lives of the people most affected by them and impact our shared conditions of living. To me, this meant trying to understand the terms of racial capitalism and the determining role of monopolistic and militaristic state violence. The two main case studies in the book are about transatlantic slavery from the vantage point of Reconstruction in the United States, and political repression and state terror in the Southern Cone of Latin America in the 1970s.

Haunting was the language and the experiential modality by which I tried to reach an understanding of the meeting of organised force and meaning, because haunting is one way in which abusive systems of power make themselves known and their impacts felt in everyday life, especially when they are supposedly over and done with (such as with transatlantic slavery) or when their oppressive nature is continuously denied (such as with free labour or national security). Haunting is not the same as being exploited, traumatised or oppressed, although it usually involves these experiences or is produced by them. What's distinctive about haunting, as I used the term (and this is not its only way, of course), is that it is an animated state in which a repressed or unresolved social violence is making itself known, sometimes very directly, sometimes more obliquely. I used the term 'haunting' to describe those singular and yet repetitive instances when home becomes unfamiliar, when your bearings on the world lose direction, when the over-and-done-with comes alive, when what's been in your blind field comes into view.

Haunting raises spectres, and it alters the experience of being in linear time, alters the way we normally separate and sequence the past, the present and the future. These spectres, or ghosts, appear when the trouble they represent and symptomise is no longer being contained, repressed or blocked from view. As I understand it, the ghost is not the invisible or the unknown or the constitutively unknowable, in the Derridean sense. To my mind, the whole essence, if you can use that word, of a ghost is that it has a real presence and demands its due, demands your attention. Haunting and the appearance of spectres or ghosts is one way, I tried to suggest, we're notified that what's been suppressed or concealed is very much alive and present, messing or interfering precisely with those always-incomplete forms of containment and repression ceaselessly directed towards us.

Haunting always registers the harm inflicted, or the loss sustained, by a social violence done in the past or being done in the present, and it is for this reason quite frightening. But haunting, unlike trauma, by contrast, is distinctive for producing a something-to-be-done. Indeed, it seemed to me that haunting was precisely the domain of turmoil and trouble, that moment of however-long duration when things are not in their assigned places, when the cracks and the rigging are exposed, when the people who are meant to be invisible show up without any sign of leaving, when disturbed feelings won't go away, when living easily one day and then the next becomes impossible, when the present seamlessly becoming 'the future' gets entirely jammed up. Haunting refers to this sociopolitical-psychological state when something else, or something different from before, feels like it must be done, and prompts a something-to-be-done.

It is in large measure on behalf and in the interests of the something-to-be-done, which may be political in the formal sense, but it is not only there that the concept's main value lies. To see the something-to-be-done as characteristic of haunting was, in a way, to limit its scope. For many people, haunting means exactly the opposite – aberrant mourning, traumatic paralysis or dissociative repetition. For better or worse, the emphasis on the something-to-be-done was a way of focusing on the cultural requirements or dimensions of individual, social or political movement and change. And one of those requirements was that the ghost him or herself be treated respectfully – its desires broached, and not ghosted or abandoned or disappeared again in the act of dealing with the haunting. Even if the ghost cannot be permitted to take everything over, a complicated requirement that's especially pertinent with living people who haunt as if they were dead. Again, for me, haunting is not about invisibility or unknowability, per se; it refers us to what's living and breathing in the place hidden from view: people, places, histories, knowledge, memories, ways of life, ideas. We'll come back to this question of the blind spot in a moment.

This particular approach to or definition of haunting – again, limited in many important ways – had, then, at its core a contest over the future, over what is to come next or later. That's to say, to the extent that a something-to-be-done is characteristic of haunting, one can say that futurity is imbricated or interwoven into the very scene of haunting itself. As I was using it, haunting is an emergent state: the ghost arises, carrying the signs and portents of a repression in the past or the present that's no longer working. The ghost demands your attention. The present wavers. Something will happen. What will happen, of course, is not given in advance, but something must be done. I think this emergent state is also the critical analytic moment. That's to say, when the repression isn't working anymore, the trouble that results creates conditions that demand renarrativisation. What's happening? How did it come to pass? What does it mean? These conditions also invite action. What do I do? Can you help? Will it get better? The something-to-be-done is something you have to try/do for yourself: while it can be shared, it can't be imposed or even given as a gift.

It was a sign of the state of the social sciences, jurisprudence and legal scholarship, and a good deal of radical thought and political activism, that it was necessary to even mention the idea of complex personhood. The basic starting point of the book was stated by Patricia Williams: 'It is a fact of great analytic importance that life is complicated.'[1] Treating that fact as analytically important – making it matter to one's knowledge practice – turns out to be harder than it seems for academic scholars. What I was trying to get at with that term was the importance of treating people with a respect that acknowledges their contradictory humanity and subjectivity. Neither victims nor superhuman agents, all people – albeit in specific forms whose specificity is sometimes everything – remember and forget, are beset by contradiction, and recognise and misrecognise themselves and others. I was looking for a language that could treat race, class and gender dynamics and consciousness as more dense and delicate than the categorical terms often imply, while also not losing sight of their brutalities. I was also trying to set out some conditions of recognition for long-lasting and effective solidiarities.

BB/RZ *Your 2004 book* Keeping Good Time *explores what it truly means to be a scholar and political activist during times of war, and a number of chapters deal specifically with activism around the prison industrial complex. Can you please explain how you see this relationship between scholarship, activism and theoretical production?*

AFG That book was put together in a moment of transition for me, or, its compilation gave permission for making a transition I was beginning: away from a work life centred in the university and its communities, towards a work life oriented to a para-academic or intellectual community in a certain segment of the art world. This transition also moved my work and me away from the United States and towards Europe.

In many ways, that very modest book was about insisting that we were at war – first with Iraq, then Afghanistan and then 'terrorism', when the global War on Terror was announced – and that educators and academics needed to have a consciousness of what that meant. That providing education during

1 Patricia J. Williams, *The Alchemy of Race and Rights* (Cambridge, MA: Harvard University Press, 1991).

wartime was a major part of our job, and that we ought to know clearly what kind of education is required in these circumstances. I was still committed to engaging and addressing sociology in the earlier pieces, and I tried to rouse my colleagues with warnings against being or becoming what C. Wright Mills called 'scared employees' in the context of the criminalisation of dissent, and of a growing law and order society where national security ties militarism abroad to policing and imprisonment at home. As you both know, I eventually gave up on that appeal. It's worth reading that 1944 Mills essay on 'the social role of the intellectual' again today – an essay he wrote during World War II while trying to avoid the draft.[2] There were very few political, rather than religious, conscientious objectors during that war (I actually wrote my history paper at Warwick on these men in England, Scotland and Wales), and Mills's reason was prescient: he believed that the war buildup would become permanent. He basically argued that the social role of the intellectual was to refuse what he called 'the job' the institution offered, and the position of the 'scared employee,' who in being ruled by a 'general fear . . . sometimes politely known as "discretion", "good taste", or "balanced judgement", remained mired in "the job"'. Political ineffectiveness was, Mills argued, symptomatic of the scared employee.

I think there are different ways to conceive the relationship between scholarship and activism, and, especially as the space for critical thought and practice shrinks everywhere, we need to nurture as many modes as possible. I've long found Chuck Morse's distinction between the radical critic and the politically engaged radical critic helpful as a guide to answering this question. He writes:

> It is the task of the radical critic to illuminate what is repressed and excluded by the basic mechanisms of a given social order. It is the task of the *politically engaged* radical critic to *side* with the excluded and the repressed: to develop insights gained in confrontation with injustice, to nourish cultures of resistance, and to help define the means with which society can be rendered adequate to the full breadth of human possibilities.[3]

The politically engaged radical critic makes a commitment to a cooperative practice with others, and to an everyday life practice which instantiates the values attached to the cooperative commitment to take such a side or a standpoint. The politically engaged radical critic has also to do all the hard 'scholarly' work that the radical critic does, too.

One area where the question you're asking becomes articulated and also enlivened – especially where I work, where we are legally prohibited from

2 C. Wright Mills, 'The Social Role of the Intellectual', in *Power, Politics and People*, ed. Irving Louis Horowitz (1944; repr., Oxford: Oxford University Press, 1963), 292–304.

3 Chuck Morse, 'Capitalism, Marxism, and the Black Radical Tradition: An Interview with Cedric Robinson', *Perspectives on Anarchist Theory* 3:1 (Spring 1999), 1.

unionising – is in the classroom, in which, for me there is still autonomy and freedom over course content. It's possible to create small, or sometimes big (I teach over 600 students in introduction to sociology), laboratories in which a lot of important unlearning and political education and guidance can take place. So too with postgraduate supervision, in which one by one, a conscientious teacher helps to train the next generation of radical scholars, hopefully helping to root out the fear that produces the scared employee and encouraging political engagement along the definitional lines Morse offers.

The university has always provided a limited and troubled space, both for critical praxis and radical scholarship – a terrain of work and struggle over the production of knowledge and the production of students. What strikes me about the situation today is that a lot of teachers and students in the elite sector of the academy want to take what they can from it – money, credentials, status, relatively autonomous labour, compared to most other professional work – in the uneven and unequal system in which they are distributed, and in which student debt and the precarity of faculty increase. But they do not want to fight to change it, to own it on different terms, to take stewardship over its future for others. That desire is not, however, acknowledged and accepted as the prize of privilege or the common sense of the exploited. Rather, it has been theorised as the height of radical thought and enabled by the dominance of social media, the cult of celebrity, the general social disrespect for intellectuals and for universities, and the elimination of slow-time anti-utilitarian research and thought. In the United States, this radical thought is completely removed from the work experiences and political organising of teachers and students working in non-elite schools, where, for example, faculty teach eight to ten courses a year (in my department we teach four), at schools with majority nonwhite working-class students. There are good reasons to poach from the university if you can, to steal what you can from it for other ends. The political questions are: Who can and who can't? What is being done with what you take and with whom? Who else is poaching, to what end, and with what consequences? What happens when there's nothing left to steal? We are facing really large complex questions about the conditions under and organisational forms in which scholarly research, writing and training are and will be defined and undertaken. These questions are not gripping, as urgent, radical scholars, and I fear for the consequences.

***BB/RZ** In your latest book,* The Hawthorn Archive: Letters from the Utopian Margins, *you write that you 'fuse critical theory with creative writing in a historical context: fact, fiction, theory, and image speak to each other in an undisciplined environment'.*[4]

4 Avery F. Gordon, *The Hawthorn Archive: Letters from the Utopian Margins* (New York: Fordham University Press, 2017), v.

How would you describe what you do, your method, in this book? What do you find compelling or theoretically useful about centring what you are calling the 'other utopianism'?

AFG Let me take the second part of the question first, as the method follows to some extent from the challenge of writing about the 'other utopianism'. The impetus for the book, which I began thinking about a long time ago, was twofold. First, was a desire to pick up where *Ghostly Matters* ended, with 'those historical alternatives' that 'haunt a given society', as Herbert Marcuse wrote;[5] to find the place where, as Patricia Williams put it, our 'longings' are 'exiled.' In this book, I call that place, after Ernst Bloch, the utopian margins.[6]

The other impetus was to challenge the twined triumphalism of the Right's 'end of history' claim and the Left's claim that the political universe had closed shut after the failures of 1968. Both positions seemed completely out of touch with the remarkable wave of anti-capitalist resistance by diverse peoples across the globe, which remained invisible to many until first the Zapatistas (in 1994), and then more widely the Seattle World Trade Organization protests (1999), woke them up. The Right's 'end of history' claim was also a 'utopian' one which went by the name 'globalisation' – the brave new Fourth Industrial Revolution, with its global assembly line, free trade and boundless privatisation – while dismissing any alternative notions of wordliness as TINA (There is no alternative), as Margaret Thatcher famously put it. The Left kept to its Marxist-inspired tradition of treating much of this opposition with the rejectionist epithet: 'That's not realistic, that's utopian!' Marcuse called it 'the merely utopian', a phrase which is often used as a bludgeon to manage proposals, people and actions that have gone too far out of bounds. Both prompts suggested the need for a more capacious language suitable for what seemed to me a significant historical moment of political and economic retrenchment and resistance to it.

There were good reasons to distrust and even dismiss the term 'utopian', although in my opinion, the main problem was not idealism and futurism, but rather the term's deeply racialised historiography and narrow set of literary, aesthetic, philosophical, historical and sociological references. To put it bluntly, the extant meaning of the term treated the genocidal settler colonialism that founded the so-called New World as a successful utopian enterprise, while absenting entirely what Peter Linebaugh and Marcus Rediker call the 'many-headed hydra' of the seventeenth-century 'revolutionary Atlantic' – those

5 Herbert Marcuse, *One Dimensional Man* (Boston: Beacon Press, 1964).

6 Patricia J. Williams, *The Alchemy of Race and Rights* (Cambridge, MA: Harvard University Press, 1991), 49; Ernst Bloch, *A Philosophy of the Future*, trans. John Cumming (New York: Herder & Herder, 1970); and *The Principle of Hope*, 3 vols., trans. Stephen Plaice, Paul Knight and Neville Plaice, 2nd ed. (Frankfurt: Suhrkamp, 1954 [vol. 1], 1955 [vol. 2], and 1959 [vol. 3]; Cambridge, MA: MIT Press, 1995). Citations refer to the MIT Press edition.

slaves, maids, prisoners, pirates, sailors, heretics, Indigenous peoples, commoners and others who challenged the making of the modern world capitalist system.[7]

There was another kind of utopianism entailed by slaves running away, marronage, piracy, heresy, vagabondage, soldier desertion, and other illegible or discredited forms of escape, resistance, opposition and alternative ways of life that continued, of course, to challenge the modern racial capitalist system over time. This 'other' utopianism lends to the term 'utopian' a very different meaning – one rooted much more in the past and the present than in an unrealistic future – and a very different notion of politics – one rooted in ongoing social struggles, in various forms of nonparticipation, and in an autonomous politics hostile or indifferent to seizing state power.

Let's come back to the significance of the past movements in your question, where you ask about historical memory and the temporality of the utopian margins. In the present, while it is always easier to see one's historical moment after the fact than in the midst of it, I think we are still in that cycle of worldwide resistance and opposition that emerged in the 1990s. The triumphalism is gone, of course, and the Left, if it's possible to even speak of such a thing, which I now doubt, is less dismissive of utopian 'hopes', even as the term 'hope' is another somewhat patronising reduction. Capitalism now lurches from crisis to crisis more frequently, and it is incapable of resolving them without ever increasing financial and military assistance from the state, even as its anti-state ideology sounds louder and louder. In this context of enhanced militarism and securitisation, the ongoing redistribution of resources from social property to private property has led to more widespread social abandonment and more entrenched inequalities within and between countries. The major capitalist powers in the West seem either not to understand or to be in denial about the decline of Western hegemony and the quiet but definitive eastward shift of the world system. The capitalist democratic state – what Ruth Wilson Gilmore calls the 'anti-state state', or most people know by the name of the neoliberal state – is also weakened, internally conflicted to the point of incapacity, nowhere more evident than in the UK's Brexit debacle.[8] The legitimation crisis that besets the viability of a capitalist democratic state is real, and the authoritarian alternative quite further advanced than the notion of a populist surge implies.

At the same time, there is widespread, daily, active and open political opposition to all this, at the scale at which people can contest it: protecting this

7 Peter Linebaugh and Marcus Rediker, *The Many-Headed Hydra: Sailors, Slaves, Commoners and the Hidden History of the Revolutionary Atlantic* (Boston: Beacon Press, 2013).

8 Ruth Wilson Gilmore, 'Forgotten Places and the Seeds of Grassroots Planning', in *Engaging Contradictions: Theory, Politics and Methods of Activist Scholarship*, ed. Charles R. Hale (Berkeley: University of California Press, 2008), 31, 36.

group of migrants from arrest, confinement and deportation; organising this strike among teachers in this city; defending this territory from oil drilling; filing lawsuits against a police department and so on; gathering in public to swear, shout, shake fists, confront the inevitably helmeted riot police. There is also widespread, daily, active, infrapolitical and even secret political opposition, which needs and wants to remain hidden. And there are also so many people, more and more in the Western wealthy countries, looking for ways to think and live on different – better terms – and doing it in small ways, whether in local collectives, or in extended family units, with illegal housing and electricity, alternative currencies, in cities and on old tribal lands.

What will happen we don't know, of course. But as more people become unable to participate in the existing economic and governing systems, they must find another way. Many people in the global South, poor people of colour in the global North, and Indigenous peoples everywhere are the most experienced at this. Solidarity, assistance, fellowship will be needed. I am not invested in the term 'utopian' – and I don't care if it's used or not. I care about what I call, in the book, 'being in-difference'. Being in-difference is a political consciousness and a sensuous knowledge, a standpoint and a mindset for living on better terms than we're offered; for living as if you had the necessity and the freedom to do so; for living in the acknowledgement, that despite the overwhelming power of all the systems of domination which are trying to kill us, they never quite become us. They are, as Cedric Robinson used to say, only one condition of our existence or being.

I think the key challenge politically, is to promote and develop that being in-difference, to learn to stop appealing to the system itself for redress, to stop believing the forces that are killing you can or will save you. This doesn't mean that we don't engage politically in struggle. It does mean preparing for being ready and available, possibly at a moment's notice, to live autonomously from the system one wants to abolish. The goal is not greater participation or assimilation into the given terms of order. The goal is to overturn that order or displace it or live otherwise than within it. The balance between withdrawal/separation and engagement in social struggle is what has to be determined. And there are, unfortunately, no clear rules for this.

As for the form/method of the book: it consists of various items, organised in files and collections, from the Hawthorn Archive. There are no chapters as in a conventional book. The Hawthorn Archive is real and it is also a device for conveying that other utopianism's mode(s) of living, for what it might mean to live in the utopian margins. It thus exists in a particular imaginative space and temporality. This temporality is not the conventional one of utopian literature – 'what might be' – nor is it quite the conditional past ('what could have been') that Lisa Lowe evokes in her brilliant book, *The Intimacies of Four Continents* (2015), although it crosses there in places. The Hawthorn Archive operates in the temporality of what was almost or not quite yet; or what was present and at the same time yet to come. It tries to represent the traces of the remains of the past, or the future yet to come, as if in the present. This is the future conditional or the imperfect past tense, a combination of the past tense and a continuous or repeating aspect, something that is unfinished. The Chimurenga Library and Pan African Space Station put the question this way: 'Can a past that the present has not yet caught up with be summoned to haunt the present as an alternative?' What would happen if we understood that what haunts from the past are precisely all those aspirations and actions – small and large, individual and collective – that oppose racial capitalism and empire and live actively other than on those terms of order. These living haunts are part of the past the present hasn't caught up with yet. This is what I mean by the idea of the utopian margins – an alternate civilisation crossing time and place, accumulating a kind of cultural and political surplus, as Bloch called it. Julius Scott called it 'the common wind.'[9]

I found it very difficult to know how best to represent this while not writing a novel. I tried to follow Monique Wittig's instruction in *Les Guérillères*: 'There was a time when you were not a slave, remember that. Make an effort to remember. Or, failing that, invent.'[10] The form of the book both remembers and invents by inviting the reader into a world situated in a liminal place – one we can call the utopian margins, where then, now and soon we are capable of, and are, living on very different terms than the various forms of enslavement, indebtedness and repression that order this one.

***BB/RZ** One theme we're interested in is historical memory, struggle and time – in this instance, as it relates to various movements active today. In a wonderful interview you conducted (in a Whole Foods with Natascha Sadr Haghighian), you explain:*

> *Even if these memories of resistance and struggle and knowing otherwise are intensely constructed and staged, they nonetheless create a force field that connects us through time and space to others, and to a power we are constantly denied and told we do not possess: the power to create life on our own terms and to sustain that creation over the long term.*[11]

This is a powerful take on both memory and the power to create life. But throughout the interviews in this book, we have also discussed a recurring erasure of history of movements or specific conversations, especially as it relates to race and

---

9 Julius Sherrard Scott, *The Common Wind: Afro-American Currents in the Age of the Haitian Revolution* (London and New York: Verso, 2018).

10 Monique Wittig, *Les guérillères* (Paris: Les Éditions de Minuit, 1969), 89.

11 Natascha Sadr Haghighian, 'Sleepwalking in a Dialectical Picture Puzzle, Part 1: A Conversation with Avery Gordon', *e-flux journal* 3 (February 2009), e-flux.com.

previous anti-racist struggles. This question is twofold: how would you explain the wilful amnesia around issues of race and anti-racist struggles? And do you think this 'force field that connects us through time and space' is a constant, or needs specific forms of excavation to be sustained?

AFG Over the years, I've had the pleasure of doing various projects with artist Natascha Sadr Haghighian, who is also a very active member of the Hawthorn Archive. The conversation you mention took place in 2009 in the large, upscale organic Whole Foods supermarket in New York's Bowery neighbourhood, next door to the New Museum, as part of a 'seminar' entitled 'Sleepwalking in a Dialectical Picture Puzzle'. We walked through the Whole Foods while being secretly filmed, talking about the commercialisation of organic food, the way Whole Foods was appropriating radical ecological and political ideas for profit and political agency. Natascha had pointed out a sign in the store that read 'Power to the People', and I was describing some of what was not signed in the store that suggested a far more radical anti-capitalist, anti-imperialist ecological approach: People's Park; MOVE; Earth First!; the Diggers, from whose 1649 manifesto against greed, private property, inequality and war I read in front of the cheese department.

Natascha raised the question of whether revealing or exposing the hidden facts or histories was effective in producing action or change. And the statement you quote was part of my answer to her.

Calling up and out, naming what's missing, is as much about haunting as it is about history. Naming the Diggers, for example, provides information many might not have, and it also creates a connection across time and space so we who are living now can work to put an end to the conditions that repeat and thus haunt. The exposure or revelation gives notice to the sedimented conditions that make putting that 'Power for the People' sign up in a megastore even possible. I'm quite interested in time, the feel of it and what form it takes in social struggles, which I find difficult to express in abstract or academic language. We tend to call this time-form memory, even if the memories are constructed and staged. You're absolutely right that the force field – the connection – must be activated. It might always be there; that's certainly my argument about the utopian margins, and Toni Morrison's argument about those 'rememories' that are always waiting for you, whether they happened to you or not.[12] But everything hinges on the encounter and what the encounter yields. There's a difference between knowing that there are continuities in forms of repression and in the struggles against them, and encountering them as a force field – as something that changes your perceptual boundaries and political compass, that prompts action, and that enables an honouring of those who came before and a necessary carrying of the struggle forward.

---

12 Toni Morrison, *Beloved* (New York: Knopf, 1987).

The wilful amnesia about anti-racist struggles and racism can be explained in part, given the direction of the discussion with Natascha, by the whitening of radical environmental politics and the history of the commons, such that the Diggers, the various maroon societies, the Seminoles, the Zapatistas and the keelboatmen, for example, appear as if in separate universes and in separate histories rather than part of one. It's striking today that despite widespread interest in and attention to climate change and global warming – all schoolchildren know these terms – environmental racism and the histories of those struggles, which necessarily addressed racial capitalism, even if they didn't name it as such, remain almost completely invisible. The lack of visibility of a critical environmental justice – as that seasoned environmental anti-racist scholar David N. Pellow has proposed, where the Movement for Black Lives, the prison abolition movement and the anti-occupation struggle of Palestinians are all considered 'environmental' or ecological – is evident and to the detriment of dealing with these catastrophic problems.[13]

At a more general level, as Cedric Robinson concisely argued, 'Racial regimes are unstable truth systems in which race is proposed as a justification for relations of power.'[14] Racial regimes, which 'masquerade' as natural and unchanging, are in reality unstable and fragile, and they shift over time as the power needs they serve change. They are unstable and fragile because they construct, rank and ontologise artificial differences among people, making them seem natural. Because in doing so they exclude an ever-present, noisy, repressed reality (we're not that!), which is always threatening to destabilise the justifications. It takes enormous work for racial regimes to function since they are constantly confronting realities that counter them in varying degrees of organised opposition. A considerable amount of that work is done by violence – by the police, the army and other organs of the repressive state. And a sufficient amount of that work is done by intellectuals, including well-meaning reformers.

BB/RZ *Indeed, in your work you attend to 'Marxism's blind spots' and note the importance of critiques coming from authors like Cedric Robinson. However, you see a focus on blind spots as coming from a 'gracious spirit of reconstruction'.*[15] *What would you say are the key features of these critiques?*

AFG 'Forged in an . . . erudite and gracious spirit of reconstruction' is how I

13 David N. Pellow, 'Toward a Critical Environmental Justice Studies: Black Lives Matter as an Environmental Justice Challenge', *Du Bois Review: Social Science Research on Race* 13:2 (2016), 221–36.

14 Cedric J. Robinson, *Forgeries of Memory and Meaning: Blacks and the Regimes of Race in American Theater and Film Before World War* II (Chapel Hill: University of North Carolina Press, 2007), xii.

15 Cedric J. Robinson, *An Anthropology of Marxism*, 2nd ed. preface by Avery Gordon (Chapel Hill: University of North Carolina Press, 2019), xi.

described the nature of Cedric's exposure of the philosophical and historical compromises Marxism made with bourgeois society in his book *An Anthropology of Marxism*, for which I wrote the preface. I'm pleased to say that this book, long unavailable and thus not well known, has been reissued by the University of North Carolina Press in the United States and Pluto Press in the UK. To simplify, the critique of Marxism in *Black Marxism: The Making of the Black Radical Tradition* focused on two main lines.[16] The first is the significance of the precapitalist history of racism within the West and its significance to the development of a constitutively racial capitalism, consistently mistaken by Marx and Marxists, and sometimes also now by well-intentioned intellectuals. Capitalism is a product of a highly racist and racialised Western civilisation, not the other way around, and Robinson is at pains to establish this point. The second line concerns Marx's claims about the specificity and dominance of the capital/(free) labour relation and his attachment to the figure of the revolutionary proletariat. Robinson critiques this intellectual and political investment and argues that it bound the development of Marxian socialism to nationalism, racism and bourgeois epistemology. The result is a way of seeing, a structure of anticipation or expectation, that could not and did not recognise Black radicalism on its own terms, but, if at all, as 'merely an opposition to capitalist organization'. A similar and expanded argument is made in *An Anthropology of Marxism*, where Marx and Engels's dismissal of precapitalist forms of socialism, female heresy and rebellion, among other outcomes, 'obliterated the most fertile . . . domain for their political ambitions and historical imaginations'.[17]

In both of these books, whether the subject is the Black radical tradition, or the European socialist tradition, the point is not merely to identify a blind field or to point out that something is missing or not seen. The list of blind spots is now rather well known, in any event: capitalocentrism, to use J.K. Gibson-Graham's term;[18] the overemphasis on a two-class model of society and a corresponding notion of class struggle and class politics; the dismissive treatment of nonindustrial labour – peasants, slaves, indentured – and of women as a class; and an economism that prevented, as Robinson writes, 'a more comprehensive treatment of history, classes, culture, race-ethnicity, gender, and language'.[19]

The point is rather to show what is living and breathing in the place blinded from view. There's always something living and breathing in the blind spot, and the question is what, or who, is there. This is, in my view, the more

16 Cedric J. Robinson, *Black Marxism: The Making of the Black Radical Tradition* (Chapel Hill: University of North Carolina Press, 2000).

17 Robinson, *Anthropology of Marxism*, 138–9.

18 J.K. Gibson-Graham, *The End of Capitalism (As We Knew It): A Feminist Critique of Political Economy* (Minneapolis: University of Minnesota Press, 2006), 80.

19 Robinson, *Anthropology of Marxism*, xiii.

important approach and one I have tried to pursue in my own work, in various ways. Robinson argues that Marx and his heirs missed an opportunity to see the rich thought and the complex struggle comprising the Black radical tradition – its collective wisdom – as worthy of theorisation and thus of generalisation. He writes, 'The difference . . . is not one of interpretation but comprehension.'[20] I think this is a very precise way of putting it.

Movements and activists, whether they make them explicit or not, assume standpoints, historiographies, terms of solidarities and what Alex Lubin calls 'geographies of liberation.'[21] These assumptions form the infrastructure of comprehension. It's not a matter of whether an individual or a movement covers everything or knows everything. This is virtually impossible; moreover, political struggles and campaigns require precision and focus to be effective. What *do* matter and are necessary are the deeper understandings, visions, values and connections – the collective wisdom, or what Haghighian calls the emotional intelligence – that are carried in specific demands and articulated in the daily operating organisational cultures in which activists and movements think and act.

BB/RZ *Moving slightly away from your writing, you have been involved longer term in cohosting a weekly public affairs radio programme,* No Alibis. *Can you talk to us about this part of your work?*

AFG A radio programme – even a radical grassroots programme like ours – is perhaps not considered political activism in the way door-to-door campaigning or organising protests are. But my most sustained political activism is the radio programme I have cohosted with Elizabeth Robinson since 1997.

No Alibis is a spin-off, created in late 1999, of an earlier radio programme Elizabeth did for a long time called *Viewpoints* with H.L.T. Quan, and which I joined in 1997. *No Alibis* is a two-hour public affairs / cultural radio programme which airs on KCSB 91.9 FM Santa Barbara. The show focuses on a range of current events in an internationalist perspective, using a semi-structured format of news (thirty minutes) and in-depth analysis of social/political issues, usually with two interview segments. On certain places and issues – Palestine, the Middle East, US imprisonment, militarism, the European border regime, Africa – *No Alibis* has been consistently reporting, long before shows like *Democracy Now!* We have a special programme in December called 'Book Tastings', in which we read excerpts of new and notable books, and in earlier years, we participated in global media projects associated with the World Association of Community Radio Broadcasters (AMARC), for which Elizabeth

20 Robinson, *Black Marxism*, 96.

21 Alex Lubin, *Geographies of Liberation: The Making of an Afro-Arab Political Imaginary* (Chapel Hill: University of North Carolina Press, 2014).

held several officer positions, such as live reporting at the World Social Forum, and Voices without Frontiers (*Voix sans fronteres*), an anti-racist and anti-xenophobia youth radio project.

I had done a little radio at university and was involved with the radio station at Boston College, but it was around music, not public affairs. When I first started doing the radio programme, I had to learn to speak intelligently to and dialogue with people all over again. Thanks to Elizabeth, it was a very good learning experience in democratic communication. KCSB and *No Alibis* have, over all these years, successfully resisted the trends towards monopolisation, standardisation and globalisation of commercial media, including the pressure on community and grassroots radio stations to mainstream programme content and station scheduling, and to professionalise the format and the sound of programmes. One of the most common ways in which the pressure to professionalise operates is in the taken-for-granted value that a 'good product' is one in which professional-sounding programmers either speak for or arrange for experts to speak for the people/listener. In this model, a good professional product does not enable people to speak for themselves. On *No Alibis*, we take political stands and stand explicitly in political solidarity. We do not ever mask our views and what we think is important. And we try to operate on the principle of self-determination – that people have the right to speak for themselves in their own language – and not on the principle of professionalisation. Experts are routinely invited on our show, of course, but we engage discussion and try to generate dialogue (or multilogue) to model a more democratic, less subservient, relationship to experts. *No Alibis* is a site where we can show other ways of seeing the world than what can be found in the mainstream media, trying to keep the imagination open, even when the course for political action seems less immediately available. Right now, for example, there is a moratorium on Trump news, unless more airspace can be reasonably justified! And a commitment to reporting on social struggles and making sure we spread the news about important initiatives and small successes. We see the programme operating in a global context, with an internationalist perspective, and so try not to treat the local and global as contradictory or contentious.

The creation of an alternative media voice is an essential political activity and an important medium of popular education, and I think Elizabeth would agree. There is, in fact, a creative, politically astute, and inclusive community and grassroots media in the United States and elsewhere. It is sustained by a set of ethical principles based on the right of all members of civil society to just and equitable access to all communications media. This media sector has been and is still under attack. The suppression of dissent, the nationalistic calls to patriotic loyalty, all the agitated and false information presented in the mainstream print, broadcast and social media are serious challenges to sustaining democratic, noncapitalist, community radio. It is important that we keep this work going.

***BB/RZ** You have been centrally involved in the prison abolition movement – can you tell us about shifts (if any) you've observed happening in the movement from its earliest days? A central concept of the movement is, of course, abolition – can you please explain to us the key ideas behind abolitionism and its importance to a multiplicity of social movements today?*

AFG The prison abolition movement in the United States has grown considerably and remarkably from its earliest (post–prison boom) days when you could count the abolitionist groups on one hand and name maybe one – the Prison Moratorium Project[22] – and the organisers of the first Critical Resistance conference thought maybe a couple of hundred people would show up. This growth reflects real organising success and also brings with it the challenges of many more people identifying with and defining what abolition means.[23]

Abolition feminism, whose best-known theoretical practitioner is Angela Y. Davis, is a part of the Black radical internationalist tradition. Although it is often associated with the movement to abolish police power and the carceral state, it names a set of positions and standpoints which understand that in order to abolish the prison system as we know it today, it is necessary to eliminate the political, social and economic conditions that produce it, to radically transform our present social order, which cannot be grasped in national or nationalist terms. As she writes, 'Prison abolition is a way of talking about the pitfalls of the particular version of democracy represented by U.S. capitalism.'[24] What's distinctive about abolition feminism is this deeper vision and the analytic, political and human connections or intersections it makes.

Perhaps the most succinct articulation of this connectedness or intersectionality is the idea of the indivisibility of justice, expressed by Martin Luther King Jr in 1963 in the letter he wrote from the jail in Birmingham, Alabama. He famously wrote: 'Injustice anywhere is a threat to justice everywhere. We are caught in an inescapable network of mutuality, tied in a single garment of destiny. Whatever affects one directly, affects all indirectly.' This notion of the indivisibility of justice – and remember very soon King himself would come to identify militarism and capitalism as what must be fought to achieve racial justice – which binds us to a network of mutuality is a way of describing solidarity or fellowship.[25] It gives us what King called standing, as well as a certain

22 Prison Moratorium Project official website, nomoreprisons.org.

23 Critical Resistance official website, criticalresistance.org.

24 Angela Y. Davis, *Abolition Democracy: Beyond Empire, Prisons and Torture* (New York: Seven Stories, 2005).

25 The text in this paragraph is reproduced, in part, from Krystian Woznicki, 'Unshrinking the World: An Interview with Avery F. Gordon about *The Hawthorn Archive: Letters from the Utopian Margins*', *Commonist Aesthetics*, June 2019.

obligation to know and to act in concert with others. This is a beautiful idea of our connection, of what we have in common – an inescapable network of mutuality, a single garment of destiny. Sometimes these connections are strong and sometimes they are weak and fractured, but they are abolition's political commons.

The intensification of police power as a mode of governance – arguably, the US is a police state – and the growth of the carceral state have activated interest among many younger people. They can see and often feel quite directly the various spatial forms of enclosure and confinement of land, people, ideas, of their capacity for so much more. They can also glimpse what Brenna has called the 'racial regimes of ownership' and the militarised infrastructure for maintenance of a highly stratified racial capitalist order.[26] There's a reach, or desire, for something else – for a life without racial capitalism, a life in which we are not enclosed by values and modes of being together based on money and exchange values, status hierarchies, violence and force, alienation, racialisation and discipline to externally imposed standards. It may be inchoate, underanalysed or inexperienced, but something of what we used to call a revolutionary impulse is more widespread than the authorities would like us to believe. That we have to build this life ourselves – it will not be given to us – is also I think partially understood, if not quite comprehended in full, and makes an already enormous job even more complex, difficult and fraught with seemingly overwhelming obstacles and challenges.

People start or enter into this process via distinct routes, picking up vocabularies, alliances, strategies and lessons, hopefully wisely and with a minimum of sectarianism. To take abolition feminism seriously, each individual, in common with others, must learn to become 'unavailable for servitude, back stiff with conviction', to use Toni Cade Bambara's words.[27] This is, in my view, the heart of the abolitionist imaginary, which understands servitude in its broadest meaning, so that the struggle to transform the world takes place immanently today through the means that embody and instantiate the values, practices and institutional formats we desire. It is also the heart of the intellectual work of organising – to link this imaginary to the capacity to build the life we need with others. It can't be done by rhetoric. It is done by the people working with INCITE! Women of Color against Violence, Critical Resistance, Survived and Punished, Oakland Power Projects and many other groups to create a portable knowledge of abolition as a way of life and a working infrastructure to reduce the role of policing and prison in our lives.

---

26 Brenna Bhandar, *Colonial Lives of Property: Law, Land and Racial Regimes of Ownership* (Durham: Duke University Press, 2018).

27 Toni Cade Bambara, *Deep Sightings and Rescue Missions: Fictions, Essays and Conversations* (New York: Vintage, 1996). See also Cherrie Moraga and Gloria Anzaldúa, 'Foreword', in *This Bridge Called My Back: Writings by Radical Women of Color*, ed. Cherrie Moraga and Gloria Anzaldúa, 4th ed. (Watertown, NY: Kitchen Table Press, 2015), xxix–xxxii.

BB/RZ *In your writing you have made the connection between militarism internationally, the prison industrial complex and the War on Terror, especially in your article on imprisonment in the context of the Abu Ghraib prison in Iraq.*[28] *What led you to make these connections? Would you frame this as the 'internationalisation' of the US prison system?*

AFG The war on terror launched by the United States in 2001 gave custodial responsibility to the Army and the Marine Corps for large numbers of prisoners of war, who were not prisoners of war but enemy alien combatants – a legal invention of the US – and civilian security threats. The Military Police Corps, in charge of prisons, were not prepared for this responsibility: military bases all had a prison or a brig, mostly used for soldiers sleeping off drunkenness, or for punishing insurbordination and so on. It was not a full-blown prison system, nor was it set up for either large numbers of prisoners of war treated according to Geneva Convention standards or for confining civilians (or soldiers) charged and or sentenced for crimes. The personnel (guards and directors), the punishment regime with its racialised sadism and normalcy of exceptional brutality, the security apparatus, and the legal infrastructure were all imported from the US civilian prison.

When the photographs of the abuse of prisoners by guards at the large Abu Ghraib prison complex and news and images of the conditions of the prisoners held at the base in Guantanamo, Cuba, went public, there was considerable attention to the normally hidden US military prison network. But most of that attention treated what was happening in those prisons as isolated instances of the abuse of state power, which obscured the relationship and the continuum between the US military prisons abroad and territorial US civilian prisons. I began writing a series of articles analysing that connection and the role of the military prison in the War on Terror – for example, 'The United States Military Prison: The Normalcy of Exceptional Brutality' and 'The Prisoner's Curse'.[29]

I did not see the military prison as the internationalisation of the prison industrial complex so much as a fungible technology or portable model in the perpetuation and expansion of a security-centred world economy. There is a vast transnational military security industry operating today – the largest business sector in the world – which underwrites a parasitic global capitalist order and an increasingly globally integrated repressive apparatus designed to

28 Avery F. Gordon, 'Abu Ghraib: Imprisonment and the War on Terror', *Race & Class* 48:1 (2006), 42–59.

29 Avery F. Gordon, 'The United States Military Prison: The Normalcy of Exceptional Brutality', in *The Violence of Incarceration*, ed. Phil Scraton and Jude McCulloch (New York: Routledge, 2009), 174–96; and Avery F. Gordon, 'The Prisoner's Curse', in *Toward a Sociology of the Trace*, ed. Herman Gray and Macarena Gómez-Barris (Minneapolis: Minnesota University Press, 2011), 17–55.

suppress and criminalise dissent and the attempts to create anti-capitalist life forms. The United States is the largest arms dealer in the world, but it hardly acts alone. In fact, the Israeli military, which has long promoted itself as the world's leader in security expertise based on its occupation of Palestine, is a major trainer of US law enforcement personnel. This is, of course, the tip of the iceberg of a set of global connections that maintain a permanent war economy, with long-term captive populations.

When the term 'prison industrial complex' was introduced, its purpose was, more than anything else, to question taken-for-granted assumptions about crime and punishment (that people went to prison because they committed crimes) and focus on the process of criminalisation (what is a crime, exactly? who exactly becomes a criminal?), and to identify the political and economic interests invested in building a seemingly self-reproducing prison system whose function had little to do with public safety. It was a powerful construct and did a good deal of the political education required of it in the US context, even though it could not and was not expected to cover everything. People today are still struggling to find the right term or terms for the expansion of criminalisation, punishment and confinement, and for what's often now called the carceral state, which shapes or 'deforms', to quote Marie Gottschalk, millions of people, many of whom have never been in a jail or prison.[30]

To my mind, privatisation of management is not the key problem or indicator for the general patterns. In the United States, around 8 per cent of all prisoners are housed in private facilities; the vast majority of those are in immigration prisons run by the federal government, which is also the fastest-growing sector of detention in the US. These private facilities are paid for by individual states or the federal government, are authorised by state authorities, and implement policies made by every branch of government – including now, rather spectacularly, by the executive branch, the president. Legally, in every way, the state is responsible for them and is the agency that contracts with private businesses. The focus on state power and on state accountability is key.

Here, I think the larger concern should be understanding the constituent role war, criminalisation (of poverty and troublemaking), punishment and confinement (whether in the workhouse, on the slave ship or the transportation ship carrying banished convicts, or on the native reservation) played historically in the making of the modern capitalist world, and in the recurring waves of primitive accumulation necessary for it to continue. Dispossession, expulsion, imprisonment and theft of land, bodies and knowledge continue in racial capitalist democracies today, and they continue to require war and militarised police

30 Marie Gottschalk, *Caught: The Prison State and the Lockdown of American Politics* (Princeton: Princeton University Press, 2016).

power to function. Without an understanding of the historical lines and the complicated patterns of a global history in which the prison is both a means of expropriation and repression and a site of subjugated knowledge, infrapolitical resistance, political conspiracy and (when possible) organised rebellion, it is difficult to grasp what's involved in fighting armed police and armies, which has been necessary in the past and is necessary again now.

BB/RZ *Shifting gears slightly for this final question, at the 2019 Venice Biennale, a work by Swiss-Icelandic artist Christoph Büchel, titled* Barca Nostra *(Our ship), was exhibited to the great consternation of some. The ship was previously a fishing vessel, en route from Libya to Italy in 2015, in which approximately 700 to 800 migrants (many of them African) died when the boat collided with a Portuguese freighter attempting to rescue those on board. The artist said the intention was for* Barca Nostra *to be a 'monument to contemporary migration'. Can you tell us about this 'artwork' and what the controversy around its exhibition represents in your view?*

AFG The first thing to note is that based on his past practice of creating provocative installations, I think it's fair to say that whatever else Christoph Büchel hoped to do, he also intended to create controversy and draw public attention to himself, as he did for his 2015 Venice project, in which he turned a church into a mosque that was closed down within two weeks after a great deal of negative media publicity. As his spokeswoman announced about *Barca Nostra*: 'As with all of his previous projects, public response – including press articles, critical essays and social media posts – is integral to the overall concept.'[31]

Büchel spent two years and 33 million euros, with the help of Sebastiano Tusa, Sicily's councillor for cultural heritage, to deal with the bureaucracy necessary to acquire the boat, salvage it (which cost 9.5 of that 33 million), move it, and display it at the world's most well-known and wealthy art exhibition. He originally claimed the process, not the boat, is the artwork, which was true in the literal sense of the work involved, although once the controversy heated up, he defended himself by making the claim you quoted above, that it was a 'monument to contemporary migration . . . representing the collective policies and politics that create such wrecks', and which, at the same time, was partial proof of the League party's Matteo Salvini's characterisation of the work as 'political propaganda'.[32]

The rusty wreck of the former Tunisian fishing boat, carrying ten times more individuals than it was built to hold and in which most of them died

31 Cristina Ruiz, 'Fierce Debate over Christoph Büchel's Venice Biennale Display of Boat That Sank with Hundreds Locked in Hull', *Art Newspaper*, 14 May 2019, theartnewspaper.com.

32 Ibid.

trying to reach Lampedusa and then other points in Europe, was hung in the Arsenale, the former Venetian shipyards, near a café, where people were constantly passing it by, without any labels displayed near the boat to explain what it was. Accompanying information was in the costly catalogue most people don't buy.

The combination of the artistic context of the Venice Biennale, which its theme – 'May you live in interesting times' – did nothing to challenge its placement, the lack of accessible contextualising information or related public programming, the exorbitant cost, the high level of media attention beyond the art press (which the work, the artist and the curators seemed to cultivate), and the seeming lack of any attention to the longer history of or the institutions responsible for the deaths of people moving without authorisation from Africa to Europe. Not to mention that the unseemly (or 'distasteful', to quote the BBC) act of exhibiting a mass grave led to considerable criticism of the work from many quarters, in varying degrees of intensity of anger.

Some of the specific criticism of the work was spot on, but overall the media debate, in which the controversy was produced and embedded, stayed close to the question of what the artist and the artwork can and cannot do in the highly commodified and appropriative art world, which can and does absorb and repackage a lot of critical ideas and impulses. It could be argued that the avant-garde work of art, situated within a larger political project and community, has been replaced by the political or radical art work, whose politics and radicality is measured by art world standards and entirely situated within it.

I don't expect the media, much less the art media, to provide a satisfying analysis of the European border regime, but I do expect it to do two things it did not. The first was to follow the money. It is virtually impossible to find reliable and detailed information on exactly where that 33 million came from and how it was spent. And while there was some good opportunity cost analysis in the blogsphere – for example, showing that the budget spent on the art work could fund two health clinics with free medication for about ten years[33] – there was little analysis or holding to account of the art institutions, curators, private donors, corporate funders and governments who enabled the work. Obviously, without this financial infrastructure, which primarily remained unnamed, Büchel could not have made the work. This is, in part, what I mean by calling it a work of political propaganda. It hides well the puppet masters.

The second element missing in the media controversy was an engagement with the many other artists working critically around the subject of the European border regime (at least one of whom, Nastascha Sadr Haghighian,

33 Alexandra Stock, 'The Privileged, Violent Stunt That Is the Venice Biennale Boat Project', *Mada*, 29 May 2019, madamasr.com.

was at Venice exhibiting, in a completely different mode, in the German Pavillion), or engaged, even more specifically, with migrant deaths at sea whose work was more sensitive or humane or emotionally moving or politically intelligent.[34] In the interests of space here, I'll just mention one project that provides a strong contrast.

Sink without Trace was exhibited in a small London gallery, P21, from June to July in summer 2019. Curated by the academic Federica Mazzara and artist Maya Ramsay,[35] this show was everything Büchel's *Barca Nostra* was not. It was organised by two women with modest means, who were involved since at least 2014 in research, art and political activism around migrant deaths at sea. It was framed not by immediate media time and state-sponsored slogans, but by this opening statement: 'Migrant deaths are not a new phenomenon, as the media and government might have us believe. They did not begin in 2015 with the death of Alan Kurdi or the so called "migration crisis".' And it was dedicated to 'all those who have perished whilst trying to reach Europe by sea, to all those who will perish in the future and to all those who have successfully made the journey'. The exhibition did not focus on the work of one famous artist, but included eighteen artists from ten countries, several of whom came to Europe as refugees. Found objects from shipwrecked vessels (Ramsay's *Countless* [*2016–19*]) were displayed, in the scale of the trace, not the monument, along with Ramsay's graphite rubbings from the graves of unidentified migrants and Victoria Burgher's fragments of foil survival blankets laminated in gold leaf, in a context that also included unsigned drawings made on migrant ships and sculptural works made by young people travelling alone and living in the Calais camps. Side by side were Forensic Oceanography's detailed scientific analysis of a 2011 case (*Liquid Traces – The Left-to-Die Boat Case* [2014]) and an elegiac ten-minute film, *Asmat: Names in Memory of All Victims of the Sea* (2014), made by Dagmawi Yimer, who made an illegal sea crossing himself, in which the names of 368 Eritreans who died off the coast of Lampedusa on 3 October 2013 are read slowly in Tigrinya. Max Hirzel's photographs of the forensic examination of the 450 bodies recovered from the vessel Büchel exhibited are set in the context of a project begun in 2011 to find the places where migrants were buried and to mark them, notifying relatives where possible. Kurdish artist Mariwan Jalal's beautiful screen prints chart his journey to the UK by sea. And more. There are intelligent, informative wall captions, as well as a small, affordable (five-pound) book with the artworks, artists' biographies and precise, thoughtful essays by the curators and postcolonial scholar Iain Chambers. The book's sales are used to raise funds for AlarmPhone, a telephone hotline for refugees in the Mediterranean Sea started by activists. The exhibition itself was free, unlike Venice, and the

34 'Journal', Deutscher Pavillon official website, Biennale Arte 2019, deutscher-pavillon.org.

35 *Sink without Trace*, exhibition catalogue, sinkwithouttrace.com.

curators note that 'after years of discussion with public galleries, who agreed on the . . . importance of the exhibition', they were nonetheless 'unable to give it space'. [36] Not one of these artists sought to 'provoke' for provocation's sake, but together the exhibition stands as a quiet collective act of aesthetic and political sabotage.

Selected Writings

Gordon, Avery F. *Keeping Good Time: Reflections on Knowledge, Power and People*. Boulder: Paradigm, 2004.

———. *Ghostly Matters: Haunting and the Sociological Imagination*. 2nd ed. Minneapolis: University of Minnesota Press, 2008.

———. 'The United States Military Prison: The Normalcy of Exceptional Brutality'. In *The Violence of Incarceration*, edited by Phil Scraton and Jude McCullough, 164–86. New York: Routledge, 2009.

———. 'The Prisoner's Curse'. In *Toward a Sociology of the Trace*, edited by Herman Gray and Macarena Gomez-Barris, 17–55. Minneapolis: University of Minnesota Press, 2010.

———. 'I'm already in a Sort of Tomb': A Reply to Philip Scheffner's *The Half-moon Files*'. *South Atlantic Quarterly* 110:1 (Winter 2011), 121–54.

———. *The Hawthorn Archive: Letters from the Utopian Margins*. New York: Fordham University Press, 2018.

———. 'Preface', in Cedric J. Robinson, *An Anthropology of Marxism*, xiii–xxxii. 2nd ed. Chapel Hill: University of North Carolina Press, 2019.

Gordon, Avery F., and Christopher Newfield, eds. *Mapping Multiculturalism*. Minneapolis: University of Minnesota Press, 1996.

Gordon, Avery F., and Ines Schaber. *The Workhouse (Breitenau Room) = Das Arbeitshaus (Raum Breitenau)*. Köln: König, 2014.

36 Ibid., 4.

Angela Y. Davis

Angela Y. Davis is a scholar, teacher, and activist/organiser. She has published books on race, class, and gender including, *Women, Race, and Class* (1981), *Blues Legacies and Black Feminism: Gertrude "Ma" Rainey, Bessie Smith, and Billie Holiday* (1998) and *Are Prisons Obsolete?* (2003). She helped to popularise the notion of a "prison industrial complex".

In 1969 she came to national attention after being removed from her teaching position in the Philosophy Department at UCLA as a result of her social activism and her membership of the Communist Party, USA. In 1970 she was placed on the FBI's Ten Most Wanted List on false charges. During her sixteen-month incarceration, a massive international 'Free Angela Davis' campaign was organised, leading to her acquittal in 1972.

When Davis retired from the University of California, Santa Cruz in 2008, she was named Distinguished Professor Emerita in the History of Consciousness and Feminist Studies. She has continued her work for prison abolition, women's rights, and racial justice.

BB/RZ *As you've written about in your autobiography, your political and intellectual formation begins in the midst of racial apartheid of Birmingham, Alabama.*[1] *It was forged through a radical high school education in New York, and then studies in French and philosophy at Brandeis University and in Paris. Your graduate studies in Frankfurt and then with Herbert Marcuse at the University of California, San Diego, and travels to Cuba, North Africa and elsewhere, were also central to your intellectual and political formation. You have created a distinctive feminist theory and praxis that incorporates Third World internationalism, Black radical traditions, Marxism and critical theory as developed by the Frankfurt School. Can you tell us what the most transformative dimensions of these different moments of study have been?*

AYD At the time I was in elementary and high school, I was not unhappy with the education I received in Birmingham, as racially segregated as it may have been. In fact, it was in large part my experiences in school that taught me early on that the regime of racial segregation, grounded in assumptions of Black inferiority, was not absolute. Our teachers taught us that counternarratives

---

1 Angela Y. Davis, *With My Mind on Freedom: An Autobiography* (New York: Bantam Books, 1978).

were possible. Thus, I learned about important Black historical figures; we frequently sang the Negro National Anthem; and I witnessed my teachers courageously speaking back to white authorities. Learning that resistance was indeed possible was an invaluable dimension of my education, and I later realised that no matter how much may have been lacking in the curriculum, I was extremely fortunate to have experienced education as resistance to the established order during the very earliest period of my formal schooling.

By the time I realised that there were major lacunae in my education and that I would have to leave Birmingham to address them, I had already developed a political sensibility and – thanks to my teachers (and my mother, who was also a teacher) – a desire to pursue education as a force for radical transformation. Thus, being exposed to such figures as Marx and Freud in the New York high school I attended – and acquiring deeper understandings of history, both of the United States and the world, that were radically different from the content of our racially biased textbooks in Birmingham – was precisely what I needed at that point in my life. Though learning French, which later led to an abiding interest in French literature, philosophy and culture, was serendipitous (the two years of intensive study of French in high school were required as a result of my lack of foreign language study in Alabama), it made me realise that I was more interested in the humanities than the sciences. Studying French literature as an undergraduate, I discovered that I was drawn to literary figures whose work also focused on philosophical ideas – Sartre and Camus, for example – and eventually, with the invaluable assistance of Professor Herbert Marcuse, I embarked on the study of philosophy. This meant that early on my philosophical orientation was grounded in critical theory, and that I never seriously considered philosophy except in relation to its potential role in social transformation.

But in all this, there was an almost total absence of an engagement with race as a legitimate category of study. Transformative moments with respect to race and racism included reading James Baldwin's *The Fire Next Time* and hearing him speak during my first year in college; hearing Malcolm X; early encounters with the Algerian Revolution, and thus reading Frantz Fanon; and educational sessions within the Che-Lumumba Club of the Communist Party, including discussions in 1968 of class, race and gender in Claudia Jones's 'An End to the Neglect of the Problems of the Negro Woman!'[2] But what has been a consistent theme in my life has been the convergence of academic knowledge and knowledge generated in the course of actively struggling for radical change in the world.

---

2 Claudia Jones, 'An End to the Neglect of the Problems of the Negro Woman' (New York: Jefferson School of Social Science, 1949).

***BB/RZ** There has been a resurgence in the past decade of debate on 'the idea of communism', and in 2017, a slew of texts examining the history and legacies of the Russian Revolution. Other celebrations marked the 150th anniversary of the publication of* Capital, *Volume 1. Few of these conferences and texts seemed to engage specifically with the Third World Marxist anti-colonial and anti-racist traditions. What are your thoughts on these recent developments and the growth of interest in Marx and Marxism?*

AYD In my mind, as long as capitalism persists in determining the future of this planet, Marxism will continue to be relevant – as critiques of existing political economies; as approaches to the philosophy of history that emphasise the impermanence of history, even as proponents of capitalism insist on representing it as the inalterable backdrop of the future; and especially as a reminder of human agency and the possibility of revolutionary transformation. Regardless of the disintegration of the USSR, and of the many problems that have been repeatedly rehearsed, I believe that the Russian Revolution will always retain its status as a monumental historical moment. But this does not mean that we fail to take account of the particular historical context both of Marx's analysis of capital and of the 1917 revolution. Those who value the Marxist tradition – and I certainly count myself among those who do – will also value critical engagements with Marxist theory based on new insights regarding the forces of history.

Although the term 'racial capitalism' as first used by political scientist Cedric Robinson was originally proposed as a critique of the Marxist tradition grounded in what he called the Black radical tradition, it can also be a generative concept for new ways of holding these two overlapping intellectual and activist traditions in productive tension. If we set out to examine the many ways in which capitalism and racism have been intertwined, from the eras of colonialism and slavery to the present (and of course, Eric Williams's *Capitalism and Slavery* emphasised this in the mid twentieth century), I think that we are not so much 'stretching Marxism'[3] as we are continuing to build upon and critically engage with its insights. Dedicated adherents to a particular way of thinking often assume that to challenge any of the associated ideas is a disavowal. In both his works of philosophy and political economy, Marx always emphasised critique – and, of course, this became the primary approach of the Frankfurt School: critical theory. What I find especially inspiring about the Marxist tradition is its emphasis on interdisciplinarity. Even as *Capital* is categorised as a work within the discipline of political economy – despite the fact that Marx considered it a *critique of political economy* – if one reads it, one discovers philosophy, literature, sociology (which was not yet an institutionalised discipline), cultural critique, and so on. What I have always

3 As Frantz Fanon proposes in *The Wretched of the Earth* (New York: Grove, 1968), 40.

appreciated is the openness of Marx's work, its implicit invitation to push it in new directions.

Unfortunately, reductionist tendencies of some contemporary Marxist literatures create an inhospitable climate for the continuation of the tradition of critique through serious engagement with new theoretical approaches associated with Black and women of colour feminisms. But new developments in global capitalism, including the increasing importance of women's labour – in manufacturing, as well as in reproductive and care labour, and especially in the global South – have pushed us to develop different categories and different methodological approaches. At a time when there is a great deal of dissatisfaction with capitalism, I think it is extremely important to expose students (either in institutionalised academic settings or in the context of movement-building education) to Marxist ideas, and especially to Marxist-inflected, anti-racist feminist approaches. Carole Boyce Davies's important study of Black woman communist Claudia Jones has inspired new research on Black women Marxists.[4]

BB/RZ *Activists involved in the Black Lives Matter movement in the United States have made alliances and expressed solidarity with Palestinians struggling against the Israeli occupation, and vice versa. This solidarity speaks to a longer history of internationalism that informed Third World Marxism and the Black Power movement. Can you reflect on the connections between and changes in these forms of solidarity over the last decades? Is there an intergenerational element present in these alliances?*

AYD I do not believe we can create viable and potent movements if we neglect the global context within which we work. Earlier communist expressions of internationalism always reminded us to be critical of the nation-state and nationalism and, of course, the refrain of 'The Internationale' – sung by socialists and communists throughout the world – contains the words 'The international working class / Shall be the human race'. Personally, I cannot imagine who I would be and how I would be thinking and acting had I not been exposed to the potential of international solidarity at a very young age. Early on in my life, I realised that the movement to free the Scottsboro Nine (led by Black communists, and the context for my own mother's politicisation) was produced through this solidarity. As I mentioned in an earlier question, I learned how to express solidarity with the Algerian Revolution while still a teenager. And, of course, my own trial on charges that initially carried the death penalty ended in victory largely due to the vast international campaign that touched people in Africa, Asia, Europe and Latin America. The Black

4 Carole Boyce Davies, *Left of Karl Marx: The Political Life of Black Communist Claudia Jones* (Durham: Duke University Press, 2007).

Panther Party and many of the other organisations promoting Black liberation in the 1960s and '70s were inspired by and created links with revolutionary struggles in the Third World.

During the 1980s in the United States, the call for solidarity with the anti-apartheid struggle in South Africa was heeded by virtually every progressive organisation in the country. This solidarity not only helped to raise the international profile of the anti-apartheid campaign, but also greatly strengthened our anti-racist movements at home. Many young Black activists associated with the larger Black Lives Matter movement began to embrace Palestine as the new South Africa, recognising that generating support for justice for Palestine would add an important internationalist dimension to the many struggles identifying with the new slogan. When Michael Brown was killed by police in Ferguson, Missouri, in 2014, the protests marked a major turning point in the movement. Importantly, activists in occupied Palestine were the first to offer solidarity and, as we know, advice regarding how to deal with the tear gas being thrown at them. The Palestinian activists had noticed, in images circulating on social media, that the Ferguson police were using the same tear gas that the Israeli military used in Palestine. The struggle that served as a catalyst for a new political turn among Black youth in the United States was also a moment defined by international solidarity, and a recognition that the militarism of US police was linked to Israel.

Over the last period, after decades of influence of the Israel lobby and after much confusion within progressive movements regarding the occupation, there is increasing recognition – including in Jewish communities – that Israel has been immune to criticism for far too long. In my own case, when I learned in January 2019 that the Birmingham Civil Rights Institute was rescinding its decision to offer me a human rights award because of my Palestine activism, I assumed that, like the firing of public intellectual Marc Lamont Hill by CNN the year before, and the attacks on Congresswoman Ilhan Omar, this would simply be one more example of the power of the supporters of Israel. However, Birmingham's Black community – including the mayor – publicly reprimanded the institute, followed by statements from individuals and organisations, many of them Jewish, throughout the country and the world. As a consequence, the top officers of the board of the institute resigned, and they announced that they wanted to offer me the prize as originally planned. I mention this example because it seems to me that it reveals an entirely new moment in our efforts to call for justice for Palestine.

Of course, this does not mean that we have emerged from this period of dangerous provincialism, which reflects the continual emphasis in public discourse on US exceptionalism. Unfortunately, many previous ties with struggles in Africa, Asia, Latin America and elsewhere in the Middle East have fallen into decline. At this moment, given the dangerous symmetry in the political circumstances of the United States and Brazil, there should be a greater awareness of racism, police violence, attacks on the environment, and so on in Brazil. While it is true that in activist, Black feminist circles, there were protests when Rio de Janeiro city councilwoman Marielle Franco was assassinated in 2018 for her anti-racist, anti-violence, pro-LGBTQ work, people in the United States – especially those who identify with the role that the Women's Marches have played in resisting the current political situation – should have taken to the streets in support of the struggles in Brazil. Of course, there are other examples as well. I have been deeply impressed for a very long time by the role of the Kurdish women's movement in fighting for democracy and simultaneously defending women's right to lead. These new Black movements, overwhelmingly led by women, a significant number of whom are queer, would greatly benefit from connections with the Kurdish women's movement.

Although most of these new movements have, understandably, emerged among youth, intergenerationality has always been an important dimension of sustainable radical movements. But the involvement of older people works, as these movements have emphasised, only if the elders refrain from assuming that they are in possession of the most relevant organising knowledge. Moreover, international outreach is linked to an understanding of the intersectionality of struggles that insists on the leadership of those who have been previously marginalised. In many instances, this means that new organisations are led by young, Black, queer women who are intentionally challenging old leadership forms that accentuate individualism and charisma, and who are introducing new forms of collective leadership.

BB/RZ *You've written about the 'fascist tendencies' that exist within liberal democracy. Can you reflect on these tendencies within the current political moment?*

AYD The outcome of the US presidential elections in 2016 would have been different if not for tendencies that are, unfortunately, best described as 'fascist'. The populism and ultranationalism that have developed within the context of liberal democratic electoral processes have influenced elections not only in the United States, but in Europe and South America. In all cases, xenophobia, Islamophobia and other racisms have played pivotal roles. The persistence of racism throughout the history of the US, from the very establishment of a democratic political order to the present, has always posed grave threats to democracy. But one might also argue – as many Marxist theorists have already done – that the class contradictions at the very heart of capitalism contain the seeds for both socialist transformation and fascist reaction. Barely a year after the Nazi Party seized power in Germany, Herbert Marcuse published an article entitled 'The Struggle against Liberalism in the Totalitarian View of the State', in which he pointed out that the transition from the liberal state to the authoritarian state is not a major rupture. He argued that liberalism 'produces' the totalitarian state 'out of itself, as its own consummation'.[5]

Fascist tendencies that have become apparent today have been produced from within the liberal democracies of Europe and the Americas. As I have said, the structural racism that has characterised the United States since the very beginning of its history has been one of the primary internal contradictions to democracy. On the other hand, every moment of considerable progress, where democracy is concerned, has emanated from Black people's struggles against racism. Political forces of conservatism and reaction have always relied on racism and, as has been evident in the recent period, the ultranationalism represented by the current president is anchored in a fascist notion of the nation that calls for exclusionary strategies that are racist and Islamophobic.

BB/RZ *From early on, you've reflected, particularly in relation to your own experiences as a fugitive and prisoner and those of your comrades and friends, on law as a racial apparatus. How do you see the law now, decades after the civil rights movement, which focused on legal reform?*

AYD Racism is embedded in US law in multiple ways, including in its long use as a repressive instrument against Black people and other racially marginalised groups. The fact that the United States is the only self-identified democratic nation that routinely uses capital punishment reflects the way that racialised forms of punishment used during slavery found their way into state and federal law. The scores of political prisoners – from Indigenous leader Leonard Peltier to Mumia Abu-Jamal and others associated with the historical Black Panther Party – the majority of whom are Black, and some of whom have been behind bars for fifty years or longer, reveals the continued racialisation of US law. That the law's subject is assumed to be an unraced, unclassed, ungendered – that is, abstract – rights-bearing subject does not, as many take for granted, guarantee equal treatment under the law. Structural racism persists despite and sometimes because of the presumed 'colour blindness' of the law.

It should not be assumed that the movement we so affirmatively refer to as the 'civil rights movement' was innocently conceptualised as a panacea by those who were its agents. Between 1955 and 1965, Southern Black (and white) activists referred to the movement they created and advanced as 'the freedom movement'. They did not believe that the law alone held the answer. They not only challenged the law; they challenged economic, political and cultural practices as well. It is interesting that the role of Black

5 Herbert Marcuse, 'The Struggle against Liberalism in the Totalitarian View of the State', in *Negations: Essays in Critical Theory* (Boston: Beacon Press, 1968), 3–42.

communists – and those, such as my own mother, who were not afraid to work with communists – in helping to create arenas on which later struggles unfolded has been entirely discounted. In many instances they challenged the law, and they also utilised the law to challenge racist economic and social inequities, and legally sanctioned racist violence, as well as lynchings, rapes and other extralegal forms of racist violence. Among them was the 1944 Alabama case of Recy Taylor, who, with the assistance of Rosa Parks (representing the NAACP) and members of the Southern Negro Youth Congress (organised by Black communists and joined by a broad array of young Black people), challenged a gang of young white men who had raped her. My own mother, I should point out, was one of the officers of the Southern Negro Youth Congress.

Less than three years after the 1948 UN Convention on the Prevention and Punishment of the Crime of Genocide, the Civil Rights Congress, also led by Black communists, submitted a petition to the UN charging genocide of Black people in the United States. Around the same time, a group of well-known Black women – including Charlotta Bass, Shirley Graham Du Bois, Eslanda Robeson, and Louise Thompson Patterson – who called themselves the Sojourners for Truth, spoke out on behalf of Rosa Lee Ingraham, who, with her son, was sentenced to death for killing a white man who had attempted to rape her. The reverberations of this case were felt throughout the world.

There are many more specific examples of activist work that predated the 1955 Montgomery Bus Boycott, usually evoked as the catalytic event for the civil rights movement. It is important, I think, to demystify the notion that movements emerge spontaneously – as if it was the single act of a woman who extemporaneously decided to disobey authorities when she was asked to move to the back of the bus. Rosa Parks was a seasoned organiser, who had already forged a long history of on-the-ground activism. And she was well aware that she was not the first Black person to refuse to sit in the back of the bus. Claudette Colvin and many others (including classmates of mine) had predated her. Moreover, voting rights activists and others who are known for their contributions to struggles for legal rights, were also involved in other arenas. Fannie Lou Hamer, for example, was a leading figure in the campaign for voting rights and for the right of Black people to fully participate in the realm of electoral politics. She is most celebrated for her role at the 1964 Democratic National Convention in attempting to unseat the all-white Mississippi Democratic Party delegation, and to seat her party – the Mississippi Freedom Democratic Party. However, she is less well known for her efforts to create the Freedom Farm Cooperative, which emphasised land, housing, education scholarships and economic liberation more generally.

This broader notion of liberation – one critical of the way race, gender, class and sexual biases are reproduced through legal practices, law enforcement, and forms of penality linked to the prison industrial complex – reflects knowledges that have been forged over time through radical political praxis. Some of the new movements that have arisen in the twentieth century recognise, for example, that racist police violence cannot be adequately addressed if one does not acknowledge the historical role of policing structures in reproducing racial hierarchies and class dominance. Abolitionist perspectives not only call for a radical critique of penal and police practices, but also of the conditions that create the larger social, economic and political context that permits these practices to proliferate.

BB/RZ *We often hear about the 'juridification of human rights' and the 'NGO-isation of politics'. Can you tell us what your understanding of human rights is, in its most expansive sense? Is there a utopian dimension to human rights?*

AYD The notion of human rights can be powerfully anti-racist, anti-capitalist and anti-sexist, depending on the context of its deployment, but if it is not critically engaged, it can also have damaging consequences that bolster neoliberalism. Most dangerous, I think, is the pernicious equation of the 'human' in 'human rights' with 'individual', and the often-unquestioned assumption that human rights are individual rights in the way civil rights are constructed within bourgeois democracies. The replication of these ideas, legitimated through international law, often occurs through the NGO structure. But human rights instruments can also be strategically employed by social movements to further feminist, anti-racist and labour-based campaigns. In virtually all progressive movements, the seductive appeal of assimilation will have to be confronted. Given the way global structures function, it will always be easier to follow paths previously carved by the defenders of capitalism and by those who see progress in the global South and in marginalised communities of the global North as consisting in bringing those on the peripheries of existing 'progress' and development inside the fold.

But human rights can also be constructed more broadly. The ideal subject of human rights does not have to be imagined as the affluent white man. What if the ideal subject were women of colour as a collective project? If the human subject is collectivised and is imagined in enduring interaction with subjects that are not necessarily 'human' – that is, other inhabitants of our planet– the call to defend 'human rights' might also entail the need to transform systems and structures that militate against the very future of living beings and their environments.

BB/RZ *You have emphasised the idea that the individual, and individual experience, is always related to a collective. Can you tell us about your understanding of the individual–collective relationship?*

AYD I think that my upbringing during the 1940s and '50s in the most racially segregated city in the United States taught me important lessons regarding the dialectical relation between individual and community. Black people would not have survived, much less flourished, under those extreme conditions of white dominance had not there been a strong sense of community. One of the interesting effects of white supremacy within Black communities was the propagation of the idea that we each represented the entire community. This fungibility at the heart of racism led to violent attacks on many Black people whose only connection to the issues that sparked lynchings was the fact that they were Black. But within our community a collective identity was evoked through constant reminders we all received that individual failures would always affect our community as well as ourselves. Of course, our individual achievements were also collective steps forward, refutations of the ideology of racial inferiority. Those who engaged in conscious efforts to advance the community were known as 'race men and women'. Personally, I always realised that my individual accomplishments were not simply my own. I realised that each time I moved forward, I was a beneficiary of collective struggle, and that, rather than assuming a self-congratulatory stance, it was my responsibility to give back.

We do not exist in the world as isolated individuals, but are connected to others in diverse ways, and it is primarily these connections that define us as individuals. This is the insight that determined how I have negotiated my way through the world, and this is how I have always interpreted my own individuality. Individualism – especially in its capitalist instantiation – militates against a real understanding of individuality. During the time I was in jail, when I saw vast numbers of women who didn't belong behind bars any more than I did, I was acutely aware of the fact that public attention was focused on me, but no one was supporting them. Thus, I was especially happy to participate from inside the jail in the development of a bail movement for the women in the New York House of Detention. Also, because of the disproportionate consideration given to my case as compared to all of the other cases of political prisoners during that period, I asked that the name of the campaign be changed from 'National United Committee to Free Angela Davis' to 'National United Committee to Free Angela Davis and All Political Prisoners'. This was an important move because when my individual case was won, no one assumed that the struggle was over – indeed, we went on to build broad campaigns to defend various political prisoners, movements against the Ku Klux Klan and their espousal of racist violence, and explicit campaigns against police violence and for prisoners' rights. This work helped to create new terrains of struggle that helped to prepare the way for prison abolitionist and Black Lives Matter movements today.

But, returning to the relationship between the individual and the community – it is especially important to reflect on the impact of neoliberal ideology over the last period and its elevation of the individual as the most important unit of society. If the individual is absolutely responsible for her/his/their condition, then poverty, homelessness and illiteracy can be explained away as individual shortcomings, rather than social and political failures. At a time when organised labour has been under continuous attack, when the welfare state (with all of its deficiencies) is a thing of the past and when human needs have been transformed into occasions for privatisation and profit, it is especially important to emphasise the social and the collective.

***BB/RZ** In an interview conducted in 1995 with Lisa Lowe, she asked you whether 'the anti-racist critique [had] successfully changed white feminism'.[6] Asking you this same question in 2019, how would you respond?*

AYD While I can't remember exactly how I answered Lisa's question about feminism and the anti-racist critique, I am sure I acknowledged the transformative effect of women of colour feminisms. But I should note that while we tend to focus critically on white bourgeois feminism, in the United States there are important histories of working-class and anti-racist white feminisms – from Prudence Crandall in the nineteenth century to Anne Braden in the twentieth[7]. So, it is misleading to simply speak about white feminism in the singular. But I think that it is equally necessary to consider the plural character of women of colour feminisms. My preference, of course, is for those feminisms that are most inclusive – anti-racist, as well as anti-capitalist. In other words, Marxist-inflected anti-racist feminisms.

I have pointed out many times that early on – in the sixties and seventies, and even the very early eighties – I was extremely reluctant to identify with feminism, because I understood the feminist movement at that time to focus so narrowly on gender that gender came to be implicitly racialised as white. Moreover, mainstream feminism tended more towards assimilation than towards radical transformation. However, the 1977 Combahee River Collective Statement had already established a framework for a more revolutionary, anti-racist feminism. And even before, beginning in 1970, the Third World Women's Alliance had called for an understanding of gender that also foregrounded race and class. The title of their newspaper, *Triple Jeopardy* (racism, imperialism, sexism), not only implied what eventually came to be known as the 'intersectionality' of justice struggles, but explicitly called for international solidarity in these struggles. I mention two important moments in an extended history of efforts to forge approaches to feminism that focus on interrelated

6 Angela Y. Davis, 'Interview with Lisa Lowe, Angela Davis: Reflections on Race, Class and Gender in the USA', in *Politics of Culture in the Shadow of Capital*, ed. Lisa Lowe and David Lloyd (Durham, NC: Duke University Press, 1997), 303–23.

7 Davis, Rodney O. *Prudence Crandall, Spiritualism, and Populist-era Reform in Kansas*. Kansas State Historical Society, 1980. Fosl, Catherine. *Subversive southerner: Anne Braden and the struggle for racial justice in the Cold War South*. University Press of Kentucky, 2006.

modes of dominance, because these are the most significant expressions of feminism today. This approach to feminism has also been taken up by poets and other cultural workers like Audre Lorde and June Jordan. The fact that 'intersectionality' may very well be the term most associated with contemporary feminism is indicative of the ways anti-racist and anti-capitalist theories and practices have shaped prevailing expressions of feminism today.

Feminisms that do not also address racism and capitalism will always misapprehend the meaning of gender equality. If gender equality is not linked to racial and economic equality, it will only basically affect relatively affluent white women. The feminisms I am referring to also entail a recognition that the narrow gender-binary structure that reflects how gender has been ideologically produced and reproduced only prevents us from understanding the fluidity and multiplicity of gender awareness, consciousness and expression. These feminisms realise that as long as racism continues to organise our social and economic lives – our educational systems, our prison systems, our housing accessibility and our job availability – gender equality will not exist. Gender equality cannot be conceptualised without foregrounding racial and economic equality. Racial, economic and gender justice are inextricably connected; one is not possible without the others.

BB/RZ *What does abolition mean, in its most expansive sense?*

AYD Contemporary abolitionist movements recognise that calls to simply reform prison and police systems will never succeed in addressing the deep, structural reasons for the persistence and proliferation of racist and repressive forms of punishment and security. Abolitionists recognise that existing systems of imprisonment and policing contain significant traces of the historical influence of slavery and exemplify the use of repressive apparatuses to extend the colonial suppression of Indigenous populations. In this sense, abolitionist theories and practices are linked to revolutionary approaches to social change, and they have developed alongside radical, anti-capitalist and anti-racist feminisms.

In the most expansive sense, abolitionist approaches acknowledge interconnections and interrelations that ultimately require us to be critical of myopic reforms – whether of prisons or police – and to always be aware of the determining effects of larger social, economic and political contexts. Thus, in the current period, when critiques of mass incarceration have entered into the mainstream, abolitionists do not assent to quick fixes that represent simple reforms as permanent solutions. We remind progressive politicians and activists that the racist and class-biased underpinnings of these repressive apparatuses are linked to capitalism, and that ultimately, they will have to be abolished. Therefore, reforms that can potentially strengthen these systems, such as building more prisons to address overcrowding, must always be challenged. The reforms that we *do* support are those that don't contribute to the permanency of the systems, but rather help to make life more habitable for the people targeted by these institutions.

Abolition is not primarily about an end to be achieved, but rather about how we conceptualise social justice issues as always interconnected and interrelated. We do not focus myopically on a single issue – say the institution of the prison – and we do not seek single and isolated solutions, but rather ask what needs to be changed about the larger society, so that we no longer need to rely on institutions that reproduce the very violence that they are supposed to minimise. So how would we reimagine a society without prisons and without institutionalised police violence? This would entail reenvisioning not only justice and security, but also economic structures, education, healthcare and so on. Justice that helps us transform social relationships, and security that acknowledges what it really means to feel safe, would require revolutionary change.

In answering the previous question about feminism, I might have pointed out that many contemporary radical feminists have embraced the concept of abolition feminism, which helps to distinguish them from 'glass ceiling' feminists, or those who are simply striving to reach greater heights without otherwise troubling the system. Abolition feminism differentiates itself from 'carceral feminism', a somewhat derogatory term for those who believe that state violence – more police and more imprisonment – is the most appropriate response to gender violence. If gender violence is ever to be eliminated, the complicated web of causes that have historically produced structures of heteropatriarchy and their embeddedness in racial capitalism for the last several centuries will have to be addressed.

BB/RZ *You have emphasised the noncommodifiable aspects of Black women's labour in the home – keeping together communities, keeping children safe. Are there commonalities here with other feminist theories and praxis? For instance, with First Nations and Indigenous women's feminisms that emphasise the centrality of land and women's central place in Indigenous communities and political formations? We have in mind here examples such as the Unist'ot'en Camp in British Columbia, where there is a protest against the liquified natural gas pipeline, or Standing Rock, where communal social provisioning has been at the heart of protest.*

AYD During the late 1960s and early '70s, largely as a consequence of the circulation of Black cultural nationalist advocacy of male supremacy, I began to think about the devalorisation of Black women's contributions more generally – especially given the popularisation of ideas associated with the 1965 Moynihan Report, which characterised the Black community as a 'tangle of pathology' at the centre of which was the 'matriarchal' structure of the Black family.[8] Because Daniel Patrick Moynihan argued that this so-called matriarchal structure of the family was a legacy of slavery, I attempted to generate a different context for thinking about Black women's role in slave communities. Thus, my first published article, written when I was in jail, was entitled 'Reflections on the Black Woman's Role in the Community of Slaves'.[9] My core argument emphasised the relationship between domestic labour and resistance. Of course, a good deal of Marxist feminist theory over the last decades has attempted to carve out a productive space for deeper understandings of reproductive labour.

Native communities and Indigenous feminisms have been at the forefront of environmental struggles and have demonstrated how we might all think more broadly about the intersectionality of social justice struggles. Feminisms grounded in native epistemologies and practices help us to incorporate an awareness of the centrality of land and water – and women's role in protecting these resources, from Standing Rock to South Africa and Palestine to Flint, Michigan.

A more expansive awareness of women's reproductive labour can also help us to more deeply grasp the historical significance of women domestic workers' participation in such movements as the anti-pass struggles in South Africa and the bus boycott in Montgomery that served as a catalyst for the mid-twentieth-century civil rights movement in the United States. It may not be accidental that Alicia Garza, one of the founders of the Black Lives Matter movement, is also a key leader of the National Domestic Workers Alliance.

Selected Writings

Davis, Angela Y. *With My Mind on Freedom: An Autobiography*. New York: Bantam Books, 1978.

———. *Women, Race and Class*. New York: Vintage, 1981.

———. *Women, Culture and Politics*. New York: Vintage, 1990.

———. *Blues Legacies and Black Feminism: Gertrude 'Ma' Rainey, Bessie Smith and Billie Holiday*. New York: Vintage, 1999.

———. *Abolition Democracy: Beyond Prisons, Torture, Empire*. New York: Seven Stories Press, 2005.

———. *Are Prisons Obsolete?* New York: Seven Stories Press, 2011.

———. *The Meaning of Freedom: And Other Difficult Dialogues*. San Francisco: City Lights, 2012.

---

8 Daniel P. Moynihan et al., *The Negro Family: The Case for National Action*, United States Department of Labor, Office of Planning and Research (Washington, DC: Government Printing Office, 1965).

9 Angela Y. Davis, 'Reflections on the Black Woman's Role in the Community of Slaves', *Massachusetts Review* 13:1–2 (1972), 81–100.

Afterword: Revolutionary Feminisms in a Time of Monsters

Lisa Lowe

The crisis consists precisely in the fact that the old world is dying and the new cannot be born. In this interregnum a great variety of morbid symptoms appear.

Antonio Gramsci, 1930[1]

As I see it, history moves from one conjuncture to another rather than being an evolutionary flow. And what drives it forward is usually a crisis, when the contradictions that are always at play in any historical moment are condensed... Crises are moments of potential change, but the nature of their resolution is not given.

Stuart Hall, 2010[2]

The struggles of our contemporary times should be thought of as productive contradictions because they constitute a rupture with past struggles, but at the same time they reside on a continuum with those struggles and they have been enabled by activisms of the past. They are unfinished activisms.

Angela Davis, 2016[3]

In our contemporary moment, cruel austerity measures deepen global economic divides, while authoritarian governments subject the poor, homeless and most vulnerable to state violence and imprisonment. Yet across the world, crowds have taken to the streets: in India, there are mass protests against the Modi government's anti-Muslim Citizenship Amendment Act and persecutions in Assam and Kashmir; while in Bolivia, people continue to demonstrate against the 2019 military coup that deposed the first Indigenous

1 'La crisi consiste appunto nel fatto che il vecchio muore e il nuovo non può nascere: in questo interregno si verificano i fenomeni morbosi piú svariati.' Antonio Gramsci, *Selections from the Prison Notebooks* (NY: International Publishers, 1971), 275–6. Gramsci's statement about the radical shift in hegemony is often translated, less precisely, as 'The old world is dying and the new world struggles to be born. Now is the time of monsters.' See Slavoj Žižek, 'Living in the Time of Monsters', *Counterpoints* 422 (2012), 32–44.

2 Stuart Hall and Doreen Massey, 'Interpreting the Crisis', *Soundings* 44 (2010): 57–71.

3 Angela Y. Davis, 2016 Steve Biko Memorial Lecture, 2 September 2016, University of South Africa, Pretoria, available at Steve Biko Foundation official website, sbf.org.za.

president, Evo Morales. Set off by an increase in the Santiago metro subway fare, over a million Chileans protest severe income equality caused by neoliberal privatisation. Haitians object to increased fuel prices, poverty and government corruption. In Lebanon, tax hikes have catalysed public outrage against unemployment, a stagnant economy, and long-standing corruption in the public sector. In Hong Kong, first colonised by the British and then by North American markets, clashes between protesters and police began as opposition to a bill that would have permitted extraditions to China, yet months of civil unrest have far outlasted the bill's withdrawal, and grown into weekly anti-government demonstrations. Tens of thousands of Okinawans gather regularly to oppose the expanded US military presence in the former Japanese colony, now the prefecture in which postwar US bases in Japan have been concentrated. In the United States, Black Lives Matter was catalysed by police violence against unarmed Black men and women – Eric Garner, Michael Brown, Trayvon Martin, Sandra Bland and others – but the movement addresses the long history of structural anti-Blackness and persistent exclusion from political and economic life. In 2016, water protectors encamped at Standing Rock Reservation to block construction of the Dakota Access oil pipeline, drawing upon long-standing Native sovereignty to build an ongoing intergenerational, hemispheric movement of Indigenous resistance. These collective, grassroots protests – across various colonial histories, regions and populations – indicate differentiated yet linked conditions of promise and peril that come together in our historical moment. At the same time, the UK Brexit debacle and the US Trump catastrophe are less populist surges than 'morbid symptoms' of imperial nation-states beset by legitimation crises. It is a time, in Antonio Gramsci's words, in which the 'old world is dying and the new cannot be born'; one in which the failure of the existing political economic order, despite its manifestation in increasing political repression, is coterminous with the birth and emergence of new ones.

Writing in a fascist prison nearly a century ago, Gramsci regarded the 1930s in which he lived as an interregnum, an in-between period during which the stabilities of former European regimes were dissolving, and the social order was on the threshold of change. Gramsci's phrasing of the radical shift in hegemony in terms of simultaneous temporalities resonates in our twenty-first century conditions: the radical fullness of the present is realised when one grasps the simultaneity of a failing prior social order and the opening of a new, emergent way of transforming the future. The ensuing chaos of the dying regime brings its own atrocities and new forms of terror, but it also makes way for a new order that we have not yet made.

The ten revolutionary feminist thinkers interviewed in this volume bring their differently situated histories and lifeworks to bear upon the current interregnum; they name the conditions of the crisis, discuss their activist and scholarly critiques of racial capitalism, patriarchy and imperialism, and share their views on how we might organise and prepare for what is to come. At the same time, they thematise the challenges of 'reading' the object of our current moment and outline the obstacles to building collectively to address its conditions. In other words, the logics of neoliberalism have so saturated public discourse that currently available political languages – of human rights, liberal freedom and individualism – are not only inadequate to name, recognise and understand the current crisis; they themselves have become serious hindrances to radical analysis, and to the creation of radical alternatives to it. The language of 'crisis' itself has been appropriated to justify the neoliberal restructuring that enables vast accumulations of wealth for the few, and imposes punishing austerity measures for the vulnerable many. However, the thinkers here remind us how we may unsettle the present by restoring our relations to the long history of revolutionary anti-racist and anti-colonial feminisms: like those of Fannie Lou Hamer, Claudia Jones and Audre Lorde, the Combahee River Collective and the Third World Women's Alliance, or the women who led and participated in the Kanehsata:ke resistance during the 1990 Oka Crisis. We could call them abolition feminists, in that they understood the connections of racial, economic and gender justice, and resolved that any feminism that sought gender justice must address racism, capitalism and imperialism, as well. Abolition feminism, as Angela Y. Davis, Ruth Wilson Gilmore, and Avery F. Gordon explain here, asserts that in order to abolish the prison system, we must eliminate the conditions that lead to and produce prisons; it is necessary to radically transform our present social and economic order, and, moreover, to create new social relations bounded neither by the nationalist terms of the current political order nor the global terms of the capitalist order. Furthermore, abolition feminists eloquently articulate that abolition does not mean merely putting an end to something; it means making something that does not yet exist. When Gilmore evokes the building of schools that was a robust part of the Black Reconstruction described by W.E.B. Du Bois, she explains: 'It is not enough to have a plan to win . . . What will you do the day after you win?' Or, put slightly differently, how do we create *now* the practical conditions for what will come after? How do we recognise and draw from the various radical visions, traditions and ways of being that may not have culminated in the seizure of state power? In her work, for example, Gordon evokes a politics that brings the radical movements of the past to bear on the present, which seeks to manifest a political future from the 'radicals, runaways, deserters, abolitionists, heretics, dreamers and liberationists'[4] whose activities may be illegible or were discredited – although their forms of resistance, opposition and escape not only challenged racial capitalism and colonialism, but provided visions of other sociality.

---

4 Avery F. Gordon, *The Hawthorn Archive: Letters from the Utopian Margins* (New York: Fordham University Press, 2017), 2.

If we take these interviews as the contemporary voices of revolutionary abolition feminism, we appreciate that they speak from widely different contexts – Black feminism, Black radical internationalism, Marxist feminism, communist movements, Indigenous struggles, anti-racist work, anti-colonial feminisms, LGBTQI movements and more – yet we observe that they converge around several key points.

The unfolding crises in India, Bolivia, Chile, Lebanon, Hong Kong, Okinawa, the United States, the UK and elsewhere are the legacy of multiple scales of colonial dispossession, enslavement and extraction; these historical divides have been weaponised by Cold War partitions and regionalisms, deepened by imperial wars and amplified by the globalisation of racial capitalism. Yet the processes are not monolithic, nor of a single structure. In certain situations, colonial powers occupy and dispossess, and, with the imposition of culture and language, seek to make the colonised into a replica of itself and its own customs, values and markers of the human. In others, a foreign power brutally constructs the subjugated as uncivilised and inhuman, as enslaveable or extinguishable, and not capable of acceding to their terms of civilisation. At times, a state extends its reach through construction of the threat of a racial enemy, while at others, it projects the colonised or neocolonised as 'victims' in need of 'benevolent' militarised rescue. Furthermore, differentiated colonial projects often converge and articulate with one another: from settler colonialism, which seeks to replace an Indigenous population in order to secure their land, disrupting their long-standing relationships to land, cultivation and nonhuman lifeworlds; to the aftermaths of the capture, sale and enslavement of African people by Portuguese, Dutch, French and British traders in transatlantic slavery; to overseas empire, which includes an expanded history of extraction, occupation and militarism in colonies 'abroad' – from European empires to twentieth- and twenty-first-century US wars, military basing and capitalist development around the world. In this sense, our contemporary condition is an assemblage of historical and ongoing operations that include political economy, racial projects, culture and ideology, and modes of governance, whose crises manifest the system's contradictions, rather than its inevitability or totality. The historical and ongoing struggles against these relations, such as those discussed by the abolition and revolutionary feminists interviewed here, are precisely the ground for rethinking the 'political', in ways that are quite different than the rights, representation or inclusions offered by nation-states, parties or capital. Yet, when dominant formations fail to assimilate these activities into their own, they vilify or dismiss them as 'feminised', 'racialised', in excess, or insignificant. On the contrary, abolition and revolutionary feminisms understand these subjugated histories not only as significant, but as the work of a still-ongoing decolonisation and social transformation – that is, the place of other social imaginaries, less acknowledged, yet actively preserved, which in turn obligate us to reconceive the sites and ends of struggle.

Feminist thinkers have long identified social reproduction as an undervalued yet crucial site in the ongoing maintenance and continuity of colonialism and capitalism. As Silvia Federici explains, the emphasis on 'productive' labour explicitly devalues and 'feminises' reproductive labours, even though capitalism has always depended upon the appropriation of a broad range of underrecognised and often unpaid social reproductive labours, both in the household and throughout the rest of social relations.[5] The abolition and revolutionary feminist thinkers interviewed here specify that collective struggles against racism or fascism are incomplete if they do not account for the totality of social reproductive labours. When facing the immediate problems of vast economic divides 'organised' by state violence and abandonment, we must appreciate that these conditions build upon a longer history of the coercion, appropriation and governance of social reproductive labours: from the Atlantic cultures of chattel slavery and coercion of enslaved Black women to birth, nurture and reproduce human beings, to the domestic labour of Black women, migrant women and women of colour to support the bourgeois family;[6] from the violent disruption of Native kinship through dispossession and allotment, to the forcible education of Native children in North American boarding schools, in the forms of households that reproduce capitalist social relations;[7] from the global restructuring of reproductive work in the international division of labour that sociologist Maria Mies has elaborated as the 'housewifisation' of the global economy, to the more contemporary 'outsourcing' of reproduction to 'surrogates' who gestate, birth and donate organs and tissues for commercial customers in North America and Europe.[8] While homes and households are primary sites for many of these operations, social reproductive work takes place in hospitals and schools, in factories and on assembly lines; it is at work in incarceration and other forms of detention, occupation and

5 Silvia Federici, *Caliban and the Witch: Women, the Body and Primitive Accumulation* (New York: Autonomedia, 2004).

6 On gender, sexuality and reproduction in the plantation household, see especially Thavolia Glymph, *Out of the House of Bondage: The Transformation of the Plantation Household* (Cambridge, UK: Cambridge University Press, 2008); Daina Ramey Berry and Leslie Harris, eds., *Sexuality and Slavery: Reclaiming Intimate Histories in the Americas* (Athens, Georgia: University of Georgia Press, 2018); on Black women's reproduction and domestic labour, see Dorothy Roberts, *Killing the Black Body: Race, Reproduction and the Meaning of Liberty* (1997; repr., New York: Vintage, 2014); Alys Weinbaum, *The Afterlife of Reproductive Slavery: Biocapitalism and Black Feminism's Philosophy of History* (Durham: Duke University Press, 2019).

7 Brenda Childs, *Boarding School Seasons: American Indian Families, 1900–1940* (Lincoln and London: University of Nebraska Press, 1998); Laura Wexler, *Tender Violence: Domestic Visions in an Age of U.S. Imperialism* (Durham: University of North Carolina Press, 2000).

8 Maria Mies, *Patriarchy and Accumulation on a World Scale: Women in the International Division of Labour* (London: Zed, 1986); Kalindi Vora, *Life Support: Biocapital and the New History of Outsourced Labor* (Minneapolis: University of Minnesota Press, 2015).

enclosure at both intimate and global scales.[9] Social reproduction includes but is not limited to the creation of human beings; it extends to the many labours and social processes that produce 'the human' as liberal citizen, and that reproduce what we might call an endless 'international division of humanity', in which race, gender and social differences are remainders of the liberal, colonial and now neoliberal processes through which 'the human' is 'freed' as bourgeois Man, while those who reproduce the conditions for that freedom are exploited and forgotten.[10]

The collective work of the thinkers interviewed here urges us to address how social reproduction builds upon the international division of labour in which formerly enslaved and colonised women have been responsible for the essential, yet unacknowledged, social reproduction of the world system. The global care chain, circuits of domestic labourers, human trafficking, transnational reproductive surrogacy and other phenomena demonstrate how social reproduction at both local and global scales builds upon legacies of colonial labour regimes. The research, writing, and activist examples of those collected here help us to acknowledge how the contemporary privatisation and commodification of social reproduction takes us far beyond the productivity of unpaid housework. Indeed, the broader range of kin labour, caring labour and all labours of human contact – communication and proximity in service work, healthcare, sex work and the entire assemblage for 'making live' – makes legible the production of value through affective labours that have never been

9 Marxist feminist theorists of the 1970s challenged the tendency of orthodox Marxism to emphasise 'productive' labour and ignore unwaged 'reproductive' labour, and focused particularly on women's housework. They argued that value is generated not only through waged work but through women's unwaged or unfree labour in the household, and observed that prioritising waged labour as a means to address economic inequality creates a labour hierarchy that naturalises the exploitation of the unwaged housework. This position grows out of Engels's *Origins of the Family, Private Property, and the State* (first edition published October 1884 in Hottingen-Zurich), in which he explained that women's subordination is not due to reproductive biology, but due to social relations of production. Yet unfree and unpaid labour has always been fundamental to colonialism and racial capitalism, and its social reproduction. Responding to feminist housework debates, Black feminists and materialist feminists of colour, like Patricia Hill Collins or Evelyn Nakano Glenn, reminded housework feminists that due to slavery and colonialism, the history of productive and reproductive labour has always been fundamentally different for Black women and women of colour, who historically perform both unpaid or underpaid 'productive' labour (often domestic service labour in the homes of white families), as well as unpaid 'reproductive' care, cleaning and nurturing within their own families. Claudia Jones discussed the 'triple oppression' of Black women as mothers, Blacks, and workers. See Evelyn Nakano Glenn, 'Racial Ethnic Women's Labor: The Intersection of Race, Class, and Gender Oppression', *Review of Radical Political Economics* 17:3 (1985), 86–108; Patricia Hill Collins, 'The Social Construction of Black Feminist Thought', *Signs* 14:4 (Summer 1989), 745–73; Claudia Jones, *An End to the Neglect of the Problems of the Negro Woman* (New York: Jefferson School of Social Science, 1949).

10 Lisa Lowe, *The Intimacies of Four Continents* (Durham: Duke University Press, 2015).

entirely outside of capitalist production, but are constru
'nonvalue' within productivist schemes.[11]

Silvia Federici has written that global capitalism is 'stru
on the free appropriation of immense quantities of labour
must appear as externalities to the market', and that these
partially subsumed forms of devalued labour are often atta
of colonised and immigrant women.[12] In this sense, we should not consider settler colonialism and racial slavery as bounded, finished historical events; to the contrary, they are formations that actively externalise and disavow their means of social reproduction, and that change over time to operate in conjunction with other means of expropriation, subjection and accumulation. In our current moment, the coexistence of vast accumulation and private property possession with wagelessness and deprivation exemplifies these operations. The blindness to social reproduction pointedly degrades women's labour, but social reproduction is evidently not exclusively limited to women's labour, and it encompasses a larger set of operations and practices: it rearticulates earlier systems of enslavement, enclosure and dispossession, and preys upon migrant lives and immigrant labour; it engages in ecological plunder that threatens to destroy the lifeways of Indigenous peoples, and robs the global South of seeds, crops, minerals, water and timber in wholly unsustainable ways.[13] In other words, while global capitalist production and accumulation depend, parasitically, on racialised, gendered social reproduction, the latter is often pushed to the background, forming an essential yet under-recognised shadow realm of expropriation.

In her interview in this volume, and in her activist and scholarly work, Ruth Wilson Gilmore insists on the need to 'jump scales' in thinking and organising, if we are to address these differentiated scales and spheres through which the work of social reproduction takes place.[14] In other words, precisely because capitalism is a differentiated unity of related, yet uneven and multiply formed processes, the work of countering and transforming it requires us not only to move from local to global, but more importantly, to

11 Michael Hardt, 'Affective Labor', *boundary 2*, 26:2 (1999), 89–100.

12 Silvia Federici, 'Feminism and the Politics of the Common in an Era of Primitive Accumulation', in *Revolution at Point Zero: Housework, Reproduction and Feminist Struggle* (Oakland: PM Press, 2012), 140. Quoted in Alyosha Goldstein, 'On the Reproduction of Race, Capitalism, and Settler Colonialism', in *Race and Capitalism: Global Territories, Transnational Histories* (Los Angeles: UCLA Institute on Inequality and Democracy, 2017).

13 Jason Moore, *Capitalism in the Web of Life: Ecology and the Accumulation of Capital* (London and New York: Verso, 2015).

14 Ruth Wilson Gilmore, *Golden Gulag: Prisons, Surplus, Crisis, and Opposition in Globalizing California* (Berkeley: University of California Press, 2007). Gilmore's use of the phrase is based on the work of Neil Smith. See Neil Smith, 'Geography, Difference and the Politics of Scale', in *Postmodernism and the Social Sciences*, ed. Joe Doherty, Elspeth Graham and Mo Malek (London: Macmillan, 1992), 57–79.

te ‘inter-scalar’ relations that link these processes. ‘Jumping scales’ ames this need to grapple with the different levels at which capital and the state work together, and to calibrate how the capital–state nexus has reorganised over time and in various places, in an asymmetrical but coordinated fashion. As she points out, this linking and movement across scales is necessary, not only because geographical space is continually partitioned and repartitioned, but also because actually living struggles cannot be totally contained by these partitions or scalar classifications. For example, in our contemporary moment, when the state actively withdraws from social welfare and invests in prisons and police, abolition movements are linking the capitalist management of prisons and schools, and organising together. Gilmore has discussed elsewhere three California teachers’ unions who recently took on prison abolition as one of their central issues, preventing both the construction of an additional prison and the further slashing of school budgets.[15]

Thus, precisely because globalised racial capitalism builds upon the histories of colonial divides and operates through newly differentiated logics and asymmetrical scales, our analytic frames and organising practices likewise cannot be limited to a single logic, issue or national framework; links and solidarities are imperative. Since ‘capitalism requires inequality, and racism enshrines it’, as Gilmore has said, it is crucial to organise across connected issues: for instance, racism and police brutality; racism and climate change; or prison buildup and migrant detention. Yet the necessity of linking is not simply a contemporary challenge; it has always been part of anti-colonial, pan-African, and communist internationalist visions. In her interview, Angela Y. Davis draws a parallel between the international solidarity of revolutionary movements across Africa, Asia, Europe and Latin America that was so crucial to the US Black Panther Party, and the current Black Lives Matter movement’s embrace of justice for Palestine. Himani Bannerji suggests that it is not possible for anti-racist feminist Marxists to view patriarchy as separate from colonialism, religion, nationalism, caste and class. Leanne Betasamosake Simpson observes the solidarity of Indigenous nations with Black activism in Toronto, the Zapatistas in Chiapas, and Palestinian struggles for freedom. Queer activists in movements such as Black Lives Matter or Queers against Israeli Apartheid (QuAIA), Gary Kinsman observes, are not merely targeting homophobia or transphobia, but are concerned with a broader critique of police violence, nationalism, militarism and capitalism; they interrogate racism in their own communities, and ask ‘*whose* national security is it?’[16]

15 Ruth Wilson Gilmore, ‘Meanwhile (Parts 1 and 2)’, lecture, November 2019, Yale University, New Haven, Connecticut.

16 Gary Kinsman, Dieter K. Buse and Mercedes Steedman, eds., *Whose National Security? Canadian State Surveillance and the Creation of Enemies* (Toronto: Between the Lines , 2000).

Vron Ware has been a powerful voice in anti-racist feminist struggles, urging white women to see their lives as always imbricated in the racism directed against Black, Muslim and immigrant communities. Avery F. Gordon evokes the indivisibility of struggles in the phrase 'network of mutuality' (195–6), from Martin Luther King Jr's 1963 'Letter from Birmingham Jail': 'Injustice anywhere is a threat to justice everywhere. We are caught in an inescapable network of mutuality, tied in a single garment of destiny. Whatever affects one directly, affects all indirectly.'

So much of existing left political thinking conceptualises 'revolution' in terms of the large-scale capture of the state, or in liberal traditions, defines 'freedom' in the narrow terms of individualism and rights granted by the nation-state. Yet the feminist thinkers interviewed here provide powerful resources with which we might think about revolution and social transformation rather differently. In Angela Y. Davis's words, 'Abolition is not primarily about an end to be achieved, but rather about how we conceptualise social justice issues as always interconnected and interrelated' (214). Davis emphasises the work of making and remaking social justice connections in the *longue durée.* Gail Lewis speaks eloquently about turning away from the seductions of individualism, and the necessary importance – whether in trade unions, the Brixton Black Women's Group, or anti-imperialist movements – of embracing collective responsibility for one another. Avtar Brah describes her work on 'diaspora' as coming out of Southall Black Sisters, a British feminist group of Asian, African and Black Caribbean women that has challenged gender-related domestic abuse, racism, and religious and community violence since its founding in 1979, not by demanding a homogeneous subject of struggle, but recognising from the outset that the national imperial state differentially racialised, gendered and governed formerly colonised subjects. Where anti-colonial nationalist and Marxist struggles have often treated gender as secondary, these feminists have not only emphasised the importance of the gendered labour of social reproduction, but regard the labours of social reproduction as crucial sites for revolutionary politics. This means not only contesting the hyper-extraction of social reproductive labour, but, moreover, revaluing the work of kinship and relation. Their work also revalues the long-standing, yet less appreciated making and sustaining of ungiven relations, remade kinships and reinvented sociality, as well as alternative visions of political community. In a 2018 essay, sociologist Ruha Benjamin focused on the practices of 'cultivating kinfulness' as an antidote to the racist violence that Ruth Wilson Gilmore has called 'the state-sanctioned or extralegal production and exploitation of group-differentiated vulnerability to premature death.'[17]

---

17 Ruha Benjamin, 'Black Afterlives Matter: Cultivating Kinfulness as Reproductive Justice', in *Making Kin Not Population*, ed. Adele E. Clarke and Donna Haraway (Chicago: Prickly Paradigm, 2018), 41–51; Ruth Wilson Gilmore, 'Race and Globalization', in *Geographies*

For Benjamin, 'cultivating kinfulness' describes the forging of relations with those who came before, appreciating the 'ancestral co-presence' of 'meta-kin' that exceeds contemporary biological relation, from Tamir Rice, Sandra Bland, Michael Brown and other recent 'Black afterlives' who have inspired social movements, to legendary African figures such as Queen Nanny, Boukman and Gullah Jack, who led fights against slavery, colonialism and imperialism. In troubling the line between the biological living and dead, Benjamin brings less legible remnants of the historical past into the present, constituting an immanent future-yet-to-come. Discussing Native Pacific activists protecting Mauna a Wākea, the highest mountain in the Hawaiian islands, from the building of the Thirty Meter Telescope, Noelani Goodyear-Ka'ōpua insists that Kānaka Maoli activists protecting ancestral connections to lands and waters should not be dismissed as fixed on the past, but rather understood as reawakening 'intergenerational pathways connecting watery bodies – human, lake, harbor – and linking ancestors with descendants' to assert Indigenous epistemologies, and to 'protect the possibilities of multiple futures'.[18] Avery F. Gordon has elaborated these dynamics through her concepts of 'haunting' and 'utopian margins'.[19] For Gordon, the haunting recurrence of the past in the present is a sign that an injustice continues unredressed; it produces a 'something-to-be-done', and illuminates a possible emergent state in which elements in the past remain and provide for something more than the present. Gordon describes this emergent space as 'what was almost or not quite yet, or was present and at the same time yet to come', evoking multiple simultaneous temporalities. In her interview, Gordon quotes the Chimurenga Library and Pan African Space Station, who put it this way: 'Can a past that the present has not yet caught up with be summoned to haunt the present as an alternative?' (189). In other words, living remnants of the past in our present may be a part of the past with which we have not yet reckoned, with which the present must still grapple to fully understand.

This volume moves us to reckon with our present time, this interregnum, as a rich amalgam of simultaneous temporalities. It is a reminder that while the present course of events is entirely capable of bringing the world to complete destruction, we are not there yet, and that other past itineraries remain unfinished – an apprehension which may help us seize the fullness of our present moment as a time in which change is still possible. This full present is a speculative space that encompasses *both* the timeline of modernity, with its aggressive drives of capitalism and war, *and* the simultaneous

---

of Global Change: Remapping the World, ed. Ron J. Johnston et al. (Oxford: Wiley-Blackwell, 1995), 261.

18 Noelani Goodyear-Ka'ōpua, 'Protectors of the Future, Not Protestors of the Past: Indigenous Pacific Activism and Mauna a Wākea', *South Atlantic Quarterly* 116:1 (2017), 186.

19 Avery F. Gordon, *Ghostly Matters: Haunting and the Sociological Imagination* (Minneapolis: University of Minnesota Press, 1997; 2nd ed., 2008); and *The Hawthorn Archive*.

condition that there may be other alternatives, barely legible, rising, inchoate, through which we might transform the inevitability and brutality of that timeline. This volume summons us to the nature of our critical analytical present, so that we may honour those who came before, and carry the struggle forward.